IN SEARCH OF LOVE

By James Clancy

A Search for Lost Relatives.
Confronting Tragedy, Joy,
Disillusionment, Distress, and Retribution.
A Family Torn Apart by Reticence
A Necessity for Responses
A Requisite for Forgiveness
A Demand for Love

Copyright © 2021 James Clancy All rights reserved

Author James Clancy

Edited by Bernard Wilds

No part of this book can be reproduced in any form or by written, electronic or mechanical, including photocopying, recording, or by any information retrieval system without written permission in writing by the author.

Although every precaution has been taken in the preparation of this book, the Publisher, Author and Editor assume no responsibility for errors or omissions. Neither is any liability assumed for damages resulting from the use of information contained herein.

ISBN 979-854-847-2564

Email: fhlanwilds@gmail.com

Health Service Executive
1st Floor, Park House
North Circular Road
Dublin 7

Dear Mr Clancy

Further to your request under the Freedom of Information Act, 1997 and 2003 for access to records held by this Executive which was received in this office on 3 April 2006. Following a search of various areas two files have been located which contain information personal to you i.e., a social file and a tracing file. An index card relating to your time spent in Saint Patrick's Mother and Baby Home has also been located...

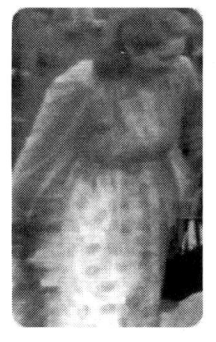

MY MOTHER

KITTY CLANCY

CONTENTS

- FOREWORD 5
- PREFACE 6
- **CHAPTER 1** 7
  - THE BEGINNING 7
  - SAINT PATRICK'S 9
  - SAINT PHILOMENA'S 13
- **CHAPTER 2** 18
  - 'BOARDING OUT' 18
- **CHAPTER 3** 29
  - SAINT JOSEPHS 29
- **CHAPTER 4** 39
  - ROAD TO FREEDOM 39
- **CHAPTER 5** 46
  - ARMY DAYS 46
- **CHAPTER 6** 56
  - BEST TIME EVER 56
- **CHAPTER 7** 65
  - CIVILIAN LIFE AND SCOUTING 65
- **CHAPTER 8** 75
  - THE ROAD TO MAKING OUT 75
- **CHAPTER 9** 84
  - COMMUNITY 84
- **CHAPTER 10** 97
  - BACK IN TIME 97
- **CHAPTER 11** 104
  - THE PRISON WORSE THAN JAIL 104
- **CHAPTER 12** 117
  - THE FINAL STRAW 117
- **CHAPTER 13** 126
  - TRIPS 126
- **CHAPTER 14** 134
  - MY HEART - MY FUTURE 134
- **CHAPTER 15** 139
  - THE CREDIT UNION YEARS 139
- **CHAPTER 16** 149
  - ANCESTRY A NEW ADVENTURE 149
- **CHAPTER 17** 166
  - UPSTAIRS DOWNSTAIRS AND COVID 19 166

THE ADVENTURES OF SEAMUS 176
ANTS AT ARMS LENGH 182
Arm's Length Management Organisation (ALMO).. 182
BROTHER RYAN REPORT 184
REFERENCE I.. 185
REFERENCE II 186
REFERENCE III 191
REFERENCES IV... 197
REFERENCE V 200
REFERENCE VI... 204
REFERENCE VII 205
ACKNOWLEDGEMENTS.. 206

FOREWORD

I met James Clancy some years ago and was intrigued by both his gentle demeanour and his cheerful attitude, his sense of humour was self-evident, he came across as a thoroughly nice man, he is!

It wasn't until I got together with Jim to assist him in writing this book about his life, his ancestry, and his search for love and more significantly to reveal to his children the true and very real story of his life that I uncovered a deeply moving portrayal of a life begot by sadness.

Revelations of truth about his childhood, his mother, a family he did not know he had, his close relationship with his brother Sean, his failed marriage, and the torment he has endured… his ill-health and the sad deaths within his family and close friends and his absolute yearning for love from his children and grandchildren, this is a life that no decent man should ever have had to endure or deserve, especially Jim Clancy.

But you would certainly wonder after reading this book, how this man still carries himself with composure and dignity throughout these years, despite all that he has endured in his life.

He believes now that he can at last right the wrongs that life has bestowed upon him and rekindle his rightful alliance with his children and grandchildren so then he may go to his 'long sleep' with peace and contentment, something at the very least he richly deserves. It is a pleasure to know this man and truly hope he realises his dream and succeeds in everything he wishes.

Bernard Wilds

PREFACE

For the first time in my life, I could go back to the beginning. I had tried several times in the late '60s to search and understand my upbringing but without success. However, I later discovered a plethora of information concerning my mother, my brother's Sean and Oliver, my childhood, and my extended family. The vaccination programmes we endured, my birthplace, and the circumstances in which my upbringing took me into two different institutions before my own boarding (fostering) out to the Greene's family in Newtown Park Blackrock.

Having told my wife Maria (whom I married in '82) of my previous attempts and astonishingly her needs and desire for my medical history, she embarked on her own quest regarding my background, consequently generating a long disparaging period in my life. I think now telling her was the biggest mistake of my life. Not all searches end up in loving reunions of newfound siblings and relatives. This searching by my wife had become an obsession, and later the revelations became a weapon that slowly gnawed away like rats at the timbers of an old house, crumbling our relationship over time to the detriment of our family life.

Proceeds of my book will go to Credit Union Futures, retaining young talent and equipping them with the relevant skills and knowledge to manage credit unions. To relieve poverty and need amongst communities in the United Kingdom and throughout the World which need such relief within the practise of "People Helping People".

James Clancy

CHAPTER 1
THE BEGINNING

The Home Saint Patrick's, the Navan Road Dublin.

> *Saint Patrick's was by far the largest of the nine Mother and Baby homes in terms of the numbers who passed through and approximately 9,000 to 12,000 women and girls went through its doors. It was also a massive 'holding centre' for unaccompanied babies and children. It was certified for 149 beds for unmarried mothers and 560 cots/beds for babies and children. Babies and children who passed away were sent for burial to the national Angel's Plot in Glasnevin Cemetery in north Dublin. There are two periods when exact numbers of deaths are known and rough estimates from other years would indicate that at least 2,000 and possibly above 3,000 babies and children died during its 81 years of operation on the Navan Road. There were several factors involved in this change of attitude including the appointment of Doctor James Deeny as the state's Chief Medical Officer. After a serious confrontation with the Sacred Heart nuns in 'Bessboro, Mother and Baby home in Cork, Dr Deeny courageously closed their M&B Home and thereby effectively laid down the law to all the M&B homes including Saint Patrick's.*
>
> *Thanks to Paul Redmond © 2015 FaceBook extract from A brief history of Saint Patrick's Mother and baby home.*

This is a view by two friends decades later visiting a school friend in Saint Patrick's I discovered on a Facebook group of St Patrick's: -

'It was a huge, scary-looking building, up a long driveway. Our sense of excitement died immediately, replaced by terror. We walked up and rang the bell. The big heavy door opened widely and we could see inside, into a very spacious hall. I'll never forget the shock of seeing many girls my age walking around, all very pregnant. The only women we knew expecting babies were old women like our mothers, never girls our age. It was like seeing a class of fifth years all enormous

.

These are my perceptions of a mother in pain! Leading to my entry to the world. Written after knowledge garnered from comments and statements made by individuals over the years.

Second Son
Spring 1950 got a new love nice lad I thought
He was smart a soldier boy
It was not long he had his wicked way
Up a back alley as the picture did play
Never! Never! Oh! Never did I see him again?
The next month it happened I'd missed and panicked
Oh! No, I'm pregnant what have I done?
God! Can't tell mum
When I showed the Master said
"Go up to the Nuns don't stick around
You've lost your job
The nuns! The nuns! they'll sort you out"
No fags, no snout, no drinks, no chocs
The sisters of charity they know how to mock
"Pray for your soul and that of your unborn"
These nuns are cruel
I can't go on, I'll do a runner
Just before dawn
Got as Far as the driveway, stopped at the lodge
"Get back you harlot! till the child is born"
The months drag past Prayers every day
Holy mass in the morning God! At the break of day
The angelus three times a day Jesus! I'm a saint
The Navan Road Saint Patrick's home
God! What a laugh More like prison
Then a maternity home for wayward single mums
Can't tell anyone especially not Dad
Or my sick Mum got to go it alone
Bring to this world My second born
April sixteen 1951 waters broke
Is it Girl or boy? not bothered
It's the nuns to sort it all out'
God the pain is awful It's worse than the first
With them nuns down in Cork Oh! God
I didn't say that! Oh God not a word!
The baby is born It's another boy Oh dear! Oh dear!
I bore a baby a baby boy
Who I know I could never, never bring up?' '
May god bless my second son' JC

SAINT PATRICK'S

Conception in the summer of 1950! What was the circumstance of conception! Lust! Love! Ignorant fumble! Willing participation! or NOT! The little tadpole oblivious of the outside world swimming to the fertile egg! Growing with no thought! When did awareness dawn! How was the news perceived in the mind! To whom did it concerns! Work Abode! Did the world know! How to cope! Seven months till the move to the Navan Road!

It all began when my expectant Mother, Kitty Clancy was admitted to Saint Patrick's home on the sixteenth of March 1951. Accounts offered by many witnesses spoke of common experiences during stays in mother and baby homes. Those who had known what to expect in terms of the natural process of birth, was the complete absence of pain medication. Believed to be deliberate since their birth pains were represented by some nuns as punishment and retribution by God for becoming pregnant out of wedlock.

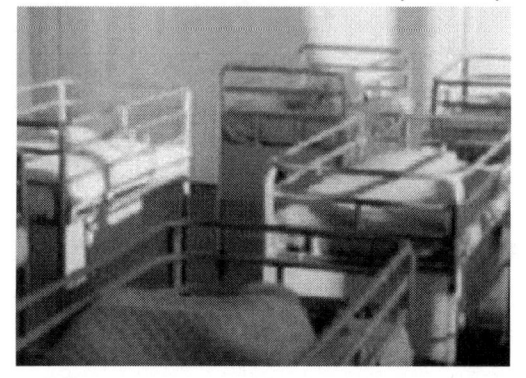

Records stated a normal delivery of a fine healthy boy 'James Clancy,' born 16th of April 1951, 7lb 7 ounces at 8 pm to Kitty Clancy in the mother and baby unit in Saint Patrick's Mother and Baby home, Navan Road Co. Dublin. Name of baby's father not given. Registered number 1538, Health service number 115810. Smallpox vaccination 6th May 1951, the triple vaccination one in February and the other two in March that same year. The medical records also state a discharging ear and chickenpox. Baptised at Saint Patrick's home on 21st April 1951. See Reference I

Kitty Clancy was discharged from the Home on 8th July 1952 (Unaware, I was dismayed at a revelation that mother was with me in the institution for all of 14 months.)

Into a new world,
Nineteen fifty-two,
Fourteen months old,
Ma was gone,
Did they find her some work?
I'm left alone to live in Saint Patrick's home,
The Navan Road,
What is to happen to that baby boy
No room for the baby son? JC

I was there till 1955 however, my mother returned in early 1953 as a repeat offender to have Sean in April of that year. The unit was run by the sisters of the daughters of Saint Vincent de Paul (later called the daughters of Charity). Charity in name but not always in nature.

The recurring thought over the years is the picture of all the babies including myself sat rocking affected my confidence and a belief that I was perhaps not a normal person and short of ability. It took until late into life many, many years to dispel those thoughts. I do recall being in a cot in the middle of lots of other cots when I was ill.

As a little boy, out of the high chair and in a huge playroom. I recall there was a sewing room at one end with glass panels and you could see girls working away on machines with a nun watching over. I have a recollection of a Christmas spent with a man and a woman at the bottom of the Sugar Loaf Mountain in County Wicklow. What I remember is the struggle I had with the trek up the mountain with the man on Christmas day. It was cold and there was a white frost on the hard ground. I only remember that one episode with them. I am thinking now that it might be possible that these people were prospective parents. It was an arrangement by the nuns as a matter of course. I certainly don't know what age I was but I was very small. It was obvious that adoption never took place. I must have been two or three at the time. Mother by this time must have returned as a repeat offender to have Sean? *(A term used for girls having a second child out of marriage)* Not much memory of this time in my life except tears and sadness.

The following is part of a post that I found in January 2020 which was picked up from *Mari Tallow Steed* one of the administers of Adoption Rights

Alliance. From my point of view, what to bear in mind to those that read this book is we as babies can reflect to the time in these homes and have mixed recollections of our time spent there.

- Magdalene Laundries and mother-baby homes were NOT the same things. They were operated by differing religious orders under different principles. Mother-baby homes were accredited and (supposedly) inspected by the State. They received capitation grants for each mother and child, in addition to whatever donations or "administrative fees" they collected from prospective adopters.
- Magdalene Laundries were privately run, never inspected, or accredited by the State, and women performed commercial work (laundry, sewing, etc.) there. All mother-baby homes had laundries, of course, and mothers may have worked in them, in addition to farm work, kitchen, minding babies, wet-nursing, sewing or any other number of assignments they may have been given.
- In many cases, mothers would have expressed an interest in doing a certain job, e.g., if they came from a farming background, they might have asked to be assigned to the farms or gardens.
- Private fee-paying patients in mother-baby homes would not be expected to "do a job" and were generally permitted to leave once their baby was born.
- Mothers from Saint Patrick's Navan Road were sent out to work in the Donnybrook Laundry.
- No babies were born in Magdalene Laundries, unless in some rare case a woman concealed a pregnancy while in the Laundry and suffered some emergency childbirth scenario. If that was the case, she would likely have been shifted to a mother-baby home.
- Of course, mothers were certainly sent on to Laundries from the homes, if they had no family/place to return to or were "repeat offenders" (multiple non-marital births). Transfers to Laundries from mother-baby homes were in the 3-5% range.

Prime Time award winning programme which uncovered the use of infants in Mother and Baby homes for medical research in the post war race to modify vaccines for polio, diphtheria, tetanus, and measles. During the making of the programme the journalists also discovered that the remains of hundreds of infants who died in these homes had been sent for anatomical dissection, without parental consent, until the 1960s. 'Anatomy of a Scandal' was an investigation into medical research and vaccine trials carried out on children and babies in Mother & Baby homes and other institutions until 1973.

Please take time to view and understand on behalf of those who never got the chance:

<u>*Prime Time Anatomy of a Scandal*</u>

Memories of a Baby from Birth
Sat rocking in a chair all of us babies sat in a square rocking ourselves
Does anyone care about us strapped in these huge high chairs? Did we do wrong?
Rocking! Rocking! all day long. No one to cuddles us, is something wrong?
Some say we're Mongol, the future will tell us it's Down Syndrome. Did we do wrong?
We all look alike, there are no mirrors, with our big round eyes,
bawling and shouting each of us for Ma' But she never comes
we are left with the nuns. Did we do wrong [JC]

SAINT PHILOMENA'S

Front Entrance to Saint Philomena's

Sent to Saint Philomena's Home,
For girls and boys, yes, a home for children,
Whose Ma has gone? JC

> *"In 1933 the nuns opened Saint Philomena's Home in Stillorgan in south County Dublin. It was "certified in pursuance of the Pauper Children (Ireland) Act 1889, for the reception of boys and girls who may be eligible to be sent to certified schools. "In this case "certified school" means "Industrial School". Saint Philomena's was used almost exclusively for children who were too old for the nursery wards in Saint Patrick's, but too young for Industrial Schools. It was later split when the boys were transferred to Saint Theresa's in nearby Blackrock. When the children reached the ages of 7 or 8, girls were normally transferred to Lakeland's Industrial School in Sandy mount while the boys were sent to the notorious Artane Industrial School on Dublin's northside."*

My date of discharge from Saint Patrick's 10/1/1955 at three years and near nine months of age. Address to where the child went from there: - Saint Philomena's Home, Stillorgan, Co Dublin.

I do remember going to the big boys play hall but do not recall the journey from Saint Patrick's home. In this hall, I am holding hands with Sister Philomena walking up and down the hall as her headdresses with wings wafting like a white swan wanting to take flight. In the afternoon, we would sit on the benches around facing the walls and go to sleep. At this stage, I do not remember much more of what we did with free time.

In baby class, I remember the toy town display, Sister Philomena encouraging play with the display and in the sand, she was great and I thought kind.

I also moved to another classroom during this time. It must have been First Infant Class. During that time but no memory really except being required to sleep for a time in the afternoon at our desks. Lunchtimes we would form a long queue to the refectory, walking along one wall on the way and then along the other wall on the way back to class. Usually, we would be passing another chain of pupils coming in the opposite direction and on their way to the refectory. At playtime, there were girls in another part of the orphanage and they had their play yard and we had ours. We could see them over the two walls that separated the yards by a path that I think led to the chapel. We all went to chapel each day together with the girls on the right and us boys on the left in the chapel, the nuns were up three or four steps at the back looking down on us all along with some grown-ups.

When I returned in later years the girls had all gone? So, girls were at Saint Philomena's in the '50s and between 1957 and 1960s when I returned, they were moved to Saint Teresa's Blackrock.

As far as I can remember I had a visit once or twice from a woman who through the freedom of information I discovered had contributed to my upkeep.

I was taken from the main hall by layperson a long way through long glass corridors and came to what appeared to be a dark tunnel of timber panelling into a very large square hall, with two bright red gigantic mahogany doors. Turning the brass rose door handle took the use of two hands. The door hanging on four brass hinges opened ever so quietly with the help of my whole body pulling in earnest.

On entry, two figures of men as black as ebony made of shiny black marble glared towards the entrance as they held the mantelpiece like Atlas or Sampson holding up the pillars of the temple. Mosaic tiles bevelled back on two sides and from the mantelpiece above towards what should have been a rip-roaring turf fire. Enormous windows were spaced evenly down the right-hand wall and across the bottom of the room all supporting oak-panelled shutters facing out to the manicured lawns and gravel drive.

Inside the lower part of the walls was forested with a line of moulded panelling enticing the imagination of small children to look for secret panels or tunnels for escape. A long highly polished dark oak table rounded at the four corners dominated the centre of the room. The legs were of the type seen supporting a grand piano on a well-polished parquet floor. A line of straight back chairs matching the table stood in regimental fashion on both sides of the table.

At the far end a woman sat with long black curly hair, she was talking to a baby who was crawling around on the floor. I remember more about the room than I do about those few visits. I was sometimes given a few sweets and some pennies, which the nuns looked after until we would go for the Sunday walk in the afternoon. *I supposed she was my mother*, but I never found out even when I met her in 1990 for the first time and only time in my life as a child and adult.

At some stage during these mixed memories of Philomena's I was moved up to the big lads' hall and started to do some jobs like sweeping the hall with a wide brush up and down. Another task was polishing the floor.

With a spoon we would splat the orange polish onto the floor making a game of the task and then spreading it in with cloths as skates. A result of our skating in the polish was falling about incurring the wrath of whoever was in charge at the time. After a while when the polish had dried, we were then required to buff it up with a block that was at the end of a long handle. The floor was lovely and shiny from the sweat that poured from our heads.

When I look back, the sight of us little boys buffing it was quite comical as we were very young and cumbersome and it was hard graft. The afternoons after school were taken up with learning Irish dancing and singing. We would have quieter games to play when the laypeople were in charge, as the nuns went off every afternoon to pray. One of the years I was learning the cords of the song "the Gipsy Rover" on a guitar and a duet of "Count your Blessings" for a fund-raising show I think we're on RTE. I do not recall how the show went, as I never thought of the guitar any further after it, but I was required to carry on the Irish dancing. Another memory was of sitting behind the big slide crying my eyes out and avoiding any contact with anyone hoping not to be seen.

I can't remember why, but I do recall others behind the big curtain at the other end playing music and dancing. I think I had done something very wrong and may have been punished. I know I sat behind the slide many times hiding, and only one lad called Nigel Mike coming to talk to me and giving me comics to read. It was my great escape in those days looking at the pictures in comics and dreaming.

Nigel Mike remains in my thoughts to this day as the friend who introduced me to the escape of picture gazing and eventually reading. I will always be grateful for the adventures through reading and developed a vivid imagination in dealing with the complexities of life. Nigel, a quiet boy, was taller than me with jet black hair and of a dark complexion.

There were trips each year with small groups of us to the seaside sponsored by the Saint Vincent De-Paul Society. I recall one such trip, which was for a week where we stayed in a big house and each nun had their very own private room next to the children's dormitory.

We had visited the circus one day here in Bray and we were sitting in the front row and the clowns came rather close to us. They were frightening. I still had the same experience when with my children visiting the circus on Cronkeyshaw common in Rochdale, in the late 1980s.

One night with a chap called Fahy we were wandering around the house, looking for adventure heading to the kitchen so we thought. On the way, we spotted Sister Veronica's door slightly ajar, so I being very brave moved forward towards the door bidding Fahy follow me, but he scurried back to the dormitory whilst I continued to creep into the room. Well, I was shocked to see a lady lying fast asleep in the bed with a head of black hair curled up like a ball. I went to look closer and closer and ended up bumping into a chair by the bed. Rosary beads fell to the floor, the lady began to move and turned to look at the chair it was Sister. I ran for my life back to the dormitory and jumped into bed with my heart going ten to the dozen. "I always thought they were different and married to GOD. She had not got her cornet on. I never saw a nun's head before in my life.

It was hard to believe she was like any other lady with short black hair and more to the point she was human.

The TV programme 'Dr Who version of the cat-like aliens wearing the cornet of the nuns always takes me back to that story, which is quite scary.

Another scary experience as a trusted big lad, I was going down to the Carmelites Convent with some other lad to collect the Holy Communion wafers for the mass. It was a long walk down the driveway with massive fields on both sides. So sometimes weather permitting we would explore the fields, the small woods in the centre of the field on the right and search in the trees for bird's nest. On arrival at the Carmelites, we would enter this small side door, which was a fraction of a bigger door part of what looked like a castle wall. Entry into a small confessional box room was quite frightening as it was dimly lit. To get served you rang a bell a small hatch would slide open and out would come a box with the wafers, and not a word was spoken.

CHAPTER 2
'BOARDING OUT'

> *Bernard and I after going over the reference documents forensically time and time again the following revelations come to light. We both discover in some of the letters by the officials from the board of assistance:*
>
> - *Frankie is also a boarded-out child.*
>
> - *That the Minister of health grants permission under article 10 of the boarding out of children regulations 1954.*
>
> - *That Doctor Brady on in his medical report; states I am a frail child but with a good mother this should improve.*
>
> - *That Ma Greene collected for both Sean and I, a clothing Voucher of £8.*
>
> - *What I find fascinating is Ma signs the contract as does grandad DUNN. Where was DA Greene when all this was going on?*
>
> - *Ma Greene requested a birth certificate for me to attend school.*
>
> - *A social worker is assigned and the local church is informed of our boarding out. The nuns are quick of the mark informing the Rathdown board of assistance that the boarding out is chargeable to them.*
>
> - *1957 Mary Greene had selected Sean and I for Boarding out. See References II*

On December 31st winding my way around the lean-to glass corridors, with one of the nuns holding my hand and the cornet on her head wafting away like a bird in flight. Her rosary beads the size of marbles hanging from her waist clicking as we rushed to where she was leading me. It was a strange feeling as we progressed from the brightness of the frozen snow-covered glass suddenly entering the narrow low dark passage at an obtuse right angle where we thought the nuns lived. To the left a narrow winding staircase I suspect led to the nuns' rooms, past the staircase was the massive entrance to the building which led to the big parlour where we the children would meet any of our visitors if we had any.

This was the same parlour with the two black men holding up the fireplace when I met the dark-haired women who gave me sweets and pennies. (Mother or Ma Greene?)

On the way to the parlour, I looked back behind us and saw one of the girls who had helped the nuns look after the smaller children, following behind us with a small boy, both were shivering with the cold.

They too came into the parlour but the girl after being thanked by the nun left. The Nun introduced me and the other boy to a huge big man with long bushy sideburns that continued under his nose like someone out of Pickwick papers. Two girls were with him the taller with a rock and roll frock and the other smaller girl a little older than me had a lollipop in her hand. The nun introduced us as the Clancy brothers that was the first time that I had known I had a brother Sean. I was now over six years old. We were told we were to go and live with the Greene's in Newtown Park.

Dymphna Greene our new big sister and cousin Helen Greene climbed up on the back of a milk float and Sean and I were lifted on by our new Uncle, "Jimmy" and we sat with our backs to the back of the driver's cabin. The journey was quite bumpy and I did not understand what was going on. We stayed at Uncle Jimmy's and Aunt Rita's till later that night. Da (Jack) Greene came to call for us along with Frankie Greene, a new brother (a year younger than me) and we were taken to 28 Castle Byrne Park to Ma Greene and Grandad Charles Dunn.

We woke on the 1st of January 1958 in a gigantic bed. From memory, we three lads slept at one end and the girls at the other for a few days or weeks, but the girls were given a room of their own when Grandad Dunn moved downstairs after Da had got a commode from work. During this period, we were known as Jimmy Greene and Sean Greene.

I went to Carysfort Mercy convent school in Blackrock Dublin, with Frankie after the Christmas holidays, my new big sister Dymphna leading the way, she was nearly finished with school. She got a job in a chewing gum factory at 14 on leaving that school following my first year.

Uncle Leo Dunn and his wife visited on Sundays when we first got there. Leo was Ma Greene's brother and they had no children as far as we were aware and even if they did, we never saw them. I remember a Sister Natty in my class.

She was very old with a weather-beaten face; she wore a different headdress that also covered all her head except the face and had the look of a penguin.

The walk home from school with Frankie was nearly always broken up with Dymphna having a fag outside and she would nearly always give us some chewing gum from the factory. The factory later in the '60s became the "Rael brook shirt factory" and the labels would read, "Made in England". I found that strange as Ireland was free of England and independent.

Ma Greene was given a clothing allowance; the request being made to the Board of Assistance on the 2nd of April 1958. This was made for my first holy communion in Saint John the Baptist on the 7th of May 1958 and I was all togged out in my new clothes and communion rosette. It was the custom in those days to call at the houses on the way home to be given coins with the promise to pray for the people. I'm sure my cousin Helen was with me and after we went to their house for tea.

Sean in September of 1958 started to go to the baby class at the convent and Frankie and I would take him until I moved to Saint John the Baptist national school. Frankie and Sean made their first holy communion together they got on better together but for some reason, Frankie and I did not. I suppose it was because I was the eldest lad and he may have felt I had taken his place. He was still the same when I returned in *1968* but that's another tale for later.

We had another big Sister Patsy she went off to England a short while after we arrived not sure what year. Patsy when she would come home from England would bring all sorts of chocolate bars we never heard of. On one of her trips back home she took me to see Tom Thumb at the pictures for my birthday.' I recall the picture was very frightening and I would dream all about the villains counting out the money. ("One for you and two for me") and so on.

Da (Jack) Greene was a very quiet man on a Friday night after work on pay day at about six o clocks we would meet him coming off the bus and he would have with him bags of chips wrapped up in newspaper and give us boys one to share and two old pence each. Once he brought a sword from work to show us and other old Knick Knacks over the years. He built a den in the garden for us from old wardrobes and doors he also got from where he worked in the auction rooms in Blackrock.

Once Ma Greene was angry with me because I was out all day with friends in Dún Laoghaire, a suburban seaside town in County Dublin. I was down by the fishing trawlers trying to nick the fish that was dropped by the trawlermen when they were unloading the boats. We got some and I took one home thinking it would keep me out of trouble, but no Ma was still mad, put the fish on a plate and put it in the meat cupboard in the pantry and said wait till your father gets home? I went to bed waiting for Da to come home and when he did, I saw him from the window stripping a length of hedge of its leaves ready to chastise me. He came up the stairs and told me to bend over Frankie and Sean was still downstairs listening to the radio with Grandad Dunn. I heard a swish as Da said this will teach you a lesson "yell" and he hit the mattress with such a belt that some of the horse's hairs and dust went up in the air. Da did it four times and said get into bed now and don't come down till morning. I found out Ma and Da had the fish for their tea that very night. I recall we called it a flatfish. I suppose it was *'plaice.'*

Grandad Charles Dunn on Ma Greene's side of the family had a hole in his nose on the right side and he was great with the stories about how it happened and stories about *Banshee's* and the like. There was no television, but around the fire in the front room, there was storytelling always by Grandad Dunn, I can still picture him with a pipe in his mouth sucking away sometimes with no tobacco.

We once took the train with all the family including Patsy and Peter, her boyfriend from England to Belfast it was because you could buy stuff there that you could not get in Dublin. Later, I went to Saint John the Baptist National School, Blackrock. This was a square stone building with high-grassed banks at the back and the right-hand side of the building. The front entrance was gated and flat with the concrete ground, the bike sheds and toilets were on the left-hand side of the building. It was a single-story building with only four classrooms and an office.

Four masters taught at the school. One Master I remember was known as the Tullamore Jew man (in later life I realised it was 'DEW MAN') and another was Mr Cuncannon he was bald and lanky. At the National school, I began to learn to be an altar boy. I enjoyed serving mass and became very good with the Latin of the mass learning it off by heart. I was allowed out of school to do special masses for Birth's marriages and deaths. And earned a few bobs in the process. I also served for the bishop when he ordained a local lad to the priesthood, Peter J Slevin. I loved the processions we did around Saint Teresa's convent, benediction, and the litanies of so many saints. I was a bit of a saint at times and was always having to go to confession for my transgressions. It was when at this school, I had an after-school job at Nelly Soden's Flower and Veg shop in Blackrock opposite where Da worked Adams auctioneers on the back road into Dún Laoghaire. It was great, I learned to do wreaths for funerals, use the big scales and weights for weighing potatoes, the smaller scales and weights for fruit and veg. When I got my first pay, I bought '20 Gold flake' for Ma thinking it would please her. At the bus stop, I thought better of it and thought she would go mad so I dumped a few in the garden behind the bus stop where a plaque on the house was acclaimed to be the residence once of, I think James Joyce. When I got home, I told Ma I found these fags on the bus. (The things we remember) I once met Robin Hood the actor Richard Greene at the auction rooms and thought he was my cousin as uncle Jimmy had a son Richard living in Manchester who I only met once in the late '50s.

I only remember one Christmas at the Greene's where we received some worn dinky toys a neighbour Dennis who had a hunch back brought them round. Some money belonging to Frankie, which he claims he was saving, had been hidden under the lino in the hall near the cloakroom. This had gone missing and Sean and I got the blame so Frankie that Christmas had got a brand-new truck with a white cab, black tyres, and blue tail boards with 9 pigs on the back. (It bugged me well into adult life). (Daft I know) We must have had more toys over the time we were with the Greene's. One of my many trips to the local shop for milk or bread in the dark was wearing my cowboy suit, especially the hat. Casting a fearsome shadow of myself with a gun and holster to avoid robbers or *banshee's* jumping out and attacking me. Once or twice, I had a fright and dropped the messages and ran all the way home and lost the change which got me in more bother.

'Forty coats' a tramp, who periodically would visit all the houses on the estate if he was doing well would sit on the grassed roundabout and all us children from around would gather and listen to his stories.

Salespeople at different times of the year would deliver free product samples to houses on the estate. Sometimes we helped and it was the first time I had seen cornflakes in small packets and got some for our hideout in the tall grass. Dymphna and John Cole, her boyfriend and future husband took us several times on the very long bus ride to the Dublin Zoo during the school holidays.

The family of O'Connor's arrived at Castle Byrne Park and were moving into number 40 across the common and we got friendly with them and helped them to move in Sean was great friends with Liam and I ended up being friends with the brothers too.

There were many great adventures in those early years at the Greene's. Fires in Arnot's with the gang at Robin Hood's den cooking the potatoes we had dug up from the nun's Saint Teresa's field and eating raw turnips. Then there were the battles with the Merrion Park gang led by the Slevin family. There were 14 children in the family and they were the leaders of that estate. Building a mud hut with sods and rocks, watering the sods so that all would bind together and a Greene sack for the entrance. This was built at the top of the long grass below a line of derelict cottages, this is where the *Banshee*'s lived and only came out at night.

We were told never to pick a comb up off the ground, as it was likely to belong to a *banshee* and she would haunt you forever if you did. Beyond the cottages were some cracking orchards which from time to time we took the liberty of reducing the need of the owners to toil away picking for themselves. In Avoca, we found a secret tunnel that led to the big house. The people in there had a phone and someone had the idea we could listen to conversations with tin cans on a piece of string tied to the phone wire above the holly tree at the exit of the tunnel. We convinced ourselves it worked and even got better results with thin wire borrowed from someone's fence. The mud hut as well as being an Aladdin's cave was a great hideout as it looked like a little hill of grass roof and all. One of our favourite past times was hunting in orchards for whatever was available regardless of the danger of being bitten by a dog or caught by big people. Once after climbing a pear tree that was tied back to a high stonewall, I was attacked by a swarm of bees and was stung head to foot. I ran all the way home and Ma Greene stuck me in the bath with some calamine and washed me all over and then put something on all the stings. Well, that put an end to that kind of venture, as basically, I became a devout coward. However, that was not the case with my little brother Sean who got into more trouble than was good for us all. One such escapade was on a motorbike after a crash when he gashed his leg open and sustained damage to his head the scars stayed with him for life.

Concerns continued to rise by neighbours whilst we were with the Greene's. We would go missing and have meals in other peoples' houses. Sean getting told off for accepting shoes and clothes from the neighbours. This gave the impression of neglect and created further concerns that we were not being cared for properly by the Greene's. Sean known as Duck by his friends when we were with the Greene's would go off with the gipsies that periodically throughout the year would visit the area and he would be riding their ponies visiting their camp. He did love being with them and he had great fun even continuing to ride motorbikes, which he fell off and got on again and again.

1960 came and Patsy was having to get married in England to Peter and they were all going to the wedding in Coventry and Sean and I was to return to Saint Philomena's for a while as Aunt Rita could not manage the three lads and her daughter for more than a day, so she would have Frankie. Patsy previously came home a couple of times with her boyfriend Peter Cole who was in the English army (ordnance corps). He was very tall and thin and spoke with a funny accent. He had to remove his hat and duck as he entered a room, I was never sure what he was saying. It was then that they were intending to get married and move to Peterborough in England. They came back a few times and Patsy had a baby girl and called her Susan. Frankie, Sean, and I bought her a few presents and a nappy, plastic pants, and baby talcum powder. Before the birth of Susan after returning from Sunday mass in Blackrock, at breakfast I received a crack across the face for suggesting she had done dirty things and that was why her belly was sticking out. During some of this time, we stayed at my cousin Helen's or went back to the home in Stillorgan. Uncle Jimmy, Helen's Da had a red handprint on his left wrist and claimed it was when the devil grabbed him. It did look like it was burnt. It happened after Grandad Dunn had passed away. Uncle Jimmy Greene let me help him with his milk rounds during the school holidays, Saturday mornings and in the evenings, he would let me collect the money from some of the houses. It was good fun and he gave me some pennies for helping. Sometimes Frankie and Sean would join in too.

When twins from up the road had died, we were made to attend their wake. We went in to say a prayer for them, they were never well and had some condition that no one knew about. The house was packed and all the men were drinking. Both lads were laid out in best suits on the bed downstairs. The women sat around the bed offering the rosary and pushing us forward to touch the twins saying, "they won't bite you." I must say, I avoided passing that house for quite some time.

The Greene's household had become very difficult, trying to establish what was happening and the eventual reasons for our return to Saint Philomena's again and again. There is a letter on the 1st of March by the board of assistance indicating a request for the removal of the Clancy children. So, the road to getting 'shut off' had already begun.

It was in April 1960 when the letters written to the Board of assistance began our return to the home. It appears the letter allegedly written by DA requesting for them to take Sean back as they can't cope with it and that I am a good boy. (See letter dated 13th April 1960). Agnes McCarthy is recommended because Mrs Greene's is unwilling to continue caring for the child that both children be transferred to a suitable foster home. (Letter dated the 29th April 1960.) This came about after complaints received from neighbours and a subsequent investigation made regarding the care of Sean and me by a Miss A. McCarthy c/o Cumberland Hotel Westland Row, Dublin. This was our social worker, as I learned much later in life. I can recall where the complaints may have come from and can still picture both houses where these had more than likely come from. Both were considered on the estate as above the rest living in the area and were both stuck up and nosey. Anyway, we stayed a bit longer because the following month I was rushed to hospital with suspected Meningitis which turned out to be influenza. *Note that the hospital has my name as James Greene.*

The period of fostering was very mixed and, in some ways, I was glad to get back to the children's home. Even at a young age I thought it was more about money and retaining a decent sized house for their family. Having said that I do not regret my time with the Greene's. At least we knew about another kind of life other than the home. I returned time and time over most of my life, the last being in 2003 after Dymphna passed away with cancer a very sad time a year after Sean had passed away.

We walked it for the last time in around 1962 from Castle Byrne Park back to Philomena's in Stillorgan. I remember pretending to hide under the bed before setting off, also on the way running in front and hiding in some new houses that were being built on the left-hand side of the road well away from the footpath. We eventually arrived at the back lane to the grounds of Philomena's and there we stayed not knowing the future, as I felt too old for the place. Philomena's had changed when we returned in early 1960's, it had become an all-boys place. The Nuns seemed bossier and a lot more women adults around. Once a few of us, a cousin of the Greene's and my friend Nigel Mike were playing cricket near rosary time we were called to rosary to line up by the girl in charge. We refused to go. I don't recall who was the ringleader.

We finished the game and then presumed the girl in charge who must have reported why we were late for the rosary. Therefore, it was some weeks before punishment was given for the incident. The use of a hurling stick is what I remember in the bathroom. A nun dished this out, with a lot of talk about being a child of the devil. As far as I can remember I was the only one punished for the incident but others may have followed later. I remember Sister Veronica and Sister Catherine as the nuns about in that period but do not recall who gave out the punishment and could not say it was either of them. I did for a long time think that I was evil.

The smell of Jay's fluid always brings back bath time and that scrubbing brush. Three baths in a row, three in each bath and beyond three rows of us naked boys queuing for the ritual of the weekly bath on a Saturday afternoon. One in and one out water either reheated or changed every so often." Cleaning both body and soul". Sister Carmel is the only Teacher I remember when at school in this period. She used to read the newspaper, the Express, whilst we the class got on with filling our copybooks with writing our name in Irish and English hundreds of times. Then at a certain time every morning, she would read I'm sure it was Rupert the bear. She used to use a hurling stick handle on the palms of her hands when dishing out punishment. There was a Sister Ursula but have no idea where she fits in. I have always thought that the Nuns were harder than the Christian Brothers!

Dymphna visited a few times until she went back to England. Mrs O'Connor from number 40 Castle Byrne Park used to visit us at Saint Philomena's with her Children and give us money. I later heard she tried to foster me on my own but was not allowed. When we moved to Tralee, she continued to send underwear and presents to Sean and me. With half a dozen children of her own, it was a very kind thing to do. I always tried to maintain contact till she died in 1991. I do send a Christmas card sometimes to her only daughter 'Drina. Patrick the husband was a TV aerial erector and had some greyhounds along with his sons he would take us to the races in his van on many a Saturday. So, life with the Greene's was quite normal for that period in Blackrock and there are fond memories.

Two days before my 8th birthday and 2 years four months since we arrived at the Greene's house Da Greene apparently wrote to have the Clancy children removed. Apparently, Sean was a handful, I on the other hand was a good lad and Mrs McCarthy who was required to do a report said we Clancy's must stay together. While letters were toing and froing between the authorities as to what to do with Sean and I, a fright went up and I was rushed to Cherry Orchard hospital with suspected meningitis. (Maria would love to have known this) It turned out to be flu. I was in Hospital for a 'long few weeks,' *'note hand written notes have my name as Greene??'* In June that year we remain under constant supervision by Mrs Agnes McCarthy as order by the powers that be from the Rathdown Board of assistance. This seems to have carried on till June 1962 where what I remember as the yoyo effect of back and forth to Philomena's began for various reasons.

By January 1963 Ma has learned how to type, hence her next letter requesting help to acquire 33 Castlebyrne Park as it has more space because where Da and Frankie are now is not big enough, although that is never mentioned in any of the letters over these years? Next time Ma reverts to a handwritten letter in March after alleging a visit to see us at the home or was it just me? As she would like me to make my conformation in Blackrock?? Heck, she was given permission to collect me? May was when she was informed, I had made the confirmation and to contact Mr McGuirk to discuss the future of Sean and myself. See Reference III. May 15th seems to be the date when the final decision was made to send us to the other end of the country, was it Ma Greene's or our fault, something none of us will ever know. But life goes on regardless. It was my visit in 1968 to 62 Brookfield places I learn that Ma Greene had left Da for Patsy's and Dymphna's

Father-in-law in Saltash Cornwall. I suppose with all these documents it reveals things we never knew.

Contact over the years has been lost as families move on but my intention after the pandemic is to try and see them all in the not-too-distant future as there is still a fondness for those years.

Dunn's Greens and Cole, early Family

CHAPTER 3
SAINT JOSEPHS

Saint Joseph's Industrial School Tralee, Co Kerry.

I am pretty sure we moved to Saint Joseph's in August 1963, however records state November a registered place of detention, where a small number of boys were also sent there for criminal offences, such as larceny, house-breaking and malicious damage.

Sean and I with three other lads Anthony Brown, Tony Calgary, and a lad from Poland or Ukraine, 'he had a round face and slightly tanned skin. I cannot remember his name but in my mind's eye, I can still picture all three who made the journey but no recollections of them after we arrived at Saint Joseph's.

Brother Ryan a big stout man with a severe-looking face picked us all up in a black taxi. At the station we were directed into a compartment on the train to Tralee. I remember him telling us about all the animals we could play with, and the trades we could learn. I can still picture the faces of those other lads on that train full of excitement. I sat back and just listened, wondering what the truth would be?

In the first week when we got there in the schoolyard, I recall the lads asking what class we would be in, we were advised "don't go in Brother Murphy's, as he is mad." Believe me, he was… as I later found out. I bravely got myself into the class above him and was ok until the brother who was elderly took ill, and I ended up in Murphy's class anyway. When Brother Ryan brought a can of sweets to the class, Brother Murphy would send to the carpenter's shop for a hammer and take a few sweets from the can and smash them with the hammer and give all in the class a bit of the sweet. You would never see that can of sweets again until another arrived from Brother Ryan.

It was thought he was selling them down in the town? Of course, there was no evidence to support this theory. One daft thing I can't forget is he used to iron his newspapers in class and then dry them on the radiators before reading them.

In the Easter holidays the following year that I had arrived at Saint Joseph's, there was a fire in Brother Murphy's classroom. I had a cowboy book and had lit a few pages with matches and threw it in the only top open sash window of his classroom, in the hope that we would not have to go back into his class for the next term. I hid in the toilet block until the alarm went off. Upon investigation, it was believed that the boiler had been exceptionally high and overheating that day. With his newspapers on the radiators that is what was believed caused the fire and not as I feared my 'Cowboy book.' It was not a major fire and was soon put out by the duty brother in the yard and some of the big lads. Brother Murphy was not pleased with the verdict and over the month questioned a lot of the lads until he found an answer he was looking for. On the way to the chapel up the winding first four steps past the lower dormitory for the six o'clock rosary, I was grabbed by the hair and taken into the lower dormitory.

There he was standing with his leather strap swinging back and forth as he let go of me snarling shouting, you're the devil that started the fire. I was leathered from one end of the dormitory to the other till I admitted my involvement, I found out that my friend Clark snitched on me. Brother Murphy never took the matter any further; he was satisfied enough with getting what he perceived as the truth. (I can still picture that cowboy annual to this day it had no pictures)

As new arrivals to Saint Joseph's Industrial school, Brother Roberts an old man would select boys to bath in a bathroom under the passageway between Brother Price's class and the kitchen. He loved to rub soap all over your body and round your private parts. He was very quiet and gentle. His face wore a big satisfactory smile all over his face when performing this ritual. It was not like at Philomena's when bathing us in Jay's fluid the nuns used a coarse-scrubbing brush that was like those used for doing the floors. With Brother Roberts, it was gentle touching which was a bit of a shock to me at the time. It 'would appear that all the new boys' went through that ritual with him. The showers on a Saturday were a very different experience. We would parade up outside the entrance to what was the shower block which also housed the laundry at the end of a long corridor, on the right to that entrance was another corridor to the left with the carpenter shop across from there was the shoemaker's further down was the darning room and then the Tailors shop leading to the exit of the buildings outside world.

Each Saturday as we were ready and according to age be marched into the shower room. We then would stand by a long-slatted bench the length of the room opposite one of the open showers, then in 'order to strip off and at the brother's command walk to the showers to wash, and then some of the brothers who were on shower duty would parade up and down asking you to turn around so that they could eye you up and down on the pretence of "have you washed properly" it was embarrassing.

Brother Manning was the brother who enjoyed stripping my clothes off in a dormitory next to the upstairs toilets near the chapel and putting on the new underclothes sent by Mrs O' Connor of Castle Byrne Park. The underwear eventually never returned after several week's washes and that was the best thing to happen. In his classroom whether fourth or fifth if you were sitting at the back he would sit on your desk and put his hand down your pants and try to get around to your front and play with your private parts. This he did quite often whilst in his class.

During the time in Brother Price's class, I recall him telling the class that love was about touching and feeling each other and we should not feel bad about this. I do not recall him ever touching me. He had his favourites like Brother Manning did. In that year in Brother Price class, I was looking forward to doing my exams, I had a liking for history, Irish, and sums, but I took ill and went into Saint Catherine's Hospital Tralee with pains in my side. I received two needles in my side and I never did get to know what was wrong with me. It was in Saint Catherine's hospital, daily a priest who visited the ward would put his hand down the sheets asking where the pain was and find his way to fiddle with my vitals. A boy in the next bed observed this, and after asking me about it told his parents. He was moved to somewhere else, but no reason was given. I had missed my exams and never got to do them. On another occasion when working in the kitchen the young new Brother in charge would get me to go up a ladder to get some pots and he would slide his hand up my pants and play. I did have the courage to object by refusing and calling him a 'knacker out loud. He had dark rim glasses and was quite tall and not much older than some of the big lads in the place.

The toilets in the yard, about 10 in a row, were up to several steps in an open building to the left of the only way out to the farm and the outside world. Half doors on the toilet newspaper hung on a nail. Sometimes brothers from time to time would check the toilets and look over to see who was in there. That was Brother Murphy's usual stunt looking for Knacker's the term used for boys playing in toilets with boys. In winter, you would not stop there very long. It was here in one of the toilets I often thought of my real mother, sometimes in tears as to where she was. I always had doubts about Sean being my brother despite him fighting my battles, tackling big lads ferociously. We were so different. Asked a lot of questions about my parents by other boys when I came up with the idea that they were killed in a car crash to avoid being called a bastard.

Left to the toilets was the shelter from the rain, and above was the big hall where band practice took place. I learned to play the trumpet from Mr Kantalin. He had long light reddish hair with his head tilted forward to the left as if he had a permanent creek in his neck. His picture remains in my mind's eye. In later years' films on a Saturday afternoon were shown and plays performed in the big hall at certain times of the year. I remember Ali Baba and the forty thieves as one play and the Mikado were another.

The hall had steep concrete steps leading up and a rough timber floor leading up to the stage. Four round pillars held up the hall on the open yard side and next to the last pillar was the tuck shop. Opened once a week on a Sunday if you had money. It was just a small room and the counter display was close to the entrance so not too many could get in at once. Next to the tuck shop was a narrow gate leading to the baker's shop and beyond that the graveyard where the 'brothers were buried. There was a rumour that a boy was buried after a 'brother had beaten him up. I never fancied going down there hence I never tried being a baker.

I did in the early stages spend time on the farm and had the daily task of milking a cow, I called her Star. I also fed the pigs and mucked out. I can't remember the brothers name he hardly spoke and when he did it was with a grunt. In later life, I could see him as a relation to one of the Addams family bent over like he had a hump on his back. After I had done some of the farming tasks like milking and mucking out the cowshed, I would serve mass before breakfast. I also sometimes served mass over at the convent across the main road from Saint Joseph's, a home for girls. I cannot remember the name but it was open to the public and the nuns with their black habits had their part with gates across where they sat away from the people. Throughout the summer most of the lads would be out saving the hay and collecting in the harvest and the reward was big pots of tea and buttered bread being brought to the fields for us all to have at lunchtime. It was hard graft and backbreaking work. Around late September it was potato picking time. Everyone did this by hand as the tractor went along the drills kicking up the potatoes for us to pick into buckets and take to the mounds and bury in straw creating three or four rows of covered potatoes.

At three o clock, each day after class, and Saturday mornings, we had to learn a trade. I eventually had had try at all the others like shoemakers, hairdressing, tailors, and laundry ending up in the carpenter's shop during the latter end of my years at Saint Joseph's. The scar on the left side of my stomach was caused by my refusal to let Richard Dunn have the tool I was using at the woodturning lathe during my time in the carpenter shop. I was being stubborn, as he continued to threaten me that if I did not give it to him… Well, the shock of him stabbing me left me dumbstruck, and I confessed that it was an accident at first but Dennis Breen the layman who taught us in the carpenter's shop, saw the incident and reported Richard to Brother Crowe, who stitched me up and Richard was sent to Saint Joseph's Danghan, which was supposed to be worse than Saint Josephs in Tralee we did accept that this was possible.

During the years, there was a time for play and from the films seen on a Saturday, we explored and used our imagination in what was a desolate place between the four walls. I was an avid reader of comics when I could get hold of them and enjoyed handball the only sport I ever really liked. I suppose that's why I also liked squash, when I joined the army in a similar game but with rackets.

Time at Saint Joseph's was challenging to say the least, keeping ahead of the lads that fancied their chances with you in more ways than one. One or two following in the ways of the Christian brothers!! I was once cornered in the confessional on the priest side by a big lad called Cyril who fondled me up and down until I had ejaculated for the first time in my life, that was in the first month at Saint Joseph's. Brother Manning also achieved the same with his wandering hand at the back of the classroom over the year I was in his class.

I leave it to the reader as to what effect this had on me for the rest of my life, as it is not easy to write about even now. One of my tasks in the refectory and kitchen was to hang out the cloth used to wipe down the tables on a rack that was screwed to a wall of the small storeroom. In the middle of the courtyard leading to the dormitories and chapel. I hung the cloth, we called them rubbers and later I discovered a window to the storeroom was unlocked. I climbed in to investigate it was obvious it was hardly ever used. It became my getaway place for thinking, crying, peace and quiet. Often when I am hanging the rubbers out, I would make up songs and sing them at the top of my voice upsetting the brothers who were praying in the chapel.

The area was a great echo chamber as it was closed in on all four sides but for a wide opening under the corridor to the dormitories on the left as you went to the chapel and dormitories. This is one of the history songs I made up after many history lessons, most of them forgotten now. I loved to sing especially in that area knowing it could irritate the brothers praying always after lunchtime and teatime. This is to the tune of "Deep in the Canadian Woods"

Here's the O'Donnell's and O'Neill's from Antrim and Tyrone
O'er Hill and glen, and bog they marched
To fight the English foe
and err the do not crush them, lord…
We'll give them a helping hand
We'll go out and give them a helping hand
to crush the English foe.

Crush the English foe
Crush the English foe
We'll go out and give them a helping hand
to crush the English foe. ᴶᶜ

When I was in the carpenter's shop, I had the privilege of going into town with the handcart to collect timber from McCowan's Timberyard on many an occasion, sometimes as many as three times a week in the school holidays. On one occasion, I would go through the market and pick up women's clothes for a planned mass breakout. It was around the time of a big feast day when extra food was becoming the norm with minerals and buns and biscuits and the tables set for a party. All the clothes were ready for those who were going on the run and stored in the special storeroom, which later I had found a key for. It was considered the best time to go, as the 'brothers would be busy drinking and less aware of lads being missing or storing food and drink for the journey. So, we all thought? On our way from the refectory Brother Price and another new Brother were waiting in the yard and calling on certain lads to go into Brother Price's classroom.

It was mostly those who were doing a runner and one or two who were not aware of the plan. In the classroom, we were told to empty our pockets and of course, the goodies were on full display. This alone was a major offence and required some form of punishment.

But when Price asked where the clothes were hidden, we knew the cat was out of the bag. Some pleaded guilty and got a couple of straps across their hands by one brother and told them to go to the dormitory. After that Price informed the other Brother, he was no longer required and to check on the dormitories. He took great pleasure in using the strap on our bare bottoms and then rubbing them with his hand after. Who told on us is a mystery to this day, he got the key to my storeroom and found all the clothes and other stuff gathered for the breakout?

My brother Sean was not involved in any of my escapades but on occasions, as I had given up fighting, he would storm in and fight on my behalf like a little terrier. Sean did not make friends easily. He did however make friends with one lad Victor Teahan as far as I can remember.

My recollection of both Sean and the other lads who came from Philomena's with me is virtually non-existent as there were a lot of boys and none were in the same dorm as me. So, I suppose we drifted apart although Sean was in the band learning piccolo, he was good at it and obviously we were on band trips together.

Brother Price ruled the roost at Saint Joseph's and was a nasty piece of work. Apart from his wandering hands over some of us boys, however, Brother Manning to the annoyance of Brother Price did try to improve things at Saint Joseph's. He started bringing better food, started films, and eventually got a television for the 'play hall. He arrived at Saint Joseph's in late sixty-three replacing another 'brother taking charge of the band with Mr Kantalin and 5th Class. He developed links with the local Saint Vincent De Paul society and got help from them for various ventures. One was the new band uniform made in the tailors' shop where Sean worked. This allowed the band to play at local events around Co Kerry.

He taught us how to march and got the bandmaster Mr Kantalin to teach us a lot of the standard Irish marching songs and some classics. Over the years, we did the Rose of Tralee festival.

Played carols whilst marching around the town at Christmas pulling a pair of reindeer, and another year a rocket made from corrugated cardboard for Santa Claus. We played throughout the year at various other places around County Kerry. Banna Strand is one I remember where Roger Casement was to meet some German boats to unload weapons for Irish freedom. I revisited the memorial site in 2009 with Eileen O'Connell who I stay with when I'm in Inch, Annascaul where Sean was brought up from the age of 14.

People will draw their own conclusions on my time at St Josephs'? I can honestly say I never would have written about those years if I had not recounted to the police, in the presence of solicitor's, the psychiatrist, and the redress board because of the accusations of my eldest. *It broke my heart!!*

Sean and I in School yard and Brother Ryan and Brother Manning & Brother from Kitchen.

> *St Joseph's was one of the institutions to be investigated by Ireland's COMMISSION TO INQUIRE INTO CHILD ABUSE launched in 1999. After reviewing extensive evidence and the testimonies of former inmates, the Commission concluded that over a period from the 1940 to 1970:*
>
> - *Physical abuse was systemic and pervasive. It only became a matter of concern when it threatened the interests of the Congregation but not when it endangered boys.*
>
> - *Predatory physical and sexual behaviour by boys on other boys was a prominent feature of life in the Institution and a source of anxiety and pain for younger boys.*
>
> - *Trade training offered limited opportunities and became irrelevant and obsolete over the years.*

CHAPTER 4
ROAD TO FREEDOM

It was Christmas 1967 I was given the present of my first razor, a sure indication I was now a big lad and, on my way to reaching the big sixteen. So, it was around my sixteenth birthday, I was called to the clothing storeroom first thing that Sunday morning after mass by Brother Ryan the Superior to get new clothes, and I knew the day had come I was getting out of Saint Joseph's for good. It was an itchy suit with a long pants shirt and tie. I felt both special and afraid, not sure what would lie ahead. It was my first day of freedom, and I paced up and down the yard till I was sent for. I'm sure I spoke to Sean and my friends Johnny Foran from Castleisland and Sean Burke who was from Tallagh in Dublin all promising to keep in touch somehow. I was called to Brother Ryan's office and saw Nicky Foran on the way obviously to see Johnny his brother. At the office, I sat outside whilst this man was speaking to Brother Ryan and having a cup of tea. After about half an hour they came out and Brother Ryan said I was to go with Mr Walsh, so I followed him out the front door down the pathway to a Morris minor and got in the back as instructed. No one spoke a word to me. I did not know what was going to happen. A few minutes later Nicky got in the front passenger seat and off we went. No one spoke till we got to our first stop. We all piled out and I was introduced to some, I later learned relatives of Mrs Walsh. I declined anything that was offered and could only think if this is where I am staying.

Next, it was Bushmount Farm, same again the same thoughts ("am I to be a Farmer's boy") same refusals of tea and food where the pigs wandered in and out of the big back kitchen. This was the Walsh's farm and it was a big huge farmhouse and a long driveway leading to the back door. I was getting more and more concerned as to what was going on and was dying for a pee. Mrs Walsh the old woman of the house, could see my predicament and guided me towards the loo, told me not to worry and all will be fine in my new home. It was now six o'clock and time for the Angelus. The clock struck and they all in the house including Nick knelt in front of the chair they were sat on and the 'Mother led the angelus. Well, I never! I did not recall doing anything like this at the Greene's or the O'Connor's or any other house except the Nuns and Brothers.

After this Mr Walsh collected some meat and we were back in the car again and on our way. My head is now spinning and I still don't know where I am going to live. We stop at another farm I learn later it's the Kelleher farm and Mrs Walsh's other sister Eilish. 'Eilish remains in my mind as a very gentle and extremely nice person. Eggs were collected here after another lot of conversations, which I could not follow, and continue to leave me in doubt as to what was going to happen to me. Finally, we ended up at La Sallette Countess Road Killarney, a detached house with a front and long back garden and the railway beyond. Nick unloaded the car, whilst Mr Walsh and I sat in the front room, wondering if this my final resting place.

Helen, Mrs Walsh gave me some supper and showed me to bed upstairs after I had eaten. So, to bed, I went sharing a room with Nicky Foran who had yet to speak to me. I tried speaking to him but he answered only in words of one syllable.

I still did not know what was to happen to me or what my future was. Since Nick was already established with this family and working for them, I thought I must be moving on to somewhere else in the morning. We were woken at 7am by Mr Walsh and went to breakfast down in the kitchen. Mr Walsh put eggs in the kettle, made a pot of tea when it was boiled and gave Nick and Myself an egg each with some toast. I was then given a biscuit tin to put some sandwiches, a jar of tea leaves, sugar and milk and a mug in and tied up with a strap. I still did not know what I was going to do. We got in the Morris Minor and off we went Nick was dropped off at this half-built house and we carried on out the Muck Russ Road. Later I was introduced to a painter Jim McCarthy and put to painting the plinth of a house in the middle of nowhere and I still had my new suit on. Jim was a nice man and he is the one who put me wise as to what was happening to me. He cleaned some of the paint off my clothes and he lent me some overalls to wear. I was with him for a couple of weeks and did eventually get around to other sites and tasks in the building trade. I went to the local Tech once a week learning joinery and roofing. Paddy Loughnan taught me plastering skills, I learnt a lot about the building trade.

Paddy after he had applied the plaster, he went to the pub to drink loads of Guinness, came back then floated off what he had done to a smooth finish. Dan Murphy the stonemason showed me how to build walls and about stonework. Mickey Callahan was the joiner I was with for a while and my first encounter was for him to pull his vitals' out and asking me to get hold, I said no and all he could do was laugh and say you are a "mono boy" so it should be no problem.

I was not with him for long, and he later apologised after a month or two when he was due to get married. One day after lunch I arrived on a site on the New Road in Killarney it was an extension to a guesthouse. The men had dug out a 15-foot hole for the foundations. Old Paddy Russell was in the bottom spreading and setting the concrete. His son young Paddy was mixing and barrowing the stuff into the hole on a nine-inch plank with ease. Booming with confidence and 'feeling, I could do anything I too grabbed hold of a barrow full of concrete and proceeded to follow what young Paddy Russell did. Old Paddy Russell spotted me and yelled out, 'I fell overhead, with the wheelbarrow following me down. I would have been killed but for Old Paddy Russell pushing the barrow away from me with his arm. I was well shaken up and Paddy's arm was swelling. We were sent to Mrs Walsh to patch us up as she was an ex-matron in one of the London hospitals in her young days. No doubt old Paddy Russell gave me my first lesson in Health and Safety and the tale has been a reminder of its importance over many years as a Supervisor at RMBC and later RBH and as Shop Steward. We worked 6 days a week. I got a full board and five shillings a week in my hand. Sundays for the first few months were spent doing the same trip around the farms to pick up produce as before and praying the rosary at Bushmount.

Once there was a celebration when the Kelleher's had a bathroom installed with all the mod cons inside a toilet, bath, and sink. There were visitors from all over. Some months later, I was receiving a wage packet in a brown envelope, as Nick had received regularly. It was about four or five pounds. Eventually, I was not required to do the Sunday trips and would look after Martin the baby son whilst Nick would look after Padraig who was two years older. I looked back and we really did not get on in any way, not even trying for the boy's sake. Nick would commandeer the radio for the top 40 on the radio and I would never get a look in. I think we both feared what we knew about each other being favoured by Brothers Price and Manning and it is relayed to others in this outside world. It had a tremendous effect on Nick what happened in the home and he never learned to deal with it and I believe he suffered all his adult life as a result. On occasions, before I had my bike, I borrowed Nicks, which never pleased him, whenever I needed to go to my weekly confession at the friary on Saturday afternoon.

One time, Nick got mad when I got back and his bike was punctured. I could not fix it because I did not know where the puncture kit was. I was napping in my bed in the outhouse; we slept in there during the holiday season, as the main house was being used as a guesthouse. He came in fists flying and Mrs Walsh heard and came to investigate, she chucked a bucket of water over us. Scolded both of us and we were to go back to confession when we got dried. I said the Friary will be closed and she told us to go to the Cathedral. The Walsh's never understood why Nick and I could not get on. I think Nick resented my presents as a *second* apprentice, because I knew he was one of Brother Price's favourites. Nick was an excellent Carpenter Joiner, and was an apprentice to an old man with a weather-beaten face called Pedergast who was a heavy drinker, an alcoholic and bad-tempered.

Nick was influenced in my view by this man in many ways and his later life took to the drink which did him no good.

On Saturdays, if the men were not working Nick and I would go to the detached house that the Walsh's were building as a future guest house opposite the "madhouse" in Killarney. Well looking back now, it was comical we were inserting 'nine bye twos' for first-floor joists and we did quite a few without saying a word to each other. The wall had only been extended up to first-floor window height that Friday, and the mortar had not hardened yet. My part was to insert the joists in the gap for the joist, which was slid to me on the previous joist laid which had yet to be secured. I was trying to balance on the unfixed joist and put the next one in the gap when Nick pushed it with a grunt, I dropped it and began to fall and I grabbed hold of the wall, the concrete blocks came away and down I went eight feet below landing on a load of cosy rap.

I was lucky yet again. Nick and I were kept apart on building sites for the rest of my time there.

Breda Ash, Helen's sister, came to live at La Sallette. Breda and myself would sit for all hours of the night talking after being to the dance in the Townhall or at the Glen Eagles and the subject of myself and Nick would come up frequently as a matter of great concern to the Walsh's'. Nothing was ever resolved and even on my return many times throughout the 45 years the wonders of our behaviour never ceased to amaze them.

Helen sadly passed away in Christmas 2014, *a sad loss to all*. Without her support in allowing me to join the British army and her interest in my welfare, I could have ended up like so many from the home.

I went to the tech in Killarney as part of my apprenticeship and my knowledge of the woodworking machines in the Carpenters shop at Saint Joseph's stood me in good stead with the teachers. John Burke ended up working and living in a hotel in Killarney and we met up again and eventually with Johnny Foran who was also living and working out at the Europa Hotel a few miles out of Killarney. We got together often as we could and when I bought my only racing bike, I would ride out to the Europa when Johnny could not make it to town on some Saturdays and Sundays.

In 1968 I tried to join the Irish army after a visit to see Sean at Saint Joseph's. Dan Hoolahan, one of my band friends, Sean told me was joining the Irish army in Dublin he was a trombone player and a friend. I never got any answers from the Irish army. John Burke was going back to Dublin to see his mum and brother and he would be going to England to a Hotel in Buckingham. Johnny Foran was being sent for training to Germany so I too got itchy feet and wanted to go back to music. So later that year the 'News of The World' had come out in Ireland and I found an advert for the British army, I applied.

The lads at work could not understand why I would want to do such a thing as they had all fled England to avoid national service. I did not understand what they were on about and eventually plucked up the courage to tell Mrs Walsh who was very concerned and left the matter on hold till there was a reply from the army in Belfast. The Walsh's eventually gave their consent and I received a travel warrant to go to Belfast.

On the day of departure, the Walsh's all came to the station to see me off. I felt a little sad, excited, and afraid of what lay ahead of me. On the train, I wondered if I had time to visit the Greene's but remembered they had left Castlebyrne Park from a letter Mrs O' Connor had sent when I was in Saint Josephs. On arrival in Dublin, I had to get to another Station and catch another train to take me north of the border so visiting Dublin and exploring was out of the question. Interestingly on the walk to the other station I had a trail of children begging to carry my case with the chant "please Mister can I carry your case" I had become a MISTER?

A report by Brother Ryan (See Reference VI) the Superior, he was not a brother we would see or talk to at all except when he would issue clothing from the storeroom between Brother Manning's class and Brother Price's. I find it ridiculous he could file a report dated 1964 about me when I had according to records been only there 7 months and not yet attended V class?

I never lost touch with the Walsh's of La Sallette and hear via email on how the family is doing from Elma who supplied the photos in this chapter.

La Sallete. The Walsh's with Nicky Foran and Myself 1967/8
Helen and Patrick Walsh, their two boys Padrig and Martin and Mary from next door And the Morris minor that brought me to a new world!

CHAPTER 5
ARMY DAYS

I stayed overnight in Belfast at the S.A.F.F.A home and went to the career's office in the morning. The Recruiting Sergeant was expecting me, and asked several questions and then sat me down for a test. He told me I could join the Queens Royal Irish Hussars as a signalman. I said I wanted to be joining a band like in the advert I had seen. He said my English test was not good enough and I did not argue. I then did my attestation:

> *I, James Clancy, swear by Almighty God, that I will be faithful to Her Majesty Queen Elizabeth II, her heirs and successors, and that I will as in duty bound, honestly and faithfully, defend Her Majesty, her heirs and successors in person, crown and dignity, against all enemies and will observe and obey all orders of Her Majesty, her heirs and successors and the Generals and Officers set over me".*

I took this oath on the 7th of August 1968. The Sergeant then gave me the bible to keep and it is still in my possession. Another travel warrant was issued and I was on board a ship to England the following day and a train to Catterick in Yorkshire for basic training. The army was an escape route that contrasted the old life of the homes which in many cases had been chaotic. Full of all kinds of physical, mental suffering, with fear and hopelessness in equal measure dominating thoughts about the future.

I must admit I was gobsmacked to see so many churches on the journey to Catterick. I was led to believe that England was a pagan country and the sight of churches left me baffled. On the train, an old lady sat beside me and we got chatting. I told her all about my life and hopes for the future. I remember her telling me she knew the bandmaster Stan Patch and that when I got to Catterick she insisted I should tell them about joining the band. This lady who was in conversation with me as far as Richmond and telling me about what to expect here in England made the journey very short. I did as she said and a sergeant from an Irish regiment got me a chance to play for the bandmaster in the next barracks where the Kings regiment was stationed.

In the meantime, there were lots of other lads arriving and we were all lined up as a new intake given uniforms etc and marched to our dormitories.

It was 10 am the next day and I was called out by the Irish sergeant and taken to the Bandmaster. He got the first trumpet part to "John Philip Sousa's "The Thunderer" for me to play and as luck would have it, I knew by heart having played it hundreds of times around County Kerry. He reported to the regiment and I was accepted that very day to be a bandsman it was a miracle.

I have never talked about that lady on the train till now and often wondered over many years if I had fallen asleep and dreamt the whole thing, but what happened in Catterick did happen and Stan Patch was expecting a very good trumpeter.

I got through the basic training, which consisted of marching, twice throwing a grenade of which I kept a pin for many years, orienteering in Wales, taking part in mock battles were one or two took it for real.

I can never forget this big huge paratrooper near killed me with his rifle (SLR). I'd be dead if I had not ducked so quickly. Something you just can't forget he was an animal and a bully. His face and body size are still embedded in my brain to this day with his gold like curly blond hair. I became a beater for some of the time whilst at Catterick during the shooting season it was a new experience that I thought was cruel and for snobs. I was still a good catholic lad and knelt by my bed to say morning and night prayers and was habitually ridiculed for it. When on one exercise we were paraded outside a church in some village and being the only Roman Catholic I was to mark time outside the church. It was the first time I was referred to as a Roman Catholic. I objected and said I wanted to go to the church and the corporal had no objections. Another surprise it was just like the mass the only difference was parishioners had wine as well as the communion another eye-opener confirming without doubt that England was Christian.

One of my last tests at Catterick was to wear a respirator, go into one of the Nissen huts, run around and take the respirator off and run around again and out the door. After my weeks of basic training was over and we had the obligatory pass out parade I took my first trip on leave back to Ireland. I had two weeks leave and had a travel warrant back to Killarney. Still, in uniform, I got the train to Holyhead and the boat to Dún Laoghaire arriving at 7:15 am still in full uniform.

I caught a bus to Blackrock and sat upstairs knowing I would be able to see clearly in advance from memory where to get off. Well, this woman was making comments about me being on the bus in British army uniform, red cap, and all. I honestly did not think I was in the wrong, but said nothing and got off at my stop. On arrival at 62 Brookfield Terrace knocked on the door and was dragged in by John Cole asking if I was mad arriving in uniform? He explained why it was so stupid and would you believe it at lunchtime we went for a drink in the Three Tunn Inn and who was there, but the woman from the bus who was a distant relative of Ma Greene. Dymphna explained who I was, and offered her a glass of stout, and all was forgiven.

It was a great feeling to be reconnecting with my foster siblings, Dymphna, and John with their first-born Kevin for it was the first chance in 1968 I had since 'leaving Saint Josephs.' John and Dymphna started with Kevin, firstborn early 60's followed by Jacky then Patricia who came to my wedding with her mum in August '82 staying at O'Mahony's. Next came Tracy and then Denise. It seemed every time I came home on leave, they had another baby. Tracy was two or three when on one of those leaves and as normal with all the children on the couch Uncle Jim would tell them a story.

Well, Tracey in her excitement grabbed hold of my hair and off it came, the fright it gave her was terrible. she screamed the house down. You see, in those days it was advisable not to have a squaddies' hairstyle so I wore a wig in those early days with the troubles up North. Mary another child was fostered at some stage before Emma who was born in the '90s as a shock on the scene.

Dymphna was diagnosed with cancer when I last visited in 2003 it was before then John and herself with Emma moved to Carlow and out of Dublin.

When I first went back in late 1968 and stayed with Dymphna, I was given my first ring, a Claddagh gold ring. It was engraved with love, of course, it got too small for my finger and then lost. I have got myself a new one since which I hope my son Treacle-Pud can have it when I achieve the 'Long Sleep.'

The 'Walsh's of Killarney' were still my legal guardians till I was twenty-one so on all my trips to Ireland I would have a travel warrant to Killarney to visit and stay with them. I also visited Saint Joseph's in Tralee to see my brother Sean but he was released to a tailor somewhere in the county in 1967. I spoke to one of the brothers about it with no joy for an address. There were not many lads left in the place and it was said that the place was going to close and lads were being moved to other homes. It was Breda Ash just by chance uncovered what had happened to Sean from a relative also called Ash who she was visiting in Inch.

Not long after I had left Saint Joseph's, people were taking some of the boys for days out and weekends and Sean was one of the lads who had this privilege. He had been out on visits a few times with the O'Connell's of Inch, Annascaul. But some months later he was boarded out to a tailor in Firies. The tailor's wife recently had a baby and he required a trainee for the business and Sean was there also to babysit when required. It was months later when the O'Connell's found out, and Kathleen, one of the girls found him in Firies and brought him back to Inch. Mr and Mrs O'Connell sent him to Milltown school and later he went on to Cork University before ending up in London. Breda Ash took me to see them and Sean on my next visit back to Killarney in the summer of '69. Breda was a mentor and a confidant to me over those early years and I could talk to her about anything she was great and a wise young owl.

After Basic Training in Catterick, it was off to Bovington, a garrison home to the Armoured Corps in Dorset the other end of the country. The garrison is a training Centre for soldiers of the Royal Armoured Corps and trade training for the Household Cavalry Regiments as well as other armoured units. My time at Bovington was an education in a lot of ways, into the world of girls, drink, and music. I was cajoled to take a girl out who worked as a waitress in the sergeant's mess. She was taller than me, slim with black curly hair and I took her to the tank museum just outside the camp.

As suggested by the lads at the time the best place to kiss was in an enclosure displaying the battle of somewhere, I no longer remember. Well, it was a disaster I tried kissing her, there was a scream and off she darted out of the enclosure down between the old tanks and guns on display like a *Banshee* who had lost her comb. 'Me green as ever, was perplexed as to what I had done that was so awful.' The lads had a great laugh at my expense pointing out that her dad was a sergeant and I could be in big trouble if he ever found out I tried to kiss his daughter. That ended my brush with girls for the foreseeable future regardless of the lads egging me on.

My first introduction to drink was at a Christmas celebration where all band members with their wives in 1968 took part. It was my first outing with so many people and we were having a Christmas meal with all the trimmings. The waiters offered wine red or white to all on my table and I declined. I explained to the lads on my table I had taken the pledge not to drink till I was twenty-one. Surprisingly they accepted this and Tony McCurry a clarinet player from Belfast in Northern Ireland offered me orange juice via the waiter and I stayed on that all night. The following morning, I could not understand why I was so ill. Another introduction was the apple juice I had not heard of before that was offered to me later to discover it was scrumpy and that too made me sick. That was the time Willy Muir jumped from the second story of the women's royal army core block to escape the officer checking the block after he was cavorting with one of the girls. He received no injuries. He was a bit crazy and loved to fight and see blood. He was a great friend of the drummer Chad McClintock also from Northern Ireland. Weymouth was not far from Bovington and at times we went there for beach parties and some would go skinny-dipping in the sea. I was too shy for that caper.

In 1969, we took part in the Royal Tournament at Earls court. Not long after I arrived at the band and a surprise music inspection there was a change of Bandmaster from Stanley Patch to P.B. Smith a flautist and composer who had previously served in the Coldstream Guards and the Ordnance Corps (Passed away in Germany in February 2018). 'Taffy Helps became Band Sergeant Major and on rehearsals in Aldershot for the Royal Tournament he wanted members of the band to tell him what they thought about him. He went to each in turn and got the most favourable response except for some of us young ones. I told him he was a little Hitler so we never got on and it put paid to me ever getting a promotion whilst he was band sergeant-major. We toured around many parts of the south of England seaside resorts, concert halls and schools giving concerts. The best I remember was playing with the Bournemouth symphony orchestra performing the 1812 Overture, a fantastic experience. In that period, the band produced two long-playing records "In Martial Mood" and "QRIH in Concert"

One of my first outings abroad with the band was to Guernsey when I was playing the cymbals as my cornet playing was marred by my inability to read music. We toured some of the shops in Guernsey and I bought my first watch as I was told they were cheaper and if I wore it on my wrist, I would not have to pay tax when we got back to the mainland. The drink flowed on the way back on the ship and the sea was choppy and the BM was the worse for wear and later it was claimed someone had spiked his drink. We did several tours in Northern Ireland before the troubles.

These tours were called K.A.P.E Tours (keeping the army in the public eye). It was around this time the band was under consideration to be going on tour to Brazil, and I was required to get a British passport and so because of my circumstance's permission had to be sought again from the 'Walsh's in Killarney which was duly granted. The trip to Brazil never happened and no reason was given to my knowledge.

Queens Royal Irish Hussars

At some stage in '1970, I was the second choice to go to the royal military school of music Kneller Hall, a mansion in Whitton, in the London Borough of Richmond upon Thames. It housed the Royal Military School of Music, training musicians for the British Army's military bands. JGK who was the first choice to improve his clarinet playing and reading could not go because of dance band commitments.

Taffy Helps was not best pleased with the new bandmaster's suggestions, as JGK had joined up in May '68 in a response to an advert in the "Melody Maker" for a guitarist for the dance band. I was next in line as I had joined up in August '68 the place was offered to me but I needed to sign up for another three years. I had to seek permission from my guardians in Killarney and told them I would sign up for another six years. This would give me a pay rise and a chance to go to the school of music. They were very concerned and I had to give assurances that it was what I wanted. After several phone calls over a few months, they gave in and signed the relevant documents. JGK was my best mate in the band. He helped me with my music and was instrumental in discouraging the other young members from making a fool out of me. I went with him to his home in Rochdale some weekends and stayed at the Gale Inn on Whitworth Road many times whilst in the army and eventually living there in '74 when I came out. With his help over those years in the band, I soon got wise to the world.

On one of those trips to Rochdale, John and I dropped off at Chelmsford folk festival where the only group I can remember from then was 'the Strawbs. John found a group of musicians having a session at night where we settled and John played the guitar and me singing a few of the Dubliners and Clancy Brothers songs. It was that weekend I met somewhat most people called Jesus freaks. I spent some time with them chatting about life, religion, and the need for peace in the world. Well, the shock to see across from them, a tent lit up with a couple performing silhouettes on the canvas of the tent with noises emanating from the direction of panting and expletives, not for print.

I think it was the last couple of weeks in August of 1970 when JGK and I went to see "my folks in Ireland" (the Greene's) and to go out with the two girls we were writing to. My cousin Helen Greene and Jennifer Robinson were close friends and we were writing to them in the late 1960's. I had shown JGK a photo of Helen and some of the contents of the letters referred to, they being like John Lennon and Yoko Ono.

Helen introduced Jennifer to me, and from her letters, we longed to see and speak to each other in the flesh. The photo she had sent showed a beautiful long-haired blond, at 18 years of age wearing a white dress. (I had that photo for many years to come) She was living with her parents in some flats in Saint Anne's Square, opposite Saint John the Baptist Church, and the national school where I went some years before.

JGK and I after visiting my Da at 62 Brookfield Place spending the night, set off to see Helen and decided on a foursome. Well, we arrived at my aunty Rita's answering the front door without her wooden leg. I thought nothing of it as I was used to seeing this, but it was a shock to JGK as I had never mentioned it before to him. We followed her down the hall and into the dining room. Aunty Rita carried on into the kitchen and put her leg on and began to make a pot of tea. We sat there making idle conversation with Aunt Rita; but JGK had not a clue what was being said. I explained that Helen was at the dentist and would not be too long. As time was passing JGK was looking more and more concerned and soon Helen arrived home.

Well, the shock Helen had lost most of her teeth and those that were left were black as the ace of spades and with respect, she did look like a huge witch. The poor girl was mortified. I quickly suggested we call later as I promised to visit the 'O'Connor's further up the road and we would call back when Jennifer arrived at about 7pm. On our way, up the road, JG voiced his concerns and we agreed to avoid the foursome and go to the Purty Kitchen in Dún Laoghaire where there was some traditional Irish music. We later went to the Crawford hotel further up towards the railway station and met up with me Da, Dymphna, Patsy, John, and Peter Cole where there was more music. JGK got talking to some Spanish girls and I joined him not long after who should turn up but Helen and Jennifer. Jennifer Robinson my second love although I never saw her again, I retained a photo of her until Maria ripped it up in one of her bad tempers as I would not rise to whatever argument at the time in the late nineties.

One does not always need photos to remind oneself of love. JGK and I stole out of the place whispering to the family goodbye and took the Spanish girls to their hostel in Sandy mount on the bus and bade goodnight never to see them again. Later in the week, JGK returned to his hometown to see his family before being posted to Germany and I was later to attend the Royal Military School of Music Kneller Hall near Twickenham London on completion of my leave. This was one of the better times of my life. I made lots of new friends from different parts of the UK and the commonwealth all lovers of music.

After the first few weeks in September at Kneller Hall I received a letter telling me that JGK was AWOL (absent without leave), well it was hard to believe as I had left him in good spirits heading home to Rochdale at the ferry in Dún Laoghaire. I rang them as soon as possible to tell them I had no idea where he was or what had happened. The military police had been in touch and his mum and dad were beside themselves with worry. At the earliest opportunity, I spent a weekend in Rochdale explaining how JGK and I had spent the holiday in Ireland and I knew nothing of his intentions not to return to camp. Had he had an accident on the boat, was it tied in with the troubles in the North of Ireland? Why would he go missing? I later in life compiled a story involving my two-little people in the involvement of JGK's disappearance somewhere in the Wicklow mountains when telling tales to the Cub Scouts, I ran in the middle to late 70s. It was many months before a phone call from himself had relieved the pain of a missing son and friend. He returned home to the Gale Inn and eventually the army was informed and he was collected and sent to Colchester for six months.

Comrades in Music & Life's Education

CHAPTER 6
BEST TIME EVER

Today, just as in days long ago, there are little people amongst us, but unless you are special human you may never see one. See 'The Adventures of Seamus'

During my time at the school of music, I had great fun convincing fellow students about my two-little people. I was quite consistent in following my routine of opening the door for them to leave the dorm, laying out their beds at night before retiring myself and removing the clogs when they were away supposedly gone away to visit relatives. Most of the lads were not sure about me at all and one day someone decided to nick the clogs from under the bed and not return them. Well, I feigned a grief-stricken fortnight not going to cornet or piano lessons going to the pub over the wall and returning late. Eventually, I was in front of the student Bandmaster of B block who was required to discipline me and I broke down and told him what had happened. This had got out to the perpetrators and the clogs were back a few days later. Of course, I got extra guard duties but it was well worth it as most of the young students believed I had two leprechauns that would do my bidding.

It was sometime later that a chap Pugsey from the other block a stout clarinet player who would remind you of Billy Bunter admitted to returning the clogs and apologised not realising what trouble it would cause my little people and me. My suspicions lay with a great trombone player 'Dual Campbell, who was a mate of Pudsey and was in the same dorm and block as me. Some lads were into witchcraft and practised some of the rituals in the washroom on the first floor of our block.

The leader is a chap from a Scottish regiment who also claimed to have had the book of shadows. This chap had black curly hair, a skinny wiry body, and piercing eyes with a darkish yellow complexion.

It was funny how the student bandmaster explained how he interrupted one of the naked sessions breaking the spell by stepping into the circle marked with chalk on the floor.

There was a lot in the papers about witchcraft around the country at the time. I admit to being very wary of the subject and stayed clear of that group.

Professor Tulip was my piano teacher, an instrument enforced on me by our regimental bandmaster and one I simply could not grasp. The problem was I could not read the bass clef as it took all my time to read the treble clef. I missed a lot of lessons and got into trouble for it. I was going to be RTU'D (returned to unit), this would be a disgrace for the regiment so the bandmaster came from Germany possibly on leave, and I don't know how but I could continue at the school and give up the piano. I do not know to this day how I got away with it but as I explained to the other students my two-little people had a hand in sorting it all out for me. Professor Hudson was my cornet tutor and I had one-hour lessons with him when at times he would fall asleep. He was a very nice man ex guards and at times liked to tell stories.

I was surprised to receive an award of 'The Concise Oxford Dictionary of Music' for progress on the cornet dated 16th September 1971. He also gave me an old book on scales for Bb instruments both are still in my possession. It was at Kneller Hall that I had my first driving lessons; it was always in the early evenings. Patsy had sponsored my provisional driving licence at the time as she lived in Strafford-on Avon at the time with Peter Cole. He was an ex-guardsman and the lessons started ok with driving around the back streets of Whitton but on later occasions, we would stop outside a restaurant inviting me to dine with him there and then. This I wondered was not normal behaviour and I thought of those times in the home when a brother was being extra kind. I decided to seek advice from Cpl Bainbridge, a fellow cornet player who oversaw our section. He advised me to stay away as this chap had been accused of soliciting young soldiers from the school. The lessons stopped and it was not until I got back to the regiment that I attempted driving again.

Another first for me at the school was I made up the words to the music of the Kneller Hall regimental march, 'the Floral Dance' and a lot of the lads joined in when we were parading around the grounds.

If you want to do some bullshit
Then come to Kneller Hall
What with fatigues and muster parades
You'll have a ruddy ball
There's no PE, walks or runs
Just scrub-outs every night
Cleaning floors and window panes
More and more bull-shite
What fine musicians they will make us all
Well, that's what they do at Kneller Hall
Besides the music, there's drill and bull
But that's to keep life from getting dull. JC

One good friend at the school of music was from the Irish Rangers Brian Coulton invited me to Aldershot many a weekend to his Aunty Brennan. I built a great friendship with this family and on Friday Brian myself and the three Brennan brothers would all head to town to the local bars and clubs. After we left the school of Music and on one leave Brian got married to Teresa, a long-standing girlfriend from Northern Ireland and I was the best man in my full Hussar uniform. That was in Wiltshire where he was stationed.

The Bride and myself. Brian & Teresa

Years later Michael had a terrible accident and was severely disabled and with some brain damage, it was heart-breaking for all the family. I rang him on the spur of the moment one day in 2003 forgetting about the accident he had. I was glad that I rang him. He managed to tell me that his mother had just passed away, he was ok and coping well.

Back with the regimental band in Germany only a few weeks and I was in bother. I bought my first car from one of Robert's brothers for only 0.50 pfennig. It was a white Volkswagen beetle and I was learning to drive it on the regimental square when someone said look the regimental Sergeant Major is coming. "Put your foot down Jim" shouted JR and that was it I panicked and stalled the engine. We were all on a charge the following Monday.

All I can remember when double marching into the CO's Office was "welcome back to the regiment Clancy and next time I'm in the band room for a concert you will sing Danny boy for me" That was Colonel O'Rourke a Dublin man. I was very lucky and the band sergeant major was not best pleased so he had me scrubbing the long corridor on my hands and knees. All the tiles were cream and had grooves going in different directions. It took over a week to finish.

I did get to sing 'Danny boy' for the CO at Christmas that year in the band club. I kept the car for a while and took it on the tank tracks instead, eventually after a couple of knocks and scrapes giving it to one of the new bandsmen Ted Stocks, who was a mechanic and a lover of motor cars.

My 21st birthday in April 1972 was the same year when the twentieth Olympics games took place in August that year. The German Olympic beer mug which I still have is a reminder of the Israeli Olympic team members that were taken hostage and eventually killed, also a German police officer. It was carried out by the Palestinian terrorist group Black September.

Snow Queen is an adventure not forgotten when the band members were required to learn how to ski. This we did one year after the other, it was in Bavaria, absolutely amazing the whole band was on the course, we stayed in an alpine house surrounded by hills and mountains. In the restroom was a crucifix in one corner of the room above the timber corner seating. It was not advisable to swear if you were sat under this crucifix as was proven on occasions when it would fall on cue, on your head.

Around on the top ledge all around the room, about 16 inches from the ceiling was placed strategically at exits and entrances strings of garlic and sprigs of Saint John's wort. Now all through my youth, I have been plagued with tales and dreams of vampires and at this time was no exception.

Tony McCurry one night after tea decided to go fishing beyond the field across from the house to a stream that was feeding a big lake further up north from the house. I went with him to see how he was going to manage without a fishing rod; besides he was egging me to join him. We went down a pathway by a fence to the stream where Tony explained he was going to tickle the fish out of the water with his fingers asking me to come and look. I did bend down and when he turned around with big red fangs protruding from his mouth, I ran for my life across the field which was like a swamp and took ages to get out. Finally, I reached the road and got to the house. The lads in the restroom asked if I had seen a ghost. I spluttered out McCurry was a vampire. Well, they laughed their heads off but I can tell you I was in a terrible state and not laughing when McCurry also returned grinning like a cat. Crosses could be seen on every mountain as we drove out to skiing resorts and did not quell my fears at all. Two weeks training sessions we were taken on a mountain where it was like a roller coaster and in order not to go over the many precipices that suddenly appeared around the many corners it was safer to fall on our backsides rather than attempt the snow plough move and click the skies together. Some of the band members were very good at the skiing lark but I preferred to ski up and down on the straight slopes. Beer drinking in the local Gasthof traditionally consisted of a two-litre glass with a small glass of wine in the bottom. The two-litre glass was passed round to one and all and the last person who reached the bottom of the beer could drink the glass of wine which I must say was exquisite.

JGK's Mum and Dad came on a visit to Germany in the seventies Dad had just bought this car for the trip it broke down whilst they were there and Ted was the man that helped them out in fixing it with new parts. Jack and Leah stayed with Cath and Frank Arscott who were recent newlywed's whilst the parts arrived and were suitably entertained by other band members during that time. I know full well they enjoyed that trip as Jack retold time and time again on our jaunts around the countryside on Saturdays before his passing in 2011. In the early '70s. they introduced the medical aspect of soldering for the bandsmen, it involved doing field medical exercises with the regiment.

After which we had to sit a test that involved 99 questions of which five of them were 'do or die, fail one of those and you failed the whole test paper no matter if the rest were all correct. You then became a class three field medical technician a posh title for a stretcher bearer. Oranges were used to practice giving injections in field conditions. There were several new band members mainly from the south of England; all good musicians one or two were from the Junior Leaders Regiment in Bovington. One chap ran the 1st Paderborn Cub Scouts since the band had moved there. Asked by Akela (Steve Down) to help with a theme night Treasure Island was my first introduction to the Scouting movement. I was to be Ben Gunn and I used the bass drum skin as my costume. I enjoyed that night and helped on many pack nights when I could with the new training scheme of Bronze, Silver and Gold Arrow awards. The early seventies in the band were interesting. Jesus Christ Superstar and Hair had just come out as a movie JGK and I started to write an alternative about witchcraft involving a lot of what was wrong with the world Vietnam Ireland Bangladesh race colour and creed.

Hence "Sea Breeze" with suspended cymbals depicting the waves swishing on the sand gently whilst the coven danced naked around the fire on the beach singing "Hail Diana, Hail Diana the goddess of love she's the goddess above" "Hail Lucifer! Hail Lucifer."

There were times when we went to rock festivals in Germany, the one in Höxter was quite some distance from camp. Three of us hitched our way to the festival on the way we slept in a shed set back off the road. We got a lift from a professor who said he was following a meteor that was expected to fall just beyond the festival site. He stopped at a village on the way, called into a shop and came back with bread round sandwich meat and bratwurst. He dropped us off outside the site and again gave us a bottle of wine and some more bread and meat thanking us for helping him with his English.

The next day was a Saturday and it was lashing with the rain. The ground was a mud bath and the two other lads went searching for" pick me ups" to get the party going. I thought it was the beer they were looking for but no as later I found it was the weed. They rolled what I thought was a few cigarettes and I had when it was offered as they cajoled it would make me feel good. I had a few of these magic cigarettes throughout the day which was making me feel great happy and melancholy and the weather was no bother at all. The following day I felt rough and realised I had been smoking dope so that is how and why I took up smoking cigarettes and they were dirt cheap with the army coupons.

Sometime later that same year I took some LSD or Speed. I was locked in my bedroom with a mate who watched over me as it was my first time with the stuff. What an 'amazing experience, psychedelic colours enhanced the music; I was on cloud nine.

In the morning, I was still high and went to the NAAFI for a pie and eating it was an experience not to be forgotten in the state of mind I was in. I later went to town to buy a carpet for my bedroom and in the shop, the rolls of carpet were turning and I could feel myself being drawn in between the rolls like a mangle squeezing the water from the washing. I did buy an orange carpet with the help of a mate who kept their eye on me for the whole of the two days. I never did touch the stuff again and have no regrets and I will always be grateful to the mate who stood by me knowing that it could have gone so bad as so many do. I would counsel against taking anything like it to anyone.

The young members of the band organised a Twelve-hour nonstop music session in the band bar-room which was in the attic of the band block shared with the C squadron. We raised a lot of money for a children's charity in the town. There was a fair bit of heavy rock, ballads, folk, and pop music. It was a great day and it was all recorded but sadly the tapes are all lost or destroyed.

The local vicar let us have an old Harmonia which was not required anymore, although it was a tremendous struggle to get it up two flights of stairs to where we young bandsmen let off musical steam busking and introducing what we thought were fantastic new sounds.

The Harmonia which I had transported to Rochdale lived with me throughout, it was stored for a time at Croft Mill Community workshops and it was here where it was smashed up by Maria with the help of Pudger in 2005. Most of it was thrown over the backyard where I was renting.

The truth is I was looking after it for JGK all those years and he never had reclaimed it. I turned some of the parts in to wedges using the key nobs as handles and presented them as gifts to JGK and members of the Keegan clan. Two of them I gave as a Unison rep at the last meeting to parting Directors of the RBH. They were being encouraged to vacate the newly formed privatisation of the housing stock to a perceived new company. The wedges I suggested would be handy to keep their next door of opportunity open.

Before my return to the regiment, I visited the Coles in Dún Laoghaire, the 'Walsh's in Killarney, and my brother Sean in Inch. Sean was at Cork University and was developing a train of thought that would leave you to think he was supporting provisional Sinn Fein.

On a return trip on the next leave, he appeared more radical which gave me concerns for both his safety and my time in the army may not be in our best interest. We had met at the Rose of Tralee festival and he was goading me about being in the British army and pretending he was a sniper. He was not serious and was indicating then that he may move to England and forget University.

I used it as an excuse to buy myself out for about £200 and the officer for C squadron tried to talk me out of it but I was determined to try civilian life and was concerned if I could manage in the "real world". JGK and I made plans to get together in Rochdale and eventually trip around Europe. That trip never happened.

Kneller Hall - Time not forgotten!

CHAPTER 7
CIVILIAN LIFE AND SCOUTING

On leaving the army in March 1974 I moved to the Gale Inn on Whitworth Road, Rochdale, thanks to Jack and Leah Keegan where I lived and worked until Jack, 'my English surrogate father' got me a bedsit to stay off Spotland Road Rochdale.

I lived with them as part of the family till JGK who had also left the forces. We bought a house later that year. I played the cornet for Milnrow brass band after an introduction by Jack and subsequently offered my first job by the 'base player who was a manager at Dexine Rubber Company on Spotland Road. Jack got me the bed-sit on Clement Royds Street not far from the factory. It was a great start to civilian life. I worked for a few years behind the bar at the Gale Inn a Bass Charrington pub on Whitworth Road. Gone now lost forever replaced with Blocks of flats that retains the' 'Gale" name. The family became a big part of my life and played a big part in helping me to deal with many incidents, adventures, tribulations that transpired since I left Her Majesty's Armed Forces and still help to this day.

Jack & Leah Keegan

Mick Bulmer a customer in the Gale Inn later in 1975 got me a job working for the gas board as a sales rep. Anyway, I did a bit of training and was put on Kirkholt, a housing estate in Rochdale, to sell gas appliances because of the change from town gas to the North Sea, with a target of some sort for the week. I was hopeless I could not for the life of me sign these people up for stuff they did not need. I spent more time nattering and drinking tea and suggesting not to be hoodwinked in buying from any of the other reps trawling the estate. All the reps would meet up in Lord Howarth for lunch and meeting with the team leader. I kept reporting I had a few sales lined up for later in the week so I only lasted a month.

I had a few years at North West Storage Company as a Warehouse foreman. The mornings began with breakfast at Gingham Diner a long caravan café at the crossroads of Oldham Road and Queensway. Sometimes the boss would come and pay for the breakfast and suggest we should be on our way to the various sites where we should be erecting steel shelving or pallet racking around the Northwest, one of the new owners, an accountant from a handbag firm frowned on my efforts as a trade union activist.

Before his arrival, however, I was instrumental in getting work for the Venture Scouts and one of their leaders. They worked hard and were grateful for the summertime work. I enjoyed working there and had use of the transport for taking the Cubs and Scouts over those years to camp at weekends and at holiday times. The owner Keith Potter was very accommodating and a good sort and fair, unlike the new fella that bought himself into the business. Keith and his wife were some of the many guests at our wedding in August '82.

It was after a trip to Leeds in 1983 in the three-ton truck fully loaded, when I got lost around the one-way system. I never got to my required destination and returned late at the depot on Vavsour Street off Crawford Street Rochdale, so it gave him the ammunition to get shut of me once and for all. I was eventually laid off due to my efforts of trying to get fellow workers to join a trade union that's my story and I am sticking to it. Throughout my working life I remained a card holding Trade Unionist, as a member of GMB, through the 70s and then NUPE and UNISION where I remain a retired member.

I had continued with the Cubs and Scouts when I left the army with the introduction by Mr & Mrs Fred and Marie Hamer to the 13th Rochdale Park Baptist Scout Group. JGK had been an acquaintance of the then Cub Scout leader Pete Hoolahan and he thought we would get on well together. The building was in a very bad state and upstairs was a dangerous place and was earmarked for demolition and to be replaced with a block of flats. Eventually, the group Scout leader Brian Leach arranged a move to the old Derby Street School where we had the use of the hall on Monday nights for the Cubs and on Friday nights Scouts and ventures Scouts met. I eventually took over the Cubs and Pete Houlihan took on the Scouts. John Mills took on the Venture Scouts and in time teamed up with the local Ranger guides and did a lot of joint ventures together.

I took part in a lot of the ventures such as climbing, abseiling, camping, fellwalking, and even went gliding a fantastic experience as silently flying like a bird over the Trough of Boland, many a camp was held in Silverdale and other Scout campsites around the northwest.

It was around this time I did my Wood badge at Gilwell Park and on completion became a member of the 1st Gilwell Scout group. Mavis Holmes from Little Hulton was part of our team. I did a tour of Scotland with Andy Anderson one of the Scout leaders from the 13th Rochdale. Whist Andy went fishing at Glencoe I set up between the hills and played my cornet and not long-playing some cows came to investigate my thoughts went to was there a bull but no, I was safe so carried on playing. Later that night we had a beach party where I sang some of my Irish and composed songs a great night was had by all. on to Fort William and then Ben Navis when I got halfway up there was a lake and we sat down to have lunch.

I was feeling rough from the previous night so thought I would just heat tomato soup however I did not eat it all and poured the rest into the lake to my surprise the lake went a pale red and as it rippled further to light pink. Andy went further up the mountain and I wandered down feeling sorry for myself. Scotland was great and a beautiful country the people were friendly but the pubs closed early. Whilst I was away Brian Owen chair of the 13th Rochdale Scout group at the time became homeless after some trouble with his wife and so I let him stay till he managed to get a place of his own with his son Denver from the Falcon patrol of 13th Rochdale Scout group.

It was around that time that I eventually went to London to see Sean, after a visit from him to my house discovering my abode from the local parish priest. I learned then he was married and living in Crystal Palace.

He had arrived with one of his mates on the way to a match in Ireland. On these jaunts up north, I don't think he ever told his wife and children when or where he was going. Sean was running a small business with Fergus who was also from Ireland and we would frequently visit the local Irish club. Liam was only two on that first visit and Emma was only a baby. It was good to catch up with my little brother who after dropping off his workmen at the various building sites would meet up later at lunchtime in the local pub. I never stayed in the pub for long as he would carry on reading his broadsheets sitting like a high intellectual in the corner.

It was 1993 when after the news of discovering Oliver, Maria and I with the children went to visit in London to let Sean know in person about Oliver the eldest Clancy. Maria was not keen on stopping the night so we returned the same day an 800-mile round trip. They came up the following year to ours and stayed a night or two. Lauren and Woppits played together and at night put a show on using the bay window as a stage with the long curtains. Sean and I went to the comrades at night and Emma was cross as she was not permitted to come with her mother so mother stayed at the house with her.

The annual ghost hunt trips to Ashworth Valley were packed full of concerns the Cubs after were eating hemlock soup being impregnated with being able to see ghosts due to the spells whilst the venture Scouts laid the trail of ghosts in the shadows and up trees and trailing across the stream that ran through the valley. Arkela faking fear and urging the Cubs to run following him to get away from the ghosts and ghouls. The Nissen hut scattered with phosphorus images of characters from the jungle book and of course Lord Baden Powell all fading away as the Cubs entered. Later the cubs were to partake of demdoc pie so to inoculate against the hemlock soup they had had before these adventures. Many a Cub camp was on various themes the one I remember most is the theme of the four nations.

We're the boys from Ireland
The boys of the Aran bog,
Although we're 'smaller in number'
We're as thick as the English lot.
The English have their fish and chips
The Scots their haggis the noo!
The Welsh their leeks and daffodils
But we like Irish stew.
Yara go on we're only joking
Yara go on we're pulling your leg
Yara go on we're only Joking
Yara go on, go on, go on, we're pulling your leg. JC

It was a district sixer camp with the theme of England Ireland Scotland and Wales and the Irish camp went to the last Grand Howl with uniforms on back to front singing "we're the Cubs from Ireland". The assistant district commissioner Cub Scout leader Margaret Witham Assistant District commissioner was not best pleased.

Around the many camp fires singing songs and telling stories about the little people who had helped me throughout my life and how they had got me out of many a scrape. I recall the comical way Harry a Scout from Milnrow escaped while running to get away from me, left me high and dry standing like a fool with my mouth open with his coat in my hand. The laughter of the other Scouts around being hilarious. The Schofield's missing on camp causing panic whilst they flew kites in another field a nightmare for any Scout leader in charge. Many an ex-Cub or Scout has since reminded me of those ghost hunts songs and the memories of their time in the Cubs thirty and forty years on when I have been having a quite pint in the club and my other drinking haunts over the last 20years. Happy memories!!

The 3rd Rochdale Cubs at Saint John's was the other group I got involved in, to progress to getting their Scouts going. We had many joint camps together teaching skills in bivouacking, fire lighting, knife, axe and saw work camp cooking storage of food tent erecting and encouraging participation in many of the proficiency badges available to achieve with the help of some experts in the many fields. The Hyles from Zion Baptist on Deeplish helped with the Cubs for a while and Pam Brocklehurst took over the 13th Rochdale Cubs from me after I got the Scouts going at Saint John's.

From 1975 to the mid 80's I got lads from a number of the Scout groups and formed the Rochdale & District Scout Band teaching drums and E-flat Calvary Trumpets on Wednesday evenings and Saturday afternoons first year at 7 Dunster avenue in the cellar using old ply church chairs. Eventually, with Peter Houlihan who took me to Oxford Street in Manchester to buy the first black snare drum, from then the district started to take us seriously. We got some old equipment from the attic of Saint Clements church Spotland Rochdale.

The rehearsals on Wednesday nights and Saturday afternoons were then permitted at District Scout Headquarters Greenbank, Rochdale, and fundraising brought in all new instruments. In those early years, we ran a lot of dances for ventures and rangers encouraging local young bands to play at these gigs for the experience. they were well attended until we ran out of places to hold them.

I at one stage got some 'talented Scouts to form a folk group, three guitar players and a lad on accordion and they performed in and around Rochdale. Steve one of the guitar players wrote some of his songs. Pete after a short break because of work commitments eventually at my request took over the Scout band in the '80s when I could no longer devote enough time as I was running Cubs, Scouts the youth club at Saint John's and planning to 'get Married. Pete was instrumental in entering the band in competition during these years with some success.

Late at night after a few jars outside Alec Wildbloods butchers, we would spend time talking into the early hours about the band, Scouts and Cubs or planning the next camp. Many a time I would call into the butchers and Alec would give me a mouthful for yapping outside his shop.

Peter and I went to Germany in his Dormobile with his Mum and Dad Peter drove all the way all the time as I did not drive at the time so it may have been in 1976. We did use several campsites on the way but on one occasion we were lost and set up on the side of the road in a layby near a small river we were lucky not to be fined as we were moved on in the morning by the local police. Tempers were frayed, many a time on that trip as the dormobile boldly went on occasions the wrong way up and down streets in one or two towns and cities.

Back in Rochdale, I had got involved in setting up the youth club for young people with special requirements and those who did not. I was very much against calling people disabled and believed in integration and not separation. It was quite successful. However, a new curate arrived at Saint John's and was not keen on the club is for all denominations and it eventually closed. So, members went to a local authority one now called Rochdale Gateway Leisure and much better than what we were offering.

But it was a great kick to see those able-bodied young people mixing with disabilities and getting on well together. Faith in young people to do the right thing is paramount to achieve a successful outcome for all regardless of perceived abilities and sharing. During the annual wakes for several years, my time was taken up running summer projects for the young people of the area via the parish along with those from the Scouts and youth club. To secure the time off work from Turner Brothers Asbestos Factory in Rochdale my (foster) Dad Jack Greene had to die twice in those years my foreman a Mr O'Brian accepted that as an excuse for my unauthorised extended absences.

One year in the late seventies Dymphna and her children came from Ireland and took part in that year's summer project along with Simon. Tracy and Julie Pattison had moved on to Deeplish Road. Julie was the youngest and my goddaughter. Simon was with myself and JGK when we went on a trip to Blackpool at the request invitation of Jack and Leah. I've never forgotten the white T-shirt we bought and put on Simon. We had printed on the front "WAR MAKES MONEY" and on the back PEACE MAKES CENTS". Often wish we had a photo of that T-shirt on Simon it was down to his ankles and lots of comments were made as we wandered around Blackpool. On our return to the caravan park, Jack laughed but Leah thought we were being silly. It wasn't until early in June 1980 that I took a trip back to Ireland and Dimps who suggested going to Barnardo's as she had found that she too was boarded out as Da had told her on his death bed. Hence on my return to England the letter from Barnardo's and other letters sent by me and received in the attempt to discover my roots. See Reference IV. Looking again at the notes and letters with fresh eyes a discovery yet again that mother was contributing to my keep and Sean's after he was born in '53.

The letters create from the written words a layer of secrecy around my mother. leaving one to think of conspiracy theories? What do you the reader think after seeing the letters?

With the summer project always the second week of the school holidays involved lots of trips out to Tandle Hill, Ashworth Valley, treasure hunts, wide games, and various competitions. The Project that year ended with a party at my house on Nicholson Street for the Dymphna family and those parents that helped supervise the project. In the early years, I had built up several friends around Scouting the McGivney's being one large family Bridie and Tom with four boys and five older girls. Brian Tom and Noel had all been in the Cubs Patrick was not but I helped him secure his first disco equipment for a gig at the Castle Inn on Manchester Road in aid of the Scout group. I ended up with a crush on Ann who was married and I would fall weak at the knees if she spoke to me. They paid for me to have a trip back to Ireland in '76 as a thank you for plastering the ceiling of the upstairs landing. There was Jean Howarth, Adrian, her son, and his Nana Clegg who ended up moving to Morecambe. The Nuttall's who lived off Deeplish road, Danny the eldest son returned a German helmet I had brought back from Germany and passed on to Treacle-Pud my son. I don't suppose he has still got it?

Lots of incidents began and finished in that first few years leaving the army. JGK had left the Army in June '74 and took up residence and part owner at Dunster avenue the sale price being £3750 bought from a bank manager and his sister who had lived there all their lives. Next door but one, was a chap from Bangladesh who late into the night would sit with me on the doorstep and he would tell me about his hopes and aspirations for his children. Two of his lads Zulfkar and Suhail joined the Cubs and were very good footballers, and they also enjoyed their participation in all the activities. Their dad made a big impression on me, strong in his religion and concerned as to how his girls would fair in this country as they would learn the western ways when going to schools and conceded it was different for the lads. Sadly, one of his daughters after the arrangement of marriage gave up on life when she reached her teens. She was a very bonny girl and a great loss to the family. I did see Mr Kajwaja many times over the years on the market in town, we spoke at times when I was on my own.

After my marriage, it became advisable for me not to show interest in other people as many a row was the cause of such happenings. I had three relationships during this time before marrying in 1982.

The first was finished as soon as it started as JGK during one of the many parties found himself in my bed with Susan a slim beautiful girl with hair as black as ebony and a body to die for. Moiré her mother looked after Susan's little girls most of the time after school and was a marvellous cook who was originally from Ireland and I would walk her home from church. That was when I met her daughter Susan.

Next was a Cub leader another Sue a big girl older than me from Swinton who I met at several Cub camps and events. She visited one weekend and took me to bed and I experienced very great pain with my vitals.

I never saw her again and I did not know what was wrong for it was my first time. I learned that reason from Jack at the Gale Inn when I told him. He advised me to see Mr Main on Drake Street who sent me for an operation at a price. After the operation, I was collected by Jack and Leah to recuperate at the Gale. It was some very painful two or three weeks but I was well looked after and any embarrassment was kept in check. It was thought in the family by some that circumcision should be done as a baby because I was a Roman catholic. I'm still none the wiser? On the many Fridays after the Scout meeting, the leaders would have sessions in the Victoria pub on Spotland road it was off to Watt's the chippy on Smith Street for the supper. I got to know Shirley who was a beautiful blond with long curly hair and the daughter of Cyril and Muriel Watts.

Shirley was then a born-again Christian and I went to her baptism, where she was 'immersed in a bath of water something I had not seen before. This was at West Saint Baptist here in Rochdale, Shirley and I went out for a while until she went away to college or university it was never serious. I think her mum and dad lived in hope that the relationship would develop further. The family was very supportive of the Scout movement here in Rochdale. I later in the 90's met Cyril as secretary of the Fusiliers old comrades' group again when the British legion wanted to relocate their prefab building for the storage of poppies next to the joiner's shop on Rugby Road.

Collage of Scouting years

CHAPTER 8
THE ROAD TO MAKING OUT

Meanwhile back at Dunster JGK had invited a chap he had met on holiday from the States to stay for a while. That was ok by me but on returning one Monday night from the Cubs which had just moved to Derby Street school, there was your man cooking a stink under the grill with some other chap who I later found out was his brother. Not jumping to any conclusions, I asked him what it was doing, and he explained they were vegetarian and were cooking it for when they travelled on. I was not convinced since it smelt a lot like what we smoked in the army. I waited a while hoping to speak to JGK but he was on a few gigs and not living there at the time. The second time I found the same thing happening but a considerable larger amount being wrapped in tinfoil. I went next door where an elderly couple lived, they had a phone and so I rang the local police, but they never came to investigate. I asked Dale who I gleaned was from Kansas, how long they were planning to stay and that I was not happy with what they were cooking.

However, they left a few days later and things got back to normal for a while. An ex-army bandsman Glen R, turned up one weekend looking for a place to stay again suggested by JGK who had given up living at Dunster avenue by this time. Glen had with him his girlfriend and his baby son and had just come up from Torquay after spending a few seasons there. Glen was a drummer from Rochdale in the regimental band and had joined at JGK's Suggestion. Glen performed gigs all over where he could get the work and like his dad picking up 'female company on the way. I recall my first trip to Rochdale with Glen Tony and JGK in 1968 when he drove from Bovington in his Morris minor, 'the passenger seat was a fruit box.' I recall his kerb-crawling around Ashfield valley, something I did not even know about.

We got on all ok and there was no bother at all, and Glen was paying rent. His Dad was a sax player and we held some good music sessions during the week there was no television at Dunster Avenue. Returning from a Scout camp on a Sunday, Glen appeared very concerned as the police had done a raid on the house looking for drugs and they would be back to talk to me Monday morning. Again, I called on Jack for his help and explained what had transpired these past couple of months.

He offered to be there first thing in the morning and true to his word he got there just as the police had arrived. They asked him what it had to do with him and they informed him I was being taken to the police station to be questioned and he was not required. He vouched for me to the police with words that declared his trust in me above others closer to him. What an experience down at the police station where weeks before I had taken the Cubs on a field trip and had many drinks in the bar with a friend who was a police constable and fellow Cub Leader. There were the good cop and bad cop routine you see on the telly but I kept to what concerned me as to why they had not acted when I rang months previously about the two yanks and they could check with the witness to it from the neighbours next door. The Customs had intercepted a parcel destined for a Dale Fetters at 7 Dunster Ave, hence the raid. In the end, I suggested I write to Dale to collect his parcel of pottery and they were dismayed at my suggestion. So that's what I did and they escorted me to the post office to post it and I went on my way up to the Gale and let them know about it all. I informed Glen what the plan was and they would catch them at the airport. More visits were made by the police and on one of the visits, Glen was informed that these culprits were known to carry guns. Understandably Glen and his family left for Torquay never to be seen again.

What followed next however, was a living nightmare. Again, on a Sunday after a Sixers camp at Ashworth valley, who should be waiting for me as I put my Yale key to the door, but Dale the bloody yank. I was in a state knowing what to do and what was I going to tell this fella about his parcel? In a panic, I welcomed him in and told him his parcel was not here and we would have to go and fetch it from a friend's house in Milnrow after I changed out of my uniform and had a brew.

On the way to town to catch a bus with this chap with me, I called at Jacqueline's shop one of Jack's daughters to get a packet of fags. Giving me the 'opportunity to pass a message to her to ring this number I had written for Rashleigh at HM Customs who oversaw the case.

Jacqueline was already aware of the case and I thought she would know what to do. No! she started to read out the message and I grabbed it off her before Dale was aware of what she was saying and left quickly before she said too much. We caught the bus to Milnrow and got off at the Tim Bobbin pub later called the Bobbin. I suggested we have a pint of Guinness here and I would go up and see Brian on Kiln Lane and collect the parcel. I don't recall the excuse I gave Dale for him to wait in the pub but he did, so off I went to Brian's to use his phone to ring Rashleigh. Brian was aware of the case and I got to use the phone I talked to Rashleigh he explained it would be a while before he could get there and to keep Dale busy till then.

Brian's wife Beryl was in bits as she had two small children and was thinking the worst could happen due to the time it would take for the police and Rashleigh to get there. I assured Brian and Beryl that in no way would I come back again and I would tell Dale you were out for the day and I would have to call back again to collect the parcel. I returned to the Tim Bobbin and explained the situation to Dale, ordered another two pints of Guinness and prayed that the police would not be a long time. After an hour or so I went to the telephone box across the road pretending to ring Brian's house to see if they were home yet. This I did a few times and Dale was getting a bit restless and followed me to the phone at one stage. I put the phone down, explained no answer and suggested a game of darts. We were just heading into the door of the Tim Bobbin again when the sirens could be heard. Dale was in front of me unaware and went towards the back of the pub heading to the toilets I followed and we were both standing at the urinal when police burst in and Rashleigh followed. Dale was arrested and bundled into the back of a police car and as they drove away, I could see the smile on Dale's face. I can still see it to this day.

Later there was a piece in one of the papers about the case and he had been jailed and later deported. One of the other reasons for moving house in case he ever came back.

It was in '75/76 when I was courting Carol which after getting engaged led me to finally move to Nicholson Street and escape all that went wrong in that house. Carol's uncle, a small man from Poland or 'was it the Ukraine' on her mother's side did some work on the house at his instance. I presumed we would marry at Saint John's but Father Spring was very concerned about me marrying a non-Catholic and suggested he would speak to my guardians who he had happened to go to school with a very good catholic family in Killarney. It was at a lads & Dads camp at Ashworth Valley that on Saturday morning Carol's dad turned up in his car, got out and stood at the top of the hill beckoning me in a commanding manner to join him. Fred Hamer, one of the dads and treasurer of the 13th Scout group gathered all the dads, expressing that I was now in trouble and would be under the thumb. We were going for lunch at the Chapel House off Ashworth Road but also a lecture as to why Carol had come home that morning crying because I would not buy a suit for the engagement. I thought it was a waste of money since we had yet to set a date for the wedding. The engagement was held in the Cyprus Tavern in Manchester organised and paid for by Carol's parents and as I was camping in Silverdale with the 13th Rochdale Scouts Pete Hoolahan the Scout leader was invited as the best man and he drove back for the party and after back to camp. Carol's father was again not best pleased. Jack and Leah Keegan were there as my adoptive English parents, Carol's sister, Adele a Cub leader 5th Rochdale and Carol's friend Adele Schofield and of course Pete Houlihan Scout leader. After moving into Nicholson Street, setting a date for the wedding became more and more pressing and I was feeling more and more pressure from all quarters.

One Sunday I was at home churning all these concerns over and over in my head and finally got the courage to ring Carol from the phone box outside the Brown Cow telling her I did not want to get married. Her dad answered the phone and was furious saying "you get over here now and tell her to her face". I got on a bus to Heywood and from the stop walked past the pub and to the bungalow where they lived. The dad let me in and said she is not in and "You will stay till she is back and explain to us all why"? He was going to beat me till his wife cut in to say that that is not the way to solve it and it was up to Carol. I waited for over an hour and eventually explained I felt it was wrong and the pressure was making me ill. After a while, I was let out of the house shaking like a leaf and with the last few shillings, I called at the pub to have a brandy. I then walked back to Ashfield Road about three or four miles and the Weavers arms and borrowed a tenner from Jose O'Mahony's after I had explained what had happened. Pauline the barmaid in the Weavers' arms Rochdale was a friend and I got to know her on my frequent visits to the pub.

After one of the many Late-night doo's, she was for some reason not able to go home and ended up with me that night. She stayed in the bed and I slept on the end, contrary to what has been said in later years I never slept with

Pauline but did see her on several occasions. I visited her mums for tea a few times and that was when I met Mark, her baby son with his big wondrous eyes and blond hair.

We did not last very long but it was to cause a lot of problems in later years when I discovered she was married to Maria's brother Michael. I had avoided relations ships for quite a while but as time passed one of the Cub's mothers latched on to me and invited me many times to her flat on Ashfield valley and she introduced me to sex urging patience and the need for foreplay. Yes, she was married and her husband was away in the gulf somewhere on oil rigs earning good money, she was always happy when he went back after his visits home on leave. Flo had a triple barrel surname and because of that, you will not see the name in print.

It was the late '70s when Mark, Pauline's son had turned up with his Nan to join the Cubs at Saint John's which I had recently taken on after the Cub leader had taken ill. Mark's aunty would collect him sometimes instead of his Nan. She appeared to be very shy and reserved. It was a job to get any conversation out of her. Her Mother Clare Jones (Marks Nan) on the other hand was quite chatty and had long experience with the Scout movement as all her sons had been Scouts and one was a leader at 37th Sudden. She offered to help with the home help badge for which I was grateful. The Cubs would turn up at her house and take part in the tasks set by Mark's Nan and end up playing in the pen after with Mark.

The Cubs enjoyed their visits as the little bantam hens clucked their way around the kitchen, annoying some of the many cats that darted out the back door to where there were a variety of ducks and more hens. The bantams had the names of kings and queens of England which tickled the young lads. Terry The eldest of Mark's uncles started to help at the Cubs' meetings held in the prefab building next to Saint John's school on McClure Rd. The Cub leaders of Rochdale had a monthly Seeonee Pack meeting at Scout headquarters and I invited Terry and Maria to what was to be a faith supper at one of the meetings. It was not a date but from then it was when Maria and I got to know each other a little better. Over that time, I suggested she begin to form a brownie group for the girls of the parish and eventually this happened after Maria had training at Saint Andrews guides and permission from the district commissioner.

Terry Turner, chairperson of the Saint John's Lourdes committee at my suggestion, invited her to join the committee as secretary as I was also involved with from the late '70s. It was one more way of seeing more of each other and we went together to various events. Many of the people who we took to Lourdes came to these events.

One girl with down syndrome had a crush on me and I would always give her a hug and a dance whenever she was around. She was very jealous of Maria and would push her out of the way, at times testing Maria's patience. We met her once or twice after the children were born in the Co-Op supermarket on Smith Street in Rochdale and ructions were caused when the children were scolded by her for playing with the toys on the lower shelves in the toy aisle. Maria was not best pleased with this girl.

Maria had 5 brothers Terry the eldest was tall and dark-haired, friendly with a reliance on some cognitive support from family members. After the death of his mother, he had a girlfriend for a short while who returned to Warrington. Living on his own he struggled to keep the animals the family had for many years and over a short period of perhaps two years they simply died. Terry was eventually housed in a small terraced house where he stayed till his passing in 1996. Trevor the second brother was Married to Dorothy with two children Richard and Russel. Trevor on many occasions over the years would call at the house against Maria's wishes with presents for my children. We were not allowed to open the door to him as Maria demanded at times so he would leave what he had brought on the doorstep.

On one or two occasions I would let him in and Maria would lock herself in the bathroom until he left, it was almost embarrassing, and I never really found a reason for the behaviour. Next comes Rodney, who Maria forbids an invitation to our wedding; Rodney was also married with children but we never met them during our marriage. He simply was a mystery and never came to our home. Maria had a tense dislike of him and her brother Roy, something to do with them searching the house after her Father Cyril who died in 1976 which came to light after Terry's death in 1996. Last, there is Michael the youngest, a jovial chap Married to Pauline who was an attraction in my life before me meeting Maria. Paul and Mark, their sons, were periodically part of our lives when our children were smaller. At times, I would when I bumped into Mark and rewarded him, for him to visit his aunty "Ria" to stop her thinking bad of his mum and dad but also to achieve some peace.

It was 1982 when the Falklands war took place, I had received my annual reserve call up records in early '82 It was a matter of concern about being sent to the Falklands as a medic, however, this did not happen due to the war ending and the reserves were not required. It was a Saturday morning in February 1981 when I had spoken to Maria's mum as she sat in her rocking chair in the kitchen asking if she was ok with me marrying Maria. To me, because her dad had passed away in 1976 it was right to ask her mum, my heart was in my mouth Maria had not told her and she was still above in bed. Claire, Maria's mum said it was fine and good luck you'll need it. I was not 100% sure what she meant by it. But anyway, after the visit by the Pope in May '82 to Heaton Park they both went to get her dress in Manchester at the latter end of the month. Maria's brother Roy who was with the police in Manchester he had me checked out, suspecting I may be an IRA man.

Trevor was in some sort of storage business who Michael called 'Walt Disney.' Rodney worked at the time in a warehouse for Tibbett & Britton. Terry the eldest lived at home relying on his mum for room and board and was unemployed but later occasionally worked for Michael who was the youngest of them all who started a security firm of his own. The months leading up to the wedding were fraught with difficulties.

Sometime in June 82, Maria's mum went into hospital being very ill and jaundice. Whilst in the hospital the brothers were convinced, she had given up on life because of Maria getting married to me. It all came out in a conversation whilst standing about in the corridor. It was first put to me that if their mum was told that the marriage was not going ahead, she would fight to stay alive. Maria was furious and insisted the marriage would not be cancelled.

It was July the 1st I had stayed with Claire overnight whilst they all went to have a rest and some sleep. I sat next to her bed and said the rosary over and over. It was sometime in the early hours of the morning she sat up in bed, looked at me, smiled, and lay back down.

She had died so the nurse said… I left and went outside to be sick and then rang Maria to let her know. The brothers were not best pleased that I had not rung them earlier. The funeral was organised by Maria and her mum had some funds to be interred in a niche in the wall at the cemetery with her husband Cyril even though this caused some problems. Two of the lads had been looking around the house on Mere Lane for something, I know not what, but it got Maria mad again and in a state. There was an extra cost to the funeral which we paid for in the end.

Now to the wedding of the year helped by some of the Lourdes crowd and the sisters at Catholic Rescue Williams Street. A fellow Scout leader Jim Gavin was my best man as Peter Hoolahan who knew me best since leaving the army was not acceptable to Maria and not being a catholic. Hence Jim Gavin a Scotsman from Glasgow and a social worker who years later was discovered as a child molester and taking photos of boys in the late '80s was later jailed in 2018 for historical child abuse dying in Prison so I was told by Terry Turner in 2020. The revelation of Jim Gavin's arrest was forever later used against me by her in-doors "Maria".

Terry and Mick Maria's brothers acted as ushers at Saint John's, Trevor was to give her away but no invite for Rodney or Roy despite my pleadings for Maria to give in at the last minute. I never understood why? Later years revealed it had something from the past and about a ring and how the two of them had acted after the death of her dad in 1976?

There was some talk by Maria about there being another girl who had kicked her mother in the tummy when she was carrying Terry giving rise in Maria's mind that there was another family from her Mum and Dads previous marriages. This haunted Maria time and time again over the years and she would drive out to various locations where there were family graves. There was some suggestion that her dad's side had been part of the Black and Tans created by Lloyd George for the Irish troubles after the great war. There is simply no evidence for this claim.

We had the hall at Saint Aiden's Sudden for the reception and the Lourdes committee ran the bar with Terry Turner Gilda Kilgallen & John Murry (RIP) where the profits went to take a disabled person to Lourdes in September of the same year. It was two o'clock in the morning when we left McGivney's and we were at Terry's to collect Rinne Maria's dog. Terry had moved his girlfriend in with her 3-year-old son. Maria was furious and insisted she had to leave and go back to Warrington and I was to pay for the taxi £50 upfront. We eventually got to bed at Nicholson Street after sorting the dog out. The next day two of the cats were brought home from Mere Lane as Maria went to check on Terry. Canon O'Connell had called to the house for a brew and a chat Just as we were about to settle down to some married activity.

It was Rochdale September wakes, when Mark, Maria's nephew, came with us on our honeymoon to our Lourdes annual trip. It was at Lourdes where we met up with Helen Walsh's of La Sallette Killarney, my previous employers before the army.

Wedding Day

CHAPTER 9
COMMUNITY

Through the church I got involved in Christmas dinners along with Dennis, from Petrus River Street who had managed a centre in Rochdale. I also started delivering second-hand furniture to those who had managed to get accommodation after being homeless. This was with the Catholic Children's Rescue Society and Sister Margaret but also with Petrus at times. Maria helped After we were married with the dinners one Christmas.

After a couple months on the dole in 1983 I went working on a temporary scheme with the Methodist Circuit in Rochdale renovating the community part of Jarvis Street church for improved community use. The interview was conducted by the Minister and a Bernard Lyons who I later discovered knew my wife via Mark her nephew. Maria had a dislike to Bernard as he was Mark's social worker and to be honest if he knew Maria was my wife, I would not have had the job as he feared a run in with Maria. We renovated and turned part in to a luncheon club and a 'number of meeting rooms. There was Frank Butterworth (RIP) the craftsman and four long term unemployed lads who received training in various skills whilst renovating the premises. John S went to Refuse collection and Mark G continued with the building trade who I met again in Royal China takeaway here in Castleton during the 2nd lock-down.

Development workers were employed to set up the community side Jenny and later Winne and the centre became a much more used building. It was in this period I had meetings with the various religious denominations of the borough to encourage joint participation and use of the building. I had the idea to have a voucher system between the communities for those from the soup run to get meals at the various luncheon clubs that I hoped would develop. I did cause some concern at one of the meetings when I declared that God was an Astronaut it was about sharing religious thought and I as always was being controversial to stimulate conversation about difference in beliefs.

It was one of the first interdenominational discussions in the borough and I learnt a lot and still have no regrets about my stance.

During that year a cooperative was formed by Mary Lamb via the All-Saint's vicar Brian Corrodingly to help long term unemployed and the homeless. I gave a hand with the soup run on Regent Street for some time. I also took part in Sr Eileen's drama group more as a senior male group leader than as any drama teacher. It was quite successful with the participants acting some real-life dramas and presenting to audiences at various venues.

After the community program at Jarvis Street with the renovation completed Jenny and Winnie were left to develop the community side and Frank and I were tasked to set up the community workshops at Drydock Mill. The shop was envisaged to assist in helping long-term unemployed to develop skills that would help them to find work.

It was quite a struggle in the beginning and the senior supervising officer "ex councillor Jack A" was reluctant to use his allotted budget for equipment. We used Frank's and mine to get started and converted the hand-held power tools to fix to tables and benches. Jack thought this was great and was convinced we did not need proper tools. I rang the safety officer to come and have a look knowing full well he would condemn them and demand we have proper equipment. The plan had worked but prior to the inspection the sanders would start up on their own so I introduced my little people by yelling to get off the machine. See 'The Adventures of Seamus'

Micheline and everyone in the room could see there was no one there. Also, Jack's Nephew was one of those long term unemployed and I constantly found him smoking and sharing dope so I suspended him. Jack had me in the office and accused me of making it up and with his secretary sat at her desk across from him I gave him a list of occasions whilst telling my little people to stop jumping about and to behave.

A sewing section was developed for the girls and a new set of problems began for supervision. I had a break for a while from the scheme as the rules of community program required on my return Frank brought me UpToDate with suggestions on who to observe and help.

There were some talented people one I can recall from Castleton Paul Mac who I found sandpapering with no interest in what he was doing. After a long chat with him I found out he was an artist and as I found out later, he was a good one, flowing with ideas. That was the start of the art department and Paul with his own team of Lads and lassies who were influenced by him positively in creating my little people in art and depicting Frank as the poison dwarf. Jack was eventually replaced new equipment and machine were bought and we moved to the top floor at croft mill where all sections became much more involved in their 6 months' time there. There were challenges with every new intake one gang from the Middleton area took to climbing on the lift and peeing on the staff from Fairfield footwear. The lunch time taken up in the pub across the road with the difficulty of accessing their ability to return to work continuously marred. Overall a great scheme and a very satisfying job…

A year passed and Maria was growing concerned that she was yet not pregnant and we embarked on the training to go into fostering with the Catholic Children's Rescue Society on Parrs Wood Road Manchester. Later that year Maria did get pregnant and we carried on with the idea, attending meetings and started looking for a bigger house. Maria had preconceived ideas on how children should be brought up which was contrary to what the trainers were delivering and became a cause of concern. In the end, we were considered not suitable for fostering or adoption in the meantime we moved to 20 Castlemere Street, a four-bedroom end terraced house owned by people we knew from church and who also had done some fostering saying the house was ideal for our intentions. We lasted three years in this house and we ended up passing the keys back to the mortgage people the house was subsiding in one corner. I had been working voluntary for the Palatine Nuns off Manchester Road off the books, and had to make a choice when the community workshops wanted me to return.

Sister Eileen got us a house on Hereford Street with Saint Vincent's Housing, they were the ones that bought 17 Nicholson Street to do up for prospective tenants. Maria at some stage informed me she lost two pregnancies before the success of Pudger, I believed her at the time but since the accusations in 2004 and the statement by the priest in 2015. It is *possible*, she was fantasising. I've thought about those miscarriages many times. My Pudger was born 10/08/1984

At Birch Hill, maternity unit Maria had a single room, and as I was there, Maria was on this epidural as the baby was overdue and it was great fun, we laughed a lot and on her way to the bathroom holding on to the epidural on a stand with wheels I would 'fall, laughing at something she would say and I was not even on the stuff. Maria could be 'really funny and she could make me laugh. We were happy. Her waters broke and we went across the hall to one of the delivery rooms. It was one of the most fascinating experiences of my life. Maria puffed on the epidural I held her hand and pushed with her when given an order to do so. There was no shouting and bawling or bad language you might see on TV. Maria never used it. The atmosphere was euphoric when the baby finally made her entrance into this world. Magic absolute magic a beautiful tiny baby girl a miracle. Later I went down to Halifax Road and had a Jameson at the pub before catching a bus home dizzy with joy and wonder, I was a 'Dad!

I recall and think about some of wonderful memories I have of Pudger. It was on one of these weekend outings in '85 with the drama group that I eventually found the set of yellow ducks for my first born which I had strongly felt the need to find. Why, I have no idea. Also, her first birthday present of a keyboard when I was supposed to buy food! The way she wiggled and giggled when it played the pre-set tune! (Twinkle, Twinkle little star) in the front room of Castlemere Street.

The tears she cried when Jack in the box suddenly popped out a present from Sr Francine one of her godmothers. Thinking back, it was with hindsight a frightening thing for one so small. Maria was concerned later about her not walking as she shovelled around on her bottom for a long time.

There was an occasion when she was rushed to the children's pavilion at Birch Hill put in a bath of water, she had a high temperature. She was kept in the hospital for about a week and was being assessed by the doctors. She was also assessed by a child specialist at the infirmary for a while. I'm not sure what that was all about. Still, she remained a wandering cheeky inquisitive baby persistently making her way up to the altar at Saint John's during the mass, causing the chuckles and cooing of the congregation at the welcome distraction of the ritual of the mass.

At Brownies in her baby walker charging up and down the hall after they had left as the tiding up after the meetings. The love bestowed by the brownies on her as soon as she entered the hall. The nativity plays she controlled at age 3 and 4 years at Hereford Street with the front room as her stage, which performing frequently with Paul her cousin and her sister Woppits before Treacle Pud was born.

Taking total control as both director and producer. The wonderful stories and imagination with her writings in her early teens. My favourite being "The ice is out to get you" all about a puddle when you walk in and are lost into a new world. 'Pudger lived I think in a dream world. When she went to Saint Cuthbert's School in Rochdale, she came home really upset that the other pupils had declared there was no such thing as Father Christmas. I told her if there are mums and dads 'there will always be a Father Christmas.

To my daughter this ditty I composed in 2002 (before accusations)

My daughter Pudger is going away from home,
To study drama and English to teach many young souls,
I hope the days on campus are full of joy
And no one, simply no one mars your future joy,
As the days turn into months and seasons into years,
I hope your dreams come true and banish all your fears.
Embrace Life! Go forward! Look ahead with glee,
Smile and you will do wonders for all whom you meet.
Oh! You fill my heart with pride and joy, each, and every day,
EEh!! I'm glad you're my daughter and I love you,
More, much more than words can ever say.
Please! Please!
Be safe and mind how you go
Keep a weather eye on others and don't go out alone.
Look! Look! To the future
And give a 'shout, if you want anything,
Then please let me help out
By phone the fax or e-mail
Or maybe you could write?
The mobile they say is handy
You could reverse the charge?
I can't undo the past
And I'm sorry
For the pain, I may have caused
You are still my daughter and I love you
Very! Very! Much. JC

When Woppits was born in July 1986 Sister Francian took care of Pudger her goddaughter as I took Maria to the hospital. It was not long before Woppits enters my world with hair as black as ebony small and tiny and not a peep out of her. Again, another fascinating experience with tears in my eyes. No Jameson for me that day as I was now the owner of a car and had to rush back to collect my firstborn from the nuns on Williams Street.

When we moved in 1987 to Hereford Street, she was still a baby and we panicked when she wandered off only to find her on the step of an end house across from the back chatting away to some little boy.

She did the same when we moved to Castleton in '93 and was found playing with one of the neighbour's toddlers around the corner in their house. Woppits as a young toddler did allow herself to be bossed around by her big sister, a stubborn baby when trying to feed her was a work of art.

If she did not like what you were giving her, she would close her mouth tight and scrunch her face up in disgust. It was the same when giving her a bottle. She was very shy as a toddler but grew to be quite good at gymnastics as she got older. On taking her to a gymnastic club at her insistence she flatly refused to go in and went all coy and shy.

Woppits loved to help with the practical things in life cooking making cakes in her little oven. Woppits played a lot with her toys and I recall searching the town for a particular spider-like toy she wanted from Father Christmas.

As she got older, she knew what she wanted and went for it. Maria was not keen on the children playing out and going in other peoples' houses. That was overcome when I was erecting a fence around the property to keep the dogs off and the children wanted to help of course.

Woppits was the only one to visit me in 2003 after a row with her mother. Woppits got her first house on Sherwood Street off Queensway, Rochdale, with her partner Rory and had a baby son in 2007. She moved around quite a lot in those days to Kirkholt and even down to Falmouth Rory had family there.

A Daughter came along in 2013. Her partner Rory left in 2015 either going back or staying in Falmouth with a new girlfriend. I always thought that Woppits would be the one that would come to my rescue at the latter end of my life. Being a practical woman, she would see through the folly of what had transpired over the years. But alas it has yet to happen?

I made efforts to create a contact back to my two youngest Treacle-Pud and Woppits by sending presents over the years after the visit from the priest in 2015 regarding Maria's request for an annulment for the marriage. He had suggested that Maria may wish to tell them the result of the annulment and I should endeavour to contact the children again. In 2020 I increased the presents to three times a year because of the struggles they may be having with the pandemic of Covid19. Treacle-Pud's partner was helpful and showed a modicum of gratitude and responded confirming the name of her fourth child a baby boy in March 2018.

Woppits: "Who is Treacle-Pud's partner?

My reply: Treacle-Pud's partner and mother of 4 grandchildren!

Woppits: Oh! I have not changed my details!

My reply: Thanks, I will send it tomorrow!

Woppits: What do you do about Pudger?

My reply: That question has bothered me for years but I have acted under advice and she is in my will of which you are one of the named executors and my solicitor. I would love to give Pudger my firstborn, but having read about her mental health problems before her marriage to Paul and because of her accusations back 2004/5 and the heartbreak of you all accepting her lies which continue to hurt. I do not want to risk any confrontation. from any quarters. I just hope she is happy. Please keep this to yourself, Sorry... Dad.

Woppits: I take it you heard about Jim Gavin going to jail!

I decided to ignore this!

Woppits: What have you read about her mental health exactly? Where do you get your information from? When we try so hard to be private and move on. You have no idea of the trauma we have all been through and continue to go through. I have tried to restart my life so many times with little or no support what so ever. We all have. But I'm not prepared to keep running any longer from anyone. I do not want you or my abusive ex-partner to turn up at our addresses because it stirs up so much anger and upset distress. Whatever you want to call it. We all have mental health issues; we didn't have the best upbringing did we. I will not allow my children to suffer the same as we did as kids. I would fight tooth and nail for my children, I do. I wouldn't let anyone hurt them. Regardless of how I was feeling. Everything we have been through has torn my family apart, homelessness, abuse, trauma, breakdowns everything that child should not have to go through. I am doing my best to hold everything together for a lot of people. I have no intention of running around telling everyone things when I know it will make situations worse for every one of my family so don't tell me to keep things to myself. When I have done for so many years."

My final reply to her question with great sadness having read her blog 'Inside a blank mind.' 'Another opportunity for reconciliation lost! Had I known any of the above, my first reaction had they maintained contact, would have been to rescue them from those awful circumstances.'

In January 1988, at 40 Hereford Street, I called across the road for Sheila Barrett to keep an eye on the children as Maria thinks she has gone into labour and I take her to Birch hill. I cannot forget the day he was born. Maria was in Hospital, Mrs Barratt from across the road of 40 Hereford Street came to tell me there were complications and I was to get to the hospital. Mrs Barrett kept an eye on Pudger and Woppits whilst I went to the nuns to see if they could help later with them. It was then I confided with Sister Eileen that Maria was going to make sure with the doctor to have no more children and she was adamant she was going to have a procedure to ensure this could happen.

My concern was partly the church's teaching and I was not averse to having more children and found it difficult to reconcile with what my wife wanted. Surprisingly Sister Eileen's view it was my wife's body and her right to choose.

When I got to the hospital the complication was not about that procedure but the umbilical cord was wrapped around the baby's neck and Maria had to have a caesarean section which had already been completed on my arrival. I cried when Treacle-Pud was placed in my arms.

My Treacle-Pud was full of laughter as a baby and as a little boy. Maria revelled in his playful ways forever telling us all how much he was like her own dad Cyril Jones. Changing his nappy was a task as he would frequently decide to discharge his water like a fountain when nearing completion managing to shower my hands and sometimes even my face. Treacle-Pud had a friend up the street who he spent many a time with and he was a cheerful child. When I left, he was fourteen and he was wishful of me staying. Years later the lies changed his views.

It was in April 2011 on one of my nightly visits to the Farewell when I first saw Treacle-Pud with his girlfriend and her Father Sean. I had greeted the landlady with a high five because I had apparently won the bonus ball and then to be confronted with strong language and high levels of abuse by Treacle-Pud who I did not recognise and had not seen for seven years. The shock unnerved me and his level of hate I found very disturbing. I pondered on the situation for a few days and decided to try and make amends via Facebook private message as follows:

> *"I'm sorry I did not recognise you last week but it has been 7 years since I saw you last, if you want to contact me then I have always been in the phone book. The lies that have been told still haunt me. I do not want any trouble… love Dad"*

And the reply came back

> *F*** you; u fat ugly old freak ur a f**kin sick peado tw** and u will neva eva see my child, ur a f**in sick nob head.*

The shock knocked me for six, I found it hard to believe. I tried again in 2015 in hope. I wrote again on Facebook:

> *It is 4 years since your foul outburst, have you ever tried to find out the truth? Checked with your School if Pudger was having counselling for the alleged abuse? No! you have not!!!*

The reply:

> *F*** you, you scumbag, I'm blocking you do not contact me again, leave us alone you f****ed up freak, just die already, trust me, we will all smile.*

He has descended into darkness, hate and anger, the 'complete opposite of what I thought he would become back when he was a small jovial boy, as Maria would remind all *"just like his grandad Cyril"*?

I am so sorry that my son has developed such hate and continues to believe the lies of his big sister. What a very sad way to live, did Maria cause this? One 'wonders? For all the wrongs that have been my journey in life through childhood, married life, and the subsequent annulment by the church, I bear no malice to anyone and 'live in hope that all will find peace and happiness.

Treacle-Pud with his partner has had four children. A daughter who passed away in June 2011. A son was born in February 2013 and another daughter in April 2016. They had another baby son around March 2018.

Treacle-Pud was reaching his thirtieth birthday on the 30th of January 2018 and as I had done for Woppits, I wished to celebrate his 30 years of life despite his reluctance to be civil with me via the Facebook messages in 2011 and 2015. It is a cause of great sadness to me.

It was all change in that year of 1988, what with the arrival of Treacle-Pud moving to Whitehall Street and the community workshops closing. It was with great regret I had to accept a position with the building service joiners' shop at Whitworth Road depot in the November. Because my attempt to secure the community workshops as a training co-operative failed. It was awarded to the NHS unit on floor 3 of Croft Mill. I had to accept a position with the building service division joiners' shop.

I was interviewed for the position of Admin support operative a title made up to gain acceptance by the staff of the shop. It was not easy I can tell you the bench hands were using the machines that in my opinion was not complying with the regulations. When I spoke to them, they took great offence and matters went to senior management for arbitration. I was re-interviewed the result was I was overqualified for the position. Those were not easy years and we moved the shop to Middleton in 1989 intending to merge the plastic window factory. It never happened but I was still an admin support officer over the window factory, Education Joiners shop, Mary Street in Heywood, and a little machine shop in Littleborough. All to be closed over the years '88 to '90 and machines sold on.

What a carry-on the window factory was moved to a unit on Red Lane the education joiners transferred to joiner's shop Middleton with the one chargehand joiner that was left. The foreman retired along with half of the older bench-hands and I was expected to run the shop where I had no respect as the Person in Charge. The gaffers buried their heads until an accident happened of which I had warned them in writing would happen as they had not appointed supervision. It just so happened the young chap two years out of his time who lost his finger lived across the road from my house. At the Shop the ambulance came and took him away along with what was left of his fingers I had collected and bagged up in ice. The ambulance informed the police and an investigation began. I had already taken the requisite photos and made out my report. The health and safety came and low and behold the management decided I was the person in charge as the supervisor. I was expecting this and put a halt to it straight away by producing my contract, duplicate logbook which I kept and passed the top copy to the gaffers weekly, also the letter informing them of a possible accident only two weeks before it happened.

I was eventually appointed senior supervisor and Jimmy Mansfield as Chargehand after much persuading to the gaffers via the HSE. It remained a tough task to monitor and supervise production introducing a training program and a relevant manual to the machines in use. Overall, the lads were a good bunch and mainly got on with the job without the need to impose strict discipline. However, one chap near set the place on fire with his smoking as he proceeds to spread Evo stick on a sheet of Formica still there was no harm done and all was needed was a good talking too. One young ambitious chap kept a log of things going on in the shop and as far as the other operatives were concerned, he was reporting back to one specific Manager of the organisation. An operative had found the book he was keeping and shared its contents to the others. He did become a thorn in the side for years to come as other members of staff were wary of him. 'Continued attempts on review of the joiner's shop viability were made every couple of years the purpose being ticking a box of outsourcing the service. Several attempts were made since 1990 the suggestion then was to move back to Rochdale with a smaller operation. That failed until Geoff a roofer suggested in 1996 after the three sites were explored that led to his suggestion that the gaffers would accept the shop moving to Rugby Road as they were council-owned and more cost-effective. The glass shop was taken on at this point a challenge where it was alleged that the stock control was a major accountability problem for many years.

In the first year, we had realised where the discrepancies were occurring and spoke to a colleague about it. we agreed to have a word with the chap and suggested he stop his deception or we would be forced to act. Unfortunately, he returned to his dishonest ways inside a couple of months with the supplier and so ended up losing his job and the supplier being informed. The shop over the many years had variation of line Managers where five of other trades and only three who were Joiners.

In closing the shop, the last Manager was an electrician manager who with respect was a very nice man but under another of many reorganisations was awarded the Joiners Shop. Since the reorganisation to Rugby Road various suggestion were made with outsourcing some on the manufacturing joinery as demanded by the Rochdale North Manager who had gained charge of the shop. Another manager on taking charge had agency staff enter the shop to augment production, and yet again another had fixing joiners collecting from contract suppliers by passing the shop granting these private providers a share of the manufacturing products. With the closure of the shop in 2009 all products and materials had been successfully outsourced. As much as it vexes me it was all done under my supervision aiding and abetting the destruction of an inhouse resource as has in my opinion occurred in so many public services. Hence, with my Cooperative and Unison head on, my delivery to the bosses in 2002 of Ant's at Arm's Length.

(The housing department being coerced in 2012 being forced out of council ownership to tenants and Workers.)

In the collage you will see Frank Butterworth my colleague and friend together we renovated Jarvis Street Methodist church here in Rochdale and supervised the Community workshops during the Community Program years in the '80s. Teaching woodwork and machining for long term unemployed people. The collage depicts Rochdale at the end of the rainbow at Platt fields Garden Show in the '80s

Collage of Community Workshops Croft Mill in mid Eighties

CHAPTER 10
BACK IN TIME

In 1990 she found my mum
She at forty-Two and I am Thirty-nine years' old
Two girls and a boy
Treacle-Pud two, Woppits four
Pudger two years more
The customhouse is where we went
The children played while the mother searched
In every book, she sought from 1921 to '51
Clancy's galore All-around Lismore
God the children and I were bored. JC

- *So, it was in 1989 when we planned to go to Ireland and Maria embarked on seeking information prior to our departure.*

- *Having returned from the two weeks in Ireland Maria takes up digging for more information Reference V as if she did not know enough.*

- *Mrs Pine refers the letter to a Sister Catherine, Maria in turn writes to the sister and continues to write 'as me' all the way to 1993.*

In 1990, on the visit to Ireland to find my mother, we visited Saint Philomena's and later in the week Saint Josephs in Tralee. Saint Philomena's buildings had not changed except it was now a day school and still, there was the place where the beggars came for some food and drink. One of the nuns showed us around the outside we were not allowed inside the building as classes were going on. Maria had asked her questions and was directed to Saint Tereasa's in Blackrock. All records she said should be there, but it was a waste of time, we were told to go away and look to our future rather than looking in the past. Our trip to Saint Joseph's was more than fruitless. It was derelict and we climbed in to get a closer look around the place I pointed out the different parts of the intuition the handball alley the nurse room the work blocks and classrooms. I think we even managed to look around the brothers ground floor quarters.

But the children were far too young to understand. The visit to the customs house was rather stressful at times and utterly boring for the children the time spent in the customs house looking at ledgers from the '40s all through the '50. Maria was in her element and ended up helping others in their search for relatives. Armed with her list of places and addresses, we were driving down south to Waterford and around Lismore looking for someone who would know my mother.

We parked up on the street just a short distance down from the parish church where Maria went knocking on someone's house and stayed for an hour believing the person was or knew my mother.

We visited many sites where 'building was going on in the belief as she was told that a brother was a builder. One visit was to a farm where a 'Jimmy Clancy lived, as we approached the dog was barking fiercely and I said there is no way we are getting out of the car. However, a Chap came out and introduced himself, when asked as Jimmy Clancy and he jokingly became known as Uncle Jimmy, absolutely no relation. Then near the bridge Ballin Maria stopping again an old man who told us up that road and take the left fork and it's on your left. We parked at the entrance to the farm we could see a cottage where Maria went and knocked. She had found my mother!

It was in 1993 when an invitation came from Frank Arscott to the QRIH regimental band reunion. I contacted JGK and decided to attend in London staying at the same hotel with everyone else. It was the first time John and I had got together since I married. Maria rang the hotel out of the blue to see if I had arrived and John answered the phone.

I had failed to say he was coming with me and it caused a lot of trouble when I got back home. That Saturday night we met up with ex-members of the band and had dinner where Prince Philp attended. The current band playing in one corner of the room whilst we chatted having dinner with past members we had served with. The weekend was completed with the march past at the cenotaph by old comrades it was a good weekend.

Later this episode in life became a stick to beat me with the claims of being a homosexual as she continuously at times used the trip to discredit me in front of the children.

Having made the effort to stay away from pubs and clubs when we moved to Sherwin Way and instead having the odd can at home this too became a source of ridicule. So, I decided to join the Comrades on Smalley Street,

Castleton, as I knew the then President Bryan Holden Treasurer of Rochdale Employees Credit Union where I was Vice president. It was around that time we had a presentation upstairs to the Credit Union founders. I originally only went once a week but from time to time would slip a pint on returning from a requested shop. I first took over bingo from Bryan Crossley in the mid to late 90's. It was then I introduced my two assistants as adjudicators in the bingo. Michelin on my right and Seanin on my left. I explained that the fact that members of the audience could not see them was irrelevant? See 'The Adventures of Seamus'. I later performed the same task at Sudden Social and later the Newtown social where presents or knickknacks were introduced as extra's with winning the money. Well! it never ceases to amaze me the anger that can be leased when errors happen or when late callers shout and they are too late. Hence for the two little people to guide me and ease the situation. Since the discovery of my mother my marriage went downhill as my mother had three before marriage and three after. It was all too much for Maria's moral high ground. It was those last 10 years when my wife accused me of being homosexual a pervert and God knows what else.

In the late 90's Pudger with the teachings of her mother developed an indifference to her dad, imitating the derogatory rants that ma-ma would impart. Whenever this occurred, I would not rise but retreat to avoid these confrontations which increased in time.

My elder half Brother Oliver who Maria discovered later in the early 90s, and met in 1994 was born in Bessboro Mother and Baby home, Bessboro Blackrock Cork, in 1946.

https://www.corkbeo.ie/news/inside-bessboroug

On Meeting Oliver, I was sort of apprehensive after all I grew up thinking I was the first born. After talking to him away from the house in the comrade's club here in Castleton for a few hours over a few pints the conversation went to his own family. His eldest was daughter who was nineteen and at college hoping to be a teacher like her mother. A son who was seventeen was at secondary school and a second son who was thirteen at the same school. Finally, a daughter who was the youngest at 10 years old and went to the same school as her mother who thought there.

First daughter and son were born in England. It was a surprise to me that Oliver was in London for a period of seven years around the same time as Sean and myself. Oliver had no heirs and graces but expressed no love for his mother describing her as cold who I understand he knew of her from a distance unlike me, who always loved her regardless. On leaving for the Airport the following day he returned to the front door to Maria warning her off contacting our mother or any of the family as it was causing stress. That did not go down well with Maria as she soon told me when I returned from the airport.

At times I have become rather jealous of my now older half-brother Oliver seeing him with the other half siblings and their families on the ever-intrusive Facebook. I must say I have always been very welcome by all whenever I got the chance to visit.

The storey goes he was fostered when he was born in the Bessboro mother and baby home in Cork and ended living not far from his mother. Oliver thinks he saw her at his wedding at the back of church but has not been certain? Oliver was fostered by the Bennet Family not far from Lismore. Two of the brothers had their own carpenters' shop which I visited with Oliver just the once. That was a great experience the walls thick with sawdust guards absent from machines.

But the talent showed in the staircase's they made were truly tremendous. It was in 1996 was when Terry passed away after some time in Hospital the niche was due in a few weeks for renewal but the cemetery had removed contents a year before the expiry date and it caused no end of trouble. Terry was to reside with his mum and dad there as well. So legal action was taken against the cemetery because the niche had been opened and the contents buried in a communal grave. Well, Maria was in a terrible state and not sleeping. You see her dad never wanted to be buried because of his experience in the war where he was in hiding from the German soldiers scouring the houses for them. He and his mate were being protected by the French family down a hole in the house. There was a newspaper cutting with the story and it was present as evidence to support the claim. After several months with solicitor involvement an agreement was reached and the lease of the niche was extended for a long period eventually satisfying Maria to some extent.

Maria over time became more quarrelsome and tended, which I excused as accidents towards me when angry. This especially took place out of sight of the children when I would not enter an argument as silence was my preferred way of dealing with conflict. It was others at work over a few years both from the main office and the joiners shop continued to point out the folly of my thinking.

Their observations of my accidental injuries time and time again declared to me to wake up to the abuse I was receiving. Overtime cuts and bruises a broken finger and the indentation of a three-pin plug in my left upper arm was exclaimed by Mark one of the bench-hands. In some ways those years brought me back with the Nuns, and Maria was one of those Nuns ridiculing me in front of the children I had to run away from the failures I had become to the family.

I began to realise I was like a dog cowering in the corner hoping to avoid all confrontation. I took to going for a drink before going home. To my way of thinking reduces the stress of work before entering the stress that homelife had become. It was our time at Hereford Street when we registered at Wellfield Surgery as it was the closest for the children and remained there from Whitehall Street through to Sherwin Way, it was there confrontations developed over time with both the staff and doctors at the surgery. Treacle-Pud was suffering from breathing problems. Maria was not excepting the diagnoses of the doctors and was according to the surgery being rather difficult.

The case was referred to arbitrators for resolving and due to the lack of what was concluded as unreasonable behaviour Maria was to be dismissed from the surgery. Consequently, the children were also removed. I had begged Maria to let me do the talking during the meeting but she flew off the handle and the doctors concluded that unfortunately my wife was mentally disturbed.

Maria insisted I was to leave the surgery as well but I refused point-blank which was very brave of me as I did not usually go against her wishes. That was the first time I stood up to her instead of giving in as I had on the many occasions when her disparaging remarks on neighbours and her confrontations with the same resulting in moves from one house to another. Our last move together to Sherwin way Castleton, was as a result of a falling out with the Head of Saint Patrick's Primary School where it was alleged Pudger was being bullied and he was doing nothing about it.

Now Maria knew the head quite well as she was secretary of the school where he was the deputy. I also knew him well and considered him both competent and a very fair quiet man. His deputy at Saint Patrick's was rather aggressive towards Maria and I had to stand in front of him to try and reduce tensions.

The move from Whitehall Street in 1993 was comical, the chap two doors away had rung the police to say we were doing a moonlight flit. It was after midnight as Maria would not let me load the van until then. The police walked straight past me and asked for Maria she was mortified and she knew it was that chap that had reported it. Of course, it was my fault because I drank with him at weekends and he worked at the same place. I had to beg for Terry to help me with some of the big stuff and she was not keen as she wished to avoid any of the siblings knowing where we were moving to.

The children were carried into the new house asleep surprised and happy in the morning to be in the house with the big garden they had visited several times the months before. Whitehall Street was rented out to a chap I knew from Scouting days who defaulted in paying utilities, and I later discovering he had a gun under the bed I was giving to a colleague from work. *The gun was disposed of discreetly by him.* April 2000 the day before my 49th birthday after continuous bouts of stomach cramps and coughing of blood I gave up smoking and began preparing for my departure from the family home.

A Dragon or Banshee?

Her tongue spat fire
When her mouth opened wide
She's a prostitute, a whore
Is your bloody Mum…
She's the cause of all our bother
I left her, I had enough
I tried not to listen
So, it could not hurt
The insults were hurled
Never meek nor mild
Full of venom hatred and Vile… JC

CHAPTER 11
THE PRISON WORSE THAN JAIL

In August 2001, I left home for a flat in one of the seven sisters blocks I had acquired near Rochdale town centre. It was a Saturday night I had slept on the couch in the dining room for over six months. Matters got worse and worse. I was nobody in the house. I felt like a dog being kicked. I was waiting for the last insurance policy to be cashed all of which I split in half with Maria. It was a Saturday and I decided to go for a drink at the Albert, and when it closed, I returned to the flat to try and sleep. It was impossible, the noise of the lift next door and the callers to the flat across was constant, with money changing hands. It was awful and Sunday morning I went back to the house and empty the flat I could not stand. *Whilst driving the car back I considered going through a wall.*

I tried so hard to mend fences and bought a new car for Maria. It was a fiat Multipla at £14K hoping it would help but no, things got worse and I was still on the couch. People both at work and the club made comments on my miserable look and commented on the injuries I had on and off over the last couple of years. On the 29th of October 2001, it was a Monday morning. I packed my clothes into a few black bags, put them in the car and said goodbye to Treacle-Pud, he was already up and out of bed.

In the first few months after I had left home, 'she who must be obeyed had been trawling around the village trying to find where I was staying. I had moved to Bryans, a three-bed with 2 reception rooms. Of course, when staying at Bryan's I parked my car anywhere but where I was staying in those first few months. The last thing I wanted was Maria turning up on the doorstep of the people I was staying with.

Bryan had recently lost his wife two or three years previous. His daughter was still at school. One of the sons was a bit of a lad and led his dad a merry dance with finances. The older son lived down Hastings and came up at Christmas. A month or two later in 2001. Woppits, my daughter contacted her cousin Lauren asking if she knew where I was, she did not. That same month finding out Sean was ill when I finally got my phone book back was a shock. I soon got the chance to ring and visit. I visited him several times in the year before his death.

Bryan did try to talk to Maria on the phone to get us to reconcile but he got short change and only managed to anger her further by discussing our business with him. Before Christmas day Maria had discovered where I was staying and dumped some of my gear as well as the children's computer, a way of discrediting me with them. I spent from October to the new year with them until someone had reported more than one adult staying at the house so I rented a new home at seven Ogden Street, six months later I had to move into no 11 as the owners wanted their place back, so the brother told me.

Because I left without notice they refused to repay the deposit. I suspect they simply could not pay it back. I am extremely grateful to Bryan for that fresh start and hope I repaid his kindness in kind. It was after a holiday in Wales that left me avoiding him in the future as we had a falling out which left him in tears and me frightened to death of him. It was as if something had taken me back in time to my childhood and I could not explain to him why I felt frightened.

It was after I had moved to no 11 Ogden Street when Oliver rang me on my land line to tell me that *mother had passed away* and the funeral was on the Sunday. I was advised not to attend as much as I may have wanted to and my finances at the time could not support instant travel.

The move to number 9 came after the death of Frank King in late 2002 the same year as my Mum in August and Sean in October. David Frank's son asked if I would be interested, I agreed to the rent and as it was a three-bedroom, I then bought three new beds in case the children wanted to stay at any time.

Maria complained many times about the house needing pointing so I got someone in to do the gable end when at one stage the neighbour was hosing it down because we did not ask for permission to go on her garage roof.

I also sent someone on two occasions to see to the hot water as the claim was that had broken down as well. I continued to pay the mortgage and bills up to 2004 as if I was still living there. Maria went to the DHS to report me as living somewhere else and ended up on the social and I being told by the DHS to stop paying for everything and to pay them instead. I have to say I was much better off and reduced my borrowing from the credit union making my life that bit easier financially. At least I was no longer drowning in debt. It was not until late November 2001 that I returned to London on hearing that Sean was ill and in hospital this was also the time that I had left home. I went down to support as often as I could his appointments at the hospital.

It was October 2002 when the news came, he had passed in his sleep and I went down for the Funeral. Stan was there helping to decorate and I was given a brush to get stuck in to the decorating of the front room. Later in the week Oliver arrived for the funeral and Eileen from Inch. One day before the Funeral I'd been to the chapel of rest and afterwards I sat in Southwark Park under a pagoda thinking of Sean and began to put together a poem. I was very conscious that all called him John and I always knew him as Sean.

I did not handle the loss very well and broke down in the car trying to hide my feelings from others in the family car. A year later with Sean's ashes we set off from London with Stan as my navigator leading the convoy in avoiding the newly introduced congestion charges. It was a winding road as the song goes and we did arrive at Inch in County Kerry all in one piece. Eileen had arranged for a commemoration on the beach near some rocks. I remember Eileen saying I should read my poem but for me at the time it was private to me, so instead I sang a hymn there on the beach which was chosen by Eileen. There were three generations of the families supporting Kathleen in this adventure what I affectionately I call my London Nadolski clan.

For it was an adventure for the 'majority of the younger generation I suppose may never be experienced again together in that way. Oliver was there with Breda and my new found half siblings Mary, Jimmy, and Mick with his partner Mary a very nice surprise for me and great for Sean I thought.

It was the greatest experience of my life of families who were inter connected in so many ways. I was always welcome down to London over the forty years and by the wider extended family. I never missed holding Sean's and Kathleen's grandchildren at some stage after they entered this world a magical privilege denied me by my own!

Many a great time was had with all sorts of celebrations throughout those years. 2019 and Covid changed that. Sidney came along and I missed the customary cuddle in my arms, Lauren and Ryan went and got married in June 2021 whilst complying to the Covid rules alas I was unable to travel because of the restrictions, however, I sent a wooden heart with a quote on both sides.

My Brother Sean 25th April 1953 to 20th October 2002.

In the words of the song in "OLIVER" the musical "Where is Love" You need look no further than The Nadolski Girls and their families having welcomed me to many a celebration over the 50 years. It never ceased to amaze me the togetherness of the generations of these families. Their participation in my brother's passing and so many of them traveling to Inch when scattering his ashes. I am immensely proud to have witnessed the infectious love bestowed on each and between all of them over those 50 odd years. I continue to miss Sean and see him always in his children and now grandchildren.

The scattering of Sean's ashes in Inch

The following is a poem I wrote in Southwark Park 29th October 2002 (The day of the funeral)

MY BROTHER SEAN

My brother Sean was not very tall
Spent two years with his mum
In the heart of Dublin Town
Till his mother had the call,
To return to her own home town
My brother Sean
Know by others as John
I was four I think he was two
St. Philomena's home Stillorgan
We were leaving as two
My brother Sean and I
Known by others as John

Back to Stillorgan with the nuns
Learning our name was not Greene
But really Clancy
Lost two sisters and a brother
Not really ours so why bother
My brother Sean and I
Known to others as John

Was it to Firies or Farenfore?
They sent him to work for a tailor
He was only fourteen years old!
He had to start to earn his board
Was this all it was to be
For my brother, Sean
Known to others as John

Off to London he did go
He met Ferguson and knew the score
They teamed together to achieve their goal
Not knowing what the future may hold
How their lives would intertwine
As the years, would pass on by
Ferguson and my brother Sean
Known to others as John

20th October 2002
Came the news he's gone in his sleep
And he did not suffer, he's gone! He's gone!
I knew then how much I loved him
Not my half brother
But my true blood brother Sean
Known to others as John

Brothers together on a milk float
New sister Dymphna to meet us
And take us to a foster home
My brother Sean and I
Known to others as John
Fostered for a couple of years or more
Can't remember now it's so long ago
Played in the long grass searched for banshees
Slipped down the drainpipe to have a feed
My brother Sean and I
Known to others as John

Tralee, we went next, Industrial school for boys
Two Black lads and a Hungarian boy
On the train with big Brother Ryan
"You'll learn a trade won't that be fine"
My brother Sean and I
Known to others as John
"Clancy your sixteen out you must go,
Go with this man, out of the home"
To where I did not Know,
No chance to say, goodbye
To my brother, Sean
Known to others as John

The O'Connell's came from Annascaul
The tailor was not happy to lose this boy
But he went back to school
To Milltown and lived in Inch
With the o' Connell's of Annascaul
It pleased my brother Sean
Known to others as John

In '75 he got wed to Kathleen
The same name I thought
As that of his mother
Liam came along
He was now a proud father
Emma followed and then Lauren,
This was the family of my brother Sean
Known to others as John

It was early in 2002 with a visit to the health centre to collect a prescription for depression *and like a miracle*, sat in the waiting room were the Mum and Dad of my best friend JGK from my army days and the reason I came to live in Rochdale. I felt great chatting once again and took them to where they had just moved into the area. I can honestly say this was my extended English family who I had known since my 18th birthday and after nineteen years of absences during my marriage, they were truly back, lock stock and barrel in my life and it was as if I had never been away.

Jack played a very big supporting role through all the trials and tribulations of my future life until his passing in 2011. Leah (Mum), his wife, passed away in 2003. I recall I went to the wrong funeral parlour to attend the funeral. It was at the Co-Op and not COOP on Manchester Rd. Jack and I spent many a Saturday touring the surrounding country calling for the odd gill at a pub from Jack's past and gazing at the road maps and the beauty that surrounds Rochdale.

From seven Ogden Street in January 2002 a rented property I was a few months later moving into eleven and by January 2003 moving to number nine where I remained till October 2009. A friend of mine who had become homeless after his divorce came to stay as he was in deep financial trouble suffering depression and not eating even when I made us some substantial meals. His daughters came to visit him and his son over the period the man was destroyed by it all. Yet again he was reported as living here and friends from the comrades found him a bedsit on station approach in Castleton.

He was eventually declared bankrupt and tragically died a year or so later. It was during this time that the lies, hatred, and harassments began. Pudger was heading to university and it breaks my heart to have put her in the situation where she felt the need to create a story that would cause so much pain and heartache. My exit from the family home on October 29th 2001 may have caused this frame of mind. She and I know in our heart of hearts that there was no truth in any of the tales that were concocted. I bear no malice and can understand that other influences may have played a part in formulating her deceit.

My greatest concern then was how would she deal with her intended career of teaching. The knowledge that this case may have eaten away in the back of her mind could not be ignored and I hoped she could find help to ease her mind. Maybe it was done in anger? Maybe she just wanted to hurt me? Maybe she was lost in a sea of anguish? Maybe it was the need to create a diversion from some other problems?

This leads me to an observation at Tesco's on Silk Street where she was at the cash machine surrounded by her siblings and mother wearing this kaftan to me looked as if she was pregnant but I could not be sure. I followed up and down the isles to try and confirm if it was the case but alas it was not possible.

A family splitting up is never easy but constant confrontation is not easy either. For the past years, I have felt every emotion possible and thought of all my children and now grandchildren constantly both morning and night with sadness. I still find it extremely difficult to believe that such a lovely, delightful, innocent, and bubbly little girl could cause so much pain and tears. Oh! Maria, why did you make this happen.

Prison of the mind!
My daughter November 2004 –
Stabbed me in the back. Why? I don't 'really know
She told the cops I raped her!
It's not true I want you to know.
I'm sad that my Princess Pudger could stoop so hatefully low
Please tell me what is the score?
Cause really, 'I don't know.' JC

Regardless of what has happened, she is still my firstborn and I was instrumental along with Maria in bringing her into this world. My feelings over the subsequent years have been up and down of disbelief, anger, a concern when pondering on news items that stir the emotions to tears of despair. I fervently hope that one day to be able to reconcile but I also fear that meeting after the absence of now so many years.

Who sowed the seed of hate? And left it to ferment
To fester in the mind of one who was so inn-o-cent
Who turned her mind? To such twisted thoughts?
A woman seeking vengeance... A woman scorned

Please tell me what is the score?
Cause really, I don't know… JC

I found a book on Amazon she wrote whilst at University in Crewe "The Second Level" in which each time I read it I wondered if she was on something or was, she disturbed? Sometime in 2010, I discovered Pudger's Blog "Inside a Blank Mind" on the Internet. It has been my only connection with her to date and I check it a few times through the years. In her blog, Pudger is about sorting her life out once and for all after many pit-falls. She states it is going to take some time to get herself in shape, another experience she writes and she is on the road again. She continues to write in her blog about her mental health and her several breakdowns over those years. Putting herself in the hospital one year by overdosing was probably as serious as things could get. She reconsiders having rushed into life before each troublesome episode; this probably was a big part of why each time she just set herself on another path towards her semi-destruction. She married in June 2012 to a chap from Uganda.

The wedding took place with a service at Tweeddale Street Mosque and the following day at Saint Joseph's in 'Heywood, with the reception at Queens Park cafeteria in Heywood. I have observed her husband Paul a few times once on Claybank Street walking past me less than three feet away and close in Tesco's, he looks at me and I wonder does he know me? Does he know the false accusations Pudger has made about me? On other occasions, I have seen him from a distance. On TV's Question time in May 2017, he made a good account of himself on Question Time following discussion on the then Manchester bombing.

In 2004 after the accusations of child abuse, I was convinced that Maria had encouraged Pudger to claim this and had a knee jerk reaction to get a divorce. Maria refused the divorce but later took control and began divorce proceedings. You would think it would be on the grounds of the alleged allegations, but in all the court papers she did not cite that as the reason. It appears she did not give the same impression to the children. We must remember this was all done after Woppits, my second daughter had run away and visited me to tell me she was getting the treatment I had received something I feared would happen. She called again on Saturday afternoon and had tea with me. But Maria had managed to convince her not to come again and her birthday card and present were returned ripped up. Sad but true!

August 2004 One night after calling bingo in Newtown another local club I escorted a young lady to near her home at the request of her father who was on holiday. I left her at the pelican crossing near my home and she went up the narrow passage close by. My wife and youngest daughter went to the young girl's house and had words with her until approximately midnight. Then at 12.15 they both came knocking on my door and the wife accused me of abusing my eldest daughter since the age of three. I could not believe that a child of mine would agree with the allegations that my wife was making and I became very concerned as to the levels my wife would go to in poisoning the children against me. These allegations were never true and I was deeply worried about the children and the role my wife appears to be indoctrinating them in.

Is it a reprisal for daring to be free?
From the bullying and taunts
The verbal abuse directed about extended family (never seen)
The venomous words spouted, perpetrated by the Bacup Banshee
Inflict torture inside our minds, that being her speciality!
Please tell me what is the score
Cause really, I don't know... JC

Late one Tuesday night in September the same year I was walking an elderly lady home as usual from the bingo, what should happen, but herself (she who must be obeyed) descended behind us like the *banshee* she had become. The fright she gave us both could have caused the old lady to faint or worse. Her descent was announced with the words "do you know he is a pervert". We tried to ignore her but she carried on "he abused his daughter and his son" I guided the old lady Lilly to her bungalow advising her to lock her door and I would ring from my house when I got in. This I did, I apologised for the incident. She was upset saying she is constantly ringing her doorbell and shouting through the letterbox. I wrongly assumed the *banshee* would have gone home when we had both locked our doors. I went back out to her and asked her to leave the lady alone and ushered her to her car. She continued to make her accusations to me. I suggested she take the matter to the police.

She did not respond and got in her car and left. As with all previous encounters I recorded them in writing for my solicitor and for future reference.

The next attack was in November 2004, my wife arrived at my home demanding to speak to me. I informed her to get in touch with my solicitors. I spoke through the letterbox but she refused to go away. So, I opened the door a fraction and secured it with my foot. I asked her what she wanted and she proceeded to call me a bastard and about my mother being a prostitute. She continued to say I had no right to deny that I had sexually abused my daughter from the age of three. She tried to force her way into the house but I managed to prevent her from getting in. She said she would phone the police. I said go ahead. She then said if she had a knife now, she would kill me. At some stage, I managed to close the door and she banged on it and eventually left. At no time, did I retaliate to any of her ravings except to say, "see my solicitors?"

I do believe that she may well try to kill me at some stage. That is why I do not open the door until I know who is there. I repeat that I am worried about the effect this may be having on the Children and concerned if she is warping their minds. I am sure that she will never give this up until she has had her revenge one way or another. If the children do not back her then God knows what will happen? (I feel they have no choice really) I wrote to my divorce solicitor that if Pudger was having counselling at school three years ago, i.e., 2001, when I was still living at home then why did the school not report the alleged abuse to the authorities, as there were two other younger children to consider and at home and the same school? Then I would have been arrested if the social and police were involved. I suggested the counselling could be disproved, as records would be kept. However, the attending solicitor said to keep that until or if it goes to court.

In January 2005 at the request of Maria I requested an interest-only mortgage of £70710 to comply with my wife's wishes to pay 30k plus the outstanding mortgage of £37.633.25. I gave it serious thought and I did not feel comfortable with the whole process. I felt that my wife should put the property on the open market to determine its true value and I was confident that she would be pleasantly surprised. Another visit from my wife by herself one Saturday in March 2005 was equally disturbing. I opened the door as I foolishly thought she wanted to discuss the coming mediation sessions mentioned in a letter from my solicitor. She put her right foot inside so that I could not shut the door.

She started again to accuse me of being a pervert worse than so and so. I told her she was lying; I also told her she was sick to make these lies up. She said that I would be punished for what I had done. I said why don't you go to the police? She got her phone out and said she would ring the police now. She did not follow through with the call. She then asked me what I had done with her stamps and brown suitcase. I told her I had done nothing with them and I did not touch them. I asked her where my youngest daughter is these days and her reply was, she is not coming near me, as she would not be safe. And it is none of my business. I started to despair and let my guard down and as she walked and looked around the front room saying" what else have you got that belongs to me" I said I have nothing. She said you gave them brats down London. She removed the Picture from the wall above the television and proceeded to go out the door with it. I said that it is mine you are stealing, she replied, "You are not fit to have pictures of your children". I let her go. Then I thought no it is mine and I will not let her take it so I followed her and told her I had paid 20 pounds for that picture and she said she would take the picture and return the frame.

I grabbed the picture from under her arm and would not let go. She grabbed at my coat and the picture fell to the ground and somehow so did I. After some effort, I got up with her still hanging to my coat and made my way back to my house with her still clinging to me. I threw the picture into my front room with my glasses and blocked her from getting into the house. I was now in a very bad state and thought I was having some sort of attack. She said something like you're in a state and I said people are watching (it was a lie) but I hoped they were. Anyway, she loosened her grip and I managed to shut the door and put the bolt-on. She banged on the window and I went to the phone and dialled 999. I thought I was having an attack of some sorts and I asked for the police. The police did not arrive until 4.45 on Sunday.

I told him all that had happened and the allegations that have been made this past year and the various incidents. I also showed him some of the letters I had written to my divorce solicitor. I asked if I could be put on the danger list to which he replied it was not likely, I told him I was afraid, as my wife had threatened to kill me or punish me in some way. The officer suggested getting a restraining order on her and to do it through my solicitor. At the time, the cost was prohibitive to get a restraining order, my solicitor advised I could not afford £1500. I had to agree.

On the 20th of April 2005 I received a card requesting I contact Detective Constable Andrew Pilling. I did this to which he requested that I make an appointment to be interviewed with regards to allegations made by my eldest daughter of sexual abuse. The appointment was made for 8.30 am on the 22nd of April 2005. Statements were taken with two police officers present and a solicitor who was recommended by my divorce solicitor.

I was placed on bail until the 19th of May 2005 I returned on the 19th and was again interviewed by the one police officer with my solicitor present. During the interview, I wondered why no one thought to check with the school as to why or was Pudger receiving counselling at school in 2002 as stated by Maria's first solicitor's letter. I sat there in the interview room with all the relative documents a pile four inches high including the reports to my solicitor handling the divorce. The solicitor handling the accusations said it was best not to make references, as it would be better to use them if it went to court. In hindsight, it may have been quicker to have let the police see the documents. But he was the solicitor and I accepted his judgment. The impression I got then that it was up to the CPS and I waited on the benches at the sergeant's counter. My solicitor left for another appointment saying he would not be far if required. I was informed that the CPS wanted the medical records of my daughters and I was to be released on bail again till the 22nd of July 2005. I attended the police station again on the 22nd of July to be ushered into a room and to be told that the CPS had not made up their minds and I was to be placed on bail again until the 23rd of September 2005. My solicitor was informed the day before what was to happen so was not in attendance. I told the officer I was not bothered about it getting in the papers I have nothing to hide and I had told my workmates so it was no secret what my daughter was accusing me of.

On the 17th of September, I wrote to my solicitor to confirm that they were aware of the date to attend the police station. I attended the police station again on the 23rd of September as requested. I was informed at the help desk that I was not required to attend and that I had received a phone call to my mobile. I had turned off my mobile that morning because I was attending the police station. The receptionist informed me to give Andrew Pilling a ring later. I later rang Andrew Pilling, the officer who informs me that bail is cancelled and he was very sorry but he had expected a result by Wednesday of that week from the CPS. I was now required to wait in this Prison of the Mind till I receive a phone call as to whether there will be any charges to face. I believe this situation to be very wrong and have been and still am very much tortured in my mind.

My understanding is that these allegations were first presented to the police in Crewe where my daughter was attending University in November 2004. A letter was written before November 2004 by Maria's first set of solicitors that Pudger was receiving counselling at school (Saint Cuthbert's) before it being reported to the police at Crewe. It was my concerned opinion at the time that Maria put Pudger up to this. It broke my heart to discover that Pudger had to give up University. I wondered when the counselling started at university was it after she reported to the Crewe Police in November 2004?

I am locked up in prison
The worst of its kind
My mind always a muddle
But I'll continue the struggle
So, one day I may cuddle
My three young ones
And escape forever
This prison of the mind
Please tell me what is the score?
Cause really, I don't know. JC

Throughout all this time Jack was there for me twice a week to talk; he listened and would be planning a drive out for the Saturday helping to keep my mind on other things. Even when he had to go into respite, we managed to take his suggested Saturday trips ending up at JGK's for coffee. Towards the end of his life getting to JGK's was too difficult as it was in the wilds of Bacup Road.

CHAPTER 12
THE FINAL STRAW

In 2005 Mary Rodack was to be the mediator whilst I agreed to the mediation, I pointed out to her that Maria is not likely to agree and may get violent as I would not agree to her lies about me abusing my eldest. I later received a letter confirming that mediation was not possible. To be honest it was a relief as a confrontation with her was the last thing I needed.

It was also in 2005 I had been to the police station in Rochdale to be interviewed to answer the accusations made by Pudger. It was about that time I was pointed to an advert in the Irish post regarding those who lived in children's homes in Ireland. There was a list of the many institutions. Sean and I had been in three that were named. The request in the advert was to hear the experiences of those who had resided in those places and should contact the firm named. Having been through the pain of retelling my journey to the police with my solicitor at my side about the three "CARE" places I had been Saint Patrick's, Saint Philomena's, and Saint Josephs it was time to seek justice. Caitriona was my appointed solicitor who furnished me with the requisite documents of the Residential Institutions Redress Act 2002, A form of authority for records and an application form to take up records concerning attendance and medical records at school.

I was to see a psychiatrist and I was to provide a written statement outlining my memories of time spent in the institutions. It took a long time to fill in the form and the outline of some of the painful memories brought tears to my eyes and the paper was dotted with teardrops each time I went back to record incidents of the time.

I think I was very lucky and I still do because I am a survivor, but others from those institutions did not survive. Some of those inmates on leaving the institutions could not cope with the outside world. The truth is many were so damaged by the so-called "CARERS Nuns, Priest and Brothers" these unfortunate young people took to drink they took to drugs they even gave up on life in many ways with some ending up in mental institutions run by the same religious orders. Yes, I was lucky and now at 70 I am still lucky I survived but the one thing I crave is that my eldest will come clean about her false allegations if not to me then to her siblings.

Received in September 2006 was the replies to the redress board by the daughters of Charity of Saint Vincent de Paul Regarding Saint Patrick's Mother and Baby Home and Saint Philomena's Home. The provisional wrote:

> "Saint Patrick's was a Home for Single Mothers and their Babies. It was owned by and under the control of the state, and was run by the daughters of Charity at the request of the state." It further states, "that Sisters who worked in Saint Patrick's, say that within the constraints of the time in terms of facilities, staffing and resources available they gave the best care that they could to the mothers, babies and young children."

The Provincial wrote on Saint Philomena's identical letter "because of the passage of time and scant information or documentation I am not in a position to provide evidence to the Redress Board." She further writes:

> "Saint Philomena's Stillorgan closed as a Residential Child Care Home in 1965. We have had inquiries made from Sisters who worked there in later years. They say that they did their very best for the children and gave them the best care they could, given the limitations of the time in terms of numbers of children in care and the facilities, staffing and resources available. They say that while facilities in those times were basic, the food was plain but wholesome and was supplemented by produce from the farm attached to Saint Philomena's. They say that corporal punishment was used by some as was acceptable at that time, but in their experience was not used excessively.

Both letters finish with:

> "I note that the making of a redress award to the applicant does not amount to a finding of criminal liability or fault on the part of the above institution or any person associated with the institution."

Now the letter from the Congregation of Christian Brothers by the Province Leader writes:

> "Brother Roberts died as a member of the congregation in good standing. Brother Manning left the congregation and resides at the address indicated in our reply of the 14th September 2006. It is assumed that he has been contacted by the Board and will make a response on his behalf."

The letter goes on to mention two lads with the surname Dunne in the relevant period and there is no information on their whereabouts. This is about a stabbing I received in the carpenter's shop by Richard. The letter states:

> "Due to the passage of time and the absence of contemporaneous objective evidence, it is not possible for the congregation either to confirm or refute allegations against deceased persons, especially in the

case of brother Roberts, when such allegations are made after their deaths. There are no records of complaints of abuse, physical or sexual having been made against Brother Roberts or Brother Manning, either contemporaneously or at any time in the course of their active careers in the service of the congregation."

It finishes with the statement:

"The congregation rejects any allegations of systemic abuse having taken place in Tralee Industrial School or that boys were inadequately fed or clothed, or denied proper medical attention or an appropriate education, or otherwise maltreated or neglected and vehemently repudiated all allegations of sexual abuse there, of pupils by staff members, or that sexual activity amongst the pupils, or abusive billing was condoned by the staff."

Low and behold Brother Manning (the Shirt lifter) has produced a report to the Redress Board headed by Jack Manning, my years in Tralee August 1963 to August 1969. The report was submitted on the 10th of November 2003. Brother JACK Manning (the first time I discovered his first name) has already been called to report because others from the Home have previously made complaints about him. I agree with a lot of what he has done but it only began after an inspection and was a slow change to the previous draconian regimes that older boys would remember. See Ryan Report.

Most of what he changed was in the latter years spent at Saint Joseph's. Brother Dowling was the Kitchen Brother who also had wandering hands. Brother Price was a nasty piece of work and it appeared to us boys that he was not keen on Manning's changes. Did Price see himself as the top dog of the brother world? I attach the report by Brother Manning. See Reference VI.

It was March 2006 when I received the appointment for an assessment by an independent expert to prepare a report on the psychological effects of the incidents experienced by me in the homes. The appointment was originally for a Wednesday in July but was then changed to a Saturday because of work commitments. Jack Keegan (my English Dad) came with me to help with directions to Altrincham Rd Wilmslow and for moral support as he was aware of my anxiety regarding the whole process. The report points to the devastation experienced when my eldest daughter had accused me of child abuse.

The report continues that I avoid getting too close to children both as a Scout leader and youth worker even my own three children because of my childhood experiences. The psychiatrist goes on to report I was pleasant and cooperative well-kempt with good eye contact and appropriate behaviour.

Further, my speech is of normal flow and content and my mood, objectively and subjectively. euthymic with no idea of harm to self or others. According to the report, I did become distressed when recalling some of the childhood experiences but clearly, I have no Post Traumatic Stress Disorder. Furthermore, there is no ongoing psychosis and my cognitive functions are intact with good insight. "Although there has not been a general adaption and global level of functioning loss Mr Clancy clearly through his childhood experiences mostly of sexual abuse has found himself very uncomfortable in his role as team leader, a youth leader in his adult life in dealing with the proximity of children". Well, I have to say all this was beyond me and 'I really at the time, did not know how these reports were going to pan out.

January 2006 was when the divorce went through the final stage. A very sad day and not a pleasant feeling at all. Later that year was when the case with the Irish government was settled and a transfer of 36,000 Euros was in my bank account. To me, it was dirt money and I did not know what to do with it and spoke to Jack who said to lock it away in premium bonds until I knew what to do.

This I did and left it there till 2009. This too was the year I had found out My Mother was living in Glenageary in South Dublin. It appeared as one of the papers I received through my solicitors in Dublin under the freedom of information act. The file which I had missed on numerous occasions going through the documents I think was left in error when so many of the papers were blank.

I started going to Sudden Social in Rochdale for some entertainment and eventually started calling Bingo on Saturday and met up with John W, the secretary and his wife Cath. John was group Scout leader of the 3rd Rochdale Scout group Cath did the home help badge for the Cubs sometimes. Of course, this was all back in the '70s and we were very good friends till after the wedding. It was great to meet up again and talk about the past. John also made our wedding cake a three-tier and it was a cracker back in '82. John died very suddenly and it was well over a year till Cath ventured back into the club with her sister Mary and Fred her brother-in-law. In time

I asked her to dance and we had a great time. I took her for a meal a few times and we met up most Saturdays.

We went to a wedding with her friends in Clitheroe and I was growing more attached. I had been to Benidorm with her for a week and some others from the club. Whilst I did not like the place, I grew very fond of Cath. I had also been to Shropshire to see her daughter Sam and granddaughter Kelsey.

Sam had been in the army and received a medal from the queen after a tour of Afghanistan or Iraq. Cath had a few grandchildren and spoke of them often as you would, this kind of depressed me as I knew I had grandchildren but would never see them. On March 17th 2009 our second planned trip to Shropshire I got cold feet and pulled out of the trip, I was feeling so guilty about my relationship with Cath, but Maria was forever in my dreams apparently from talking in sleep. I suppose it was very silly but Cath was very understanding, accepting that my head was a mess. I regret very much letting her down and I must admit after so many years I miss her. I have spoken to her since when walking in the park or on the street. I constantly wish I could snog the face of her but won't because I fear both rejection and the commitment required if that makes any sense.

October 2009 was when I moved into my new home Alan got the new bed for me from someone, he knew earlier that year. It was on the way to collect it when an oriental chap and his sister or girlfriend ran into the back of me at some traffic lights. They were mortified and swapped insurance but I told them if no damage no need to worry. He rang me a week later and was very relieved when I suggested he donate to his favourite charity, this he did as I had a call from the charity thanking for the donation. I trust and always have had great faith in young people to the best they can in life for themselves and others given the chance.

With the help of Keith Janice and Jacqueline and John from the Keegan clan, helping with furniture and fixings, all the repairs and the installation were done. I drank myself to sleep at night for the first 15 years. Mornings were the worst, I would wake up as normal, then my thoughts come to think of my children as it does to this day. I'm busy during the day, but when morning comes, I wake up and remember the hurt every single morning.

Years on and on despite the pain of the lies that fester and pass through the first thoughts of the day, I miss them and now my grandchildren.

In 2014 the exercise for the annulment of the marriage had a depressing effect on me and a lot of my anger was spent on those people who were exercising their right to vote for a new committee to run the Credit Union chapter. The emails I had fired out berating those people who stood was unforgivable and I have been so sorry for my actions.

Maria seeks an Annulment from the church I suspect via her parish priest in Heywood. My first letter informing me arrives in March 2014 and asks if I am the man concerned and if I wished more information. This was a shock! My thoughts were, 'what is she up to now after so long? Of course, I want more information. More letters arrived over March, April, May, to answer questions and then read the statements from Maria but you could not take the documents away you had to read in front of the interviewer and respond according to your thoughts. I continued to object to the whole process at every stage and refused to sign anything or make promises not to discuss it with others. I did discuss with some people and was offered advice.

Two people offered to be witnesses but I felt they did not know about the marriage and they would be only offering opinions after the event which would not be relevant to the period in the marriage. I did take the advice to record any future meetings.

On June, 5th 2014 I kindly answered questions in connection with the annulment petition requested by my ex-wife to the Diocese of Salford Tribunal. The lady asking the questions was very kind and professional and requested I would not disclose or discuss the matter outside this process and presented me with a bible to swear to it. I politely told her that I had no intention of keeping it quiet or secret and I would be discussing it with friends as that is how I have managed to survive these past thirteen years and I am very grateful to all that have listened and helped me get through one of the worst times of my life.

June 2015 was the arrival of this letter stating:

> *Thank you for the time you took to answer the questions of this tribunal in the matter of the application of your former spouse for a declaration of invalidity of marriage. The presiding judge has determined that the grounds on which the case is to be instructed are:*

- *Grave lack of discretionary judgment – Petitioner*
- *Inability to assume the essential obligations of marriage – Petitioner*
- *Grave lack of discretionary judgment – Respondent*
- *The law allows you 10 days to challenge the grounds now established. Should you wish to do so you should write to me indicating your objection and the reasons for it?*
- *The law allows you 10 days to challenge the grounds now established. Should you wish to do so you should write to me indicating your objection and the reasons for it?*

(This is Church Canon Law and nothing to do with civil law.)

A recording I took of the meeting using my phone really because I could not remember what was said or what I read. It took just over three hours and I have no regrets in deciding to do this after my first meeting in June 2014 with the same person. There was a lot of silence as I read the reports and I have edited the silence out so the recording is reduced to just over an hour and a half. See Reference VII.

December 15th a Priest from the Salford diocesan Tribunal came to explain the result of the sentence regarding the annulment. The priest was in a hurry and said we had under an hour. He began with the process of the annulment he explained that he was an independent person and was not involved in the decision-making so he could not talk about the ins and outs of anything that has gone on he was just here to report the facts and if there is anything I would like him to report back then he would take notes and do so. He then required me to sign to agree I had seen him and I would keep the contents confidential. I refused to sign and said that I have not signed any agreement throughout the process; at every stage, I did not agree that the church should be doing this. He accepted my right not to sign and proceeded to explain what he called the Sentence and findings of the tribunal.

He says and I quote:

> *"In terms of the details of why they granted the annulment it had nothing to do with you in the sense of you were open to being married and understood the obligations to marry. Would that be a matter of extra understanding you knew what you were entering into because of your marriage? As far as you are concerned the church is saying you had come to terms with married life. So, they speak of a grave lack of discretionary judgement on the part of the respondent now you are the respondent, the petitioner was your former wife, you know, and on your side of things it has come back as what they call non-constant so the decision was that you, so the nullity was granted because of you, it was*

granted because of the great lack of discretionary judgement on behalf of your wife if that makes sense."

I retorted "meaning that she didn't agree to be married"

Priest; "No she agreed but she wasn't either logically able or mentally able to take on the obligations of marriage. That's what they have said."

I said "when you go back over it, when her mother was poorly and subsequently died or before she died, she refused to give up the idea of getting married to an Irish man. All the brothers encouraged her to do so, but she refused 'to point-blank. So how could she turn around and claim all that later, it is ridiculous.'

I interrupt with "so basically there saying she was tapped!" Em!

Like, it says she was enabled to assume the essential obligations of marriage, and that she made a reactionary judgement that means she was not fully aware of what she was mentally entering. Her judgement at that point and she should never have made those vows too. She wasn't freely able to enter the marriage contract. So, it says you were, but she wasn't and that's why the nullity was granted you see, because of the church's kind of perception of your former for?? That is a principle or do you think still going back to that day that she knew what she was doing?

I reply sadly "Oh Yes! Honestly, I do!"

The priest goes on to explain that I was not in the wrong and they have said using the professional services the church contacted the service of a local clinical psychologist to access her. So, the ruling was that she was not in the right mental state to enter a marriage. He says I may not have seen this, as she may be functioning reasonably well while internally there is emotionally a kind of chaos taking place. Looking back on all the trials and tribulations we both endured I do feel very sad that this has been the outcome and I am sure it is not what she will want to hear or tell our children. So, I will for the foreseeable remain in this prison of the mind. However, at times I'm up and down anger seeps into my mind. At times, I want revenge but interactions with people I know and can talk to and soon I'm forgiving yet again.

Doubts creep in as to whether the church will give her the same reasons for the annulment because I do not think she will like their clinical assessment. I fear there may be a confrontational reaction later in time.

In 2016 and no confrontation so I assume she has been told perhaps a variation of the annulment different to this recording which I took so I could remember for this book.

For weeks, I spent listening to this recording trying to understand my feelings which were full of sadness and tears at the outcome and disbelief of the church's interpretation after the reports of the clinical psychologist. I still cannot believe it?

My trust, what little I had retained was completely obliterated from the Holy Roman Catholic Church. Who yet again with pompous piety dismissed its teachings taking me back to the 28th of August at Saint John's and the marriage mass conducted by Canon O'Connell that sunny Saturday afternoon?

Exiting the church to the hymn "Now as I start upon my chosen way", to this day bringing a tear to my eye. The woman who advocated hating liars was lying all those 24 years of marriage and according to the tribunal due to mental health issues? RUBBISH! Absolute RUBBISH!

There are times I get tired of thinking, the children, and their children, I look forward to a quiet passing, to stop the sadness I feel, and wonder how it would have been if Pudger had not told those awful lies, where did she get the idea from? I wanted to give her the same present as the others had, but her blog and constant reminders by others of the hurt cautioned me against it unless it reignited the mental health issues professed in her blog. I hope she will accept what is offered in my passing. Well, it won't matter because I will have gone from this world.

CHAPTER 13
TRIPS

After Sean's funeral in 2002 I took a trip to Dublin as I had been told Dymphna was in Hospital and not very well. I went straight to the hospital from the plane and met up with John Cole, her husband. Frankie Greene, my foster brother was also there with a scowl on his face as much to say "what are you doing here" Since my return in 1968 to the Greene's on a short leave from the army Frankie has always treated me with a distance. Dymphna moved down to Carlow to recuperate and I visited as often as I could. It was on her advice that I took a Christmas holiday to Malta in 2004. Well, I was sat with two women on the plane from Manchester who was half cut and they managed to spill their drinks all over me. Oh, dear, I stank of drink and had to stay that way till I got to the hotel where I showered and changed. The trip was about doing something different and I had booked some sightseeing trips. I was sitting out on the veranda when I spotted a woman, the spit of Patsy, my foster big sister who I had not seen since my wedding to Maria in '82. She had come up from Peterborough and stayed at Mrs Mahoney's on Ashfield Rd. I approached her to check if I was right but she was too young so I asked if she was Susan, her daughter who I had not seen since she was a child. I was so wrong she was a stranger and happily, she did not take offence. Was its wishful thinking on my part. I don't know but the mind plays tricks at times?

Whilst not a complete disaster the second half I took ill and could not leave my room for a few days. Malta was interesting. One trip was in a glass boat where we could see the fish below swimming around some debris lying on the seabed. One of the sites that fascinated me was the buildings looking like they were built with sand blocks with flat roofs. A church I visited had a bomb to the left-hand side as you went in. It had been from World War two. Whilst it was an interesting trip I would not be going again as my mind wandered a lot to what my children were up to.

2016 is the year of Woppits 30th birthday. I am fixated on recognising her birthday in July but do not have a clue where she lives. I saw on Facebook she had gone to Falmouth, down south with the two children and her partner. Around August 2015 her partner no longer was her friend on

Facebook and she had gone back to her 'maiden name on Facebook. I talked to Jackie and Janice week after week seeking their points of view. I tried to search on the net but no joy whatsoever. By May I am adamant regardless of people's thoughts I'm going to find her address and send a gift to mark her time on planet earth. I eventually towards the end of June had a tracing company get me the address. Well, they got me the address within a couple of days. She was back in Heywood. I was not sure where it was so I drove out with my Sat Nav to check the address. Well, I could not believe it but there was a row of the same number lettered from A65 to L65. I had to email the firm to let me know which letter Woppits was.

I had already paid them but to be fair they made great efforts to search for the letter of the property she was living at. The tracing agency was adamant that that was her address to date.

Periodically I ventured to both ends of the road over the coming weeks. I parked outside the Catholic Church on many occasions close to the local RC primary school. I noticed Woppits was wearing a works ID that said staff on one of her photos with the children in the car. Checking online for playgroups and schools I eventually realised she might work for the primary school. So, I parked on the street close by and eventually spotted her. Her birthday had passed and having spotted her I was no nearer seeing where she lived. After the funeral of Julian, I took a turn for Heywood and asked Julian to help me out and by design, there was Woppits and the two children heading to their house set back a bit of the road. I checked it out later that night and got to send the present. This was the trip myself and Martin made to Belfast in 2017 for the world conference on credit Unions where we stayed at the famous Queens University for three or four days. We missed having our pa from Killarney Credit Union who knew the Walsh's of La Sallette Countess Road.

The visit of our Romanian Credit Union friends to Liverpool, Manchester and Lancashire in June and November of 2015 turned out to be a fantastic and overwhelming experience.

Martin Logan from Voyager Alliance Credit Union and I from Metro Moneywise volunteered to meet with Paul Jones from John Moore's University at the John Lennon airport to welcome the visitors to Liverpool.

There were 14 Northwest credit unions involved that put on such tremendous receptions and speakers at the various events. The Romanians were overwhelmed with the kindness and warmth of the welcome and they did want our Credit Union people to visit them in Romania in return. The exchange visit organized by the National Association of Credit Unions of Employees in Romania under the motto "Improving Lives through credit unions" was held later in April 2016. Participants: credit unions from North West of England and credit unions from counties Arges, Brasov, Bucharest, Dolj, Hunedoara, Mures, Prahova, Valcea as well as territorial credit unions. It was a real example of friendship and was just what being in the Credit Union movement is all about. I gave a presentation on Metro Moneywise Credit Union and my role on the supervisory committee. We learnt so much from one another and our Romanian friends and colleagues. It is a lovely country, with great people and the hospitality was second to none. I came home feeling very privileged, inspired, and proud to have taken part in such an amazing trip. I decided there and then to take a trip to other European countries and booked a trip on the Danube taking me to Hungry, Slovenia and Austria for my birthday in 2017.

Setting off from Castleton 11 am Thursday 10th of November 2017 morning with a lift to the station from Keith for the adventure on the MS Nordyls and the experience of the Norwegian fjords, the Northern lights were with a mix of eager and apprehensive thought. The train Journeys to London were pleasant and shortened with the reading of Death of an Addict. On the underground to Victoria, offers of help with my case up and down steps from young people secured my faith in them, yet again as good citizens. Victoria Station was a nightmare trying to get on the correct platform for the train to Horley where I was to stay overnight. My thanks to the lady on the ticket barriers for her help in eventually getting me on the correct train after two hours of up and down from the platform to platform.

The plane to Bergen was again not too long with the continued reading of my book from Castleton Library. Arriving at the ship or car ferry I became, at last, a guest on an explorer and working cargo Ship that calls at ports delivering the mail, what looked like kitchen worktops, supermarket goods, locals journeying back and forth to work or wherever they needed to be. The MS Nordyls are modern Ships with an intimate friendly atmosphere with a small gym, a sauna on deck two which I took advantage of most days. The ships weaved their way through channels with islands of all shapes and sizes on either side as you relax in the multi seated panorama lounge. I spent time clicking away with my little digital camera where it perplexed me to see many of my photos experiencing the presence of UFOs.

The second night out at sea was rough and I spent an hour or so over the sink and on the toilet.

Was I pleased they were strategically placed, still it was not too long before I could get to sleep in the bed not conducive to an obese person? At the various ports, I had a most pleasant time observing the loading and unloading and on occasion a walk off the boat to visit very near sites or perhaps being nosey. I did find an Art shop not sure which town or city it was in but I spent a good half hour there before returning to the ship. Many a time was spent near the café on deck to observe the Sea and some of the islands we passed, but I never saw any wildlife that had been advertised in many of the brochures. It may be that these are part of the excursions of which I felt were too expensive to be worth the money especially those requiring a coach trip in the dark. Still, Chandra Patel who I met earlier in the week went on quite a few of these trips, some she said were ok, and some not so good. Chandra and I had a 'good few laughs during the cruise and exchanged photos. Then there was the family from Devon with 90-year-old Margaret with her sixty-year-old sister Sheila and her daughter Sara and then her daughter Grace who was going on the dogs with her grandmother, Great grandmother and mother stayed on the boat.

They left the ship at Kirkenes in the north as they felt it was enough for Margaret. Also, I met there aboard, were the twins from Yorkshire and four more all ex-leaders from the Scout movement from around the English-speaking world who all sat for lunch together as it was open dining. I gave them a few of my little ditties. I did take to having a walk all around the ship on deck five on several occasions telling myself it kept me fit. This is not a cruise with vast open water stretching to the horizon either side for hours at a time. Having said that at times, the ship veered out to sea and I'm told are visited by gannets, puffins and other seabirds going about their daily business, but normally I was in bed for 10 pm.

The evening meal was a set dining and I was allocated table 28 where I was joined by Rita and Taufique Mujtaba from Essex a man and wife and Donna from Melbourne who worked as a postie. We had some wonderful conversations Taufique worked for UNICEF for many years and had some very interesting tales to tell.

Rita was alongside him at all his postings. Wonderful people I thought, they reminded me of another Bangladesh family whom I was friendly with back in 1974 on Dunster Ave.

It also reminded me of the song I co-wrote with JGK in our army days about peace in the world with the conflicts of the time not much has changed in the way of conflicts.

Let's all sing for the freedom of the people
Peace in our time and peace throughout the land.
Let's all sing for the freedom of the people.
Let's get it all together hand in hand.
What do you think of the problem in Ireland?
the Bengali people or the Vietnamese,
Do you think they are equal, higher, or lower?
what do you think about YOU?
Let's all sing for the freedom of the people
Peace in our time and peace throughout the land
let's all sing for the freedom of the people
let's get it all together hand in hand
What do you think of people with black skin?
With white skin or red skin or skin of any hue.
Do you think they're equal to higher or lower?
What do you think about YOU? JC

Well in January 2018, having given Thomas his thirtieth birthday present, I felt it was time I treated myself and after my experience on the ship with the sauna I decided to search on the internet and eventually purchased one. What a disaster! It was a kind of tent where your head stuck out of the top and you zipped yourself in. I erected it quite easily, plugged it in and switched it on and put the chair inside to sit on. After a few seconds, the chair collapsed and I was on the floor, keeled over on to my side on to the right-hand heater which was now KAPUT. Luckily, I could get hold of the remote and switch off the heat. I laid there for a while wondering what to do. Given my physique, I struggled to get up.

A day or two later I complained to the supplier about the chair who was in Germany, he said it was meant only for 10 stone. (I don't believe it!!) In the meantime, I reset the whole thing up again with two of the heating panels not working using a timber stool with four legs to sit on. It was quite nice but the two panels were needed and so the firm promised to send replacements. I told them under no circumstance to send another chair. Well, the panels they sent had the wrong fittings so I had enough and packed the lot back in the box, but what a palaver to try and return the box. I was still trying to deal with that via parcel force and DHL with the return slip I received from AMAZON towards the end of February (yes! I know about tax avoids, shame on me). Anyway, I have now got a sauna single room more solid and it looks like an extra wardrobe in the bedroom but with a glass door and it takes my weight. The door could be a bit wider to accommodate my cocoon, but I get there and revel in Classic FM for half an hour or so most days but I soon reverse it once a week.

I joined Peter Hoolahan at Wardle conservative club for his 70th birthday. Andrew Gardiner who was one of the ex-Scouts was there as well, also Adele Peter's daughter who had tracked me down on Facebook, and Wendy the wife who had recognised me and Janet Swallow her sister. I went to visit him on several Thursdays during 2018/19 talking over old times about the Scouts, our families, and the many changes we have seen over the years. He was a keen rugby player and now like myself requires the aid of a stick after heart problems a while back.

Geoff Livesey who I have known since the late '80s through work, unions and Metro Moneywise was also a rugby player along with Peter over those early years Geoff also was involved in Scouting. Peter died in December 2020.

I attended his funeral and sat outside the crematorium to listen to what was being said as the only close family of 22 in number were allowed in.

Peter died of a heart attack on Monday of the 7th and as I said to his wife Wendy It was a very fitting tribute to Peter. It also suggests that we are all heading that way some sooner than others. For myself that trip I look forward to quite often what I call 'that long sleep.'

It is forty-nine years since JGK and I were in Ireland together so we tried to go in May 2019 to the west coast Cleggan in Galway. 'Wal' dropped John off at mine in Castleton and I was having a stressful time trying to enter the postcode for the boat and Wal had a go as well with no success. we remained perplexed as to what was wrong and John who sits on the passenger's side and mentions the Sat Nav may only support England maps. 'The Sat Nav was set for England `GOBSHITE!!" Well, I knew that was not the case and subsequently was put in the UK and a pleasant journey to the boat was had. The same can be said for the crossing. One of the most peaceful and enjoyable two weeks away from the hustle and bustle of life. I enjoyed the driving but at times my sciatica would kick in and be extremely painful. At the cottage, the sun was shining and I got my face burnt. It was John's 70th Birthday on the 7th of May whilst we were there and he did a power presentation of the trip when we got back. We stayed at Lacey cottage in Rossadillisk Cleggan Bay the cottage was built in memory of those who perished in the bay 1n 1927. It sticks in my mind as the year of my mother's birth in Lismore. On the rest of the days from driving around the sky road, I had chosen my favourite spot to park up and read and listen to my music, very peaceful and relaxing. It was also my paddling spot and exploration for shells for Lily-Mae's resting place at home in the cemetery.

One trip out was to Omany Island where the tide determined when you could drive across John was not keen but I decided I would do it on my own. On reaching the island the driving paths were rather narrow and perspiration did flow from my forehead and down my face as I endeavoured to tackle the contours of the track that like a ribbon twisted up, down and around winding bends to the other side on the island where I decided to take a photo to confirm I reached the end of the track. Heading back before the tide came in, I came across a White Swan floating on some water and this took me back to the story of the Four White Swans of King Lir. I sat there for a while with gentle classical music in the background and reminded myself of that story of how the children of king Lir were transformed into four white swans and they were required to travel for 300 years to each of the four corners of the known earth.

Having revelled in the memory it was time to get on to the winding track and across the sand where John would be wandering on the mainland. After that adventure, I chanced to take unplanned roads leading uphill and down dale the sights were marvellous and many a rest stop was taken to take in the wonderous views. An included a trip to Galway Salthill to meet my half-siblings possibly for the last time, I certainly enjoyed spending the time with them and John and Jimmy got on splendidly.

Trips galore!

CHAPTER 14

MY HEART - MY FUTURE

It was August 28th 2019, 37 years since the day I got married, I was to attend a fraud awareness session with several Credit Union people. I caught the 8:45 train to Manchester Victoria and the Tram to Piccadilly arriving at N04 Piccadilly Place. It was a very interesting day, a lot of what I had heard over the past thirty years in the movement. I wondered as a director of the association if I should say a few words of thanks but Dave from the NW forum jumped in which pleased me as I was only there on behalf of Moneywise CU. On the way back to the station for the Tram, I was a little out of breath but thought that was nothing new and put it down to the excellent feed that we had at lunch.

Arrived back in Castleton and had a few jars at the Newtown club, got home at 5:30 to watch channel five news, only to find Boris had prorogued parliament. I was furious and wrote on my Facebook page "this is Dictatorship" GET HIM OUT signing the petition that I had from Labour. At the same time, my chest was getting very tight and I was having a toothache and me with no teeth. After a while, I checked the systems on the NHS web site. Yes, it looks as If I was having problems with my heart. Should I ring someone and think to myself this is the curse of the Bacup *Banshee* it will pass. I thought of the children and the grandchildren and felt do I need to carry on or look forward to the long sleep. Tired of thinking about them and other unfinished projects on my mind. I decided to have some tea and walk around for a bit it seemed to ease. So, I thought I'd sleep on it at the end of the night and decide in the morning. Most of the night was spent catching up on emails and resisting to check on the historical society website progress, but nothing appeared to be happening so I left it.

The next day after what was an up and down night to the day after a breakfast of Porridge and berries. I had an appointment at the surgery regarding my feet and hosiery but the wrong nurse was there so I had to stay at home to receive a fresh appointment for the 12th of September. I was experiencing further tightness in the chest in the afternoon and was still getting angry about Johnson's announcements and all the other rotten things that had happened to me over the years.

I decided to make a DVD for Woppits my daughter just in case with her name and current address. The purpose was to transfer all the documents regarding the case Pudger had lied about to the police. The book I had been writing about my life and the annulment case I had recorded secretly when meeting with the church officials from the Salford RC Cathedral. By the time of going to bed, the tightness in the chest had gone. I decided to leave the shopping till after my appointment with the Chiropractor at 10 to three the next day. The person checked the pulse on my feet and it was very fast. She was concerned and asked for the district nurse who also was concerned. They rang the concerns in and an Ambulance arrived and off I went, after they did their checks in the ambulance on the stretcher to the nearest hospital Crumpsall. Whilst I had an 'inclination of a heart job, I was not that bothered. At the hospital A & E, I was seen By Dr Georgina receiving all the abbreviations one hears on the telly when watching Holby City. Looking around I observed while waiting for results and other checks a small nurse stepping up on a typist chair with all the wheels to unlock a medicine metal cabinet the doors opening out and below another uniformed person trying to get at forms below the counter. H&S was not the priority here.

It was about 9:30 to 10 pm when I arrived in H3 Ward bed 11 for my three-night stay under monitors and supervision. The nurses were great at a range of levels. Now on a rake of tablets and even needles in the stomach apparently, I had a few heart attacks over the past week and low sugar levels. Friday was a difficult night for sleep. Sent Janice (who is like a sister to me) a text with all my needs what a cracker she has been. My phone being nearly out of credit and charge I was wondering if she would receive all the messages but as always, she came through.

The nurse in charge was Emma who was very friendly and everyone was her Darling which amused me no end, but I kept my gob shut. Janis arrived with Keith and I had all that I requested. When they left, I charged my phone and got on the internet with my notebook to read my emails.

One from Megan saying she was not able to catch up on the history site, another from Nina co-op college if we would do a presentation on the 11th for the Nepal visitors.

I emailed her explaining where I was and not sure if I would be around to be there, but pleased that Martin had replied he would do it on returning from Canada. I copied Martin into my reply and he rang me first thing from Canada at 8 am, 4 pm UK time, that was nice of him. He asked if I had rung Frank, but I said I did not want to bother him and he would only remind me there are two 'Fs' in Duffy. I'll ring him when I get home. I did not want him to feel the need to come in and see me.

Later, I got moved to bed 21, which should be named bay 21, as bed no 11 came with me Strange but true. There were only two of us left so they were making it a lady's ward. What a noisy night oh dear up and down peeing. Monday started ok until the Doctor said I was not going home, oh heck I'd just sent emails telling people I was. So, the morning was spent checking a new text to all I was going to another ward for heart jobs and perhaps to Fairfield to have colours in my veins to see what is going on and perhaps from thereafter X-ray to an OP. Watched the one o'clock news and had soup and tuna butties for lunch the usual checks and would you believe it my chest went tight at exactly 3:15 after the consultant had explained why I was going upstairs to Cardiology or Fairfield for procedures. It's nearly half six and still waiting. The heart attack at 3;15 lasted about 15min an ECG and a spray got me ok again but now all plans were changed.

After I had been to do my ablutions, I asked if it was ok to go for a walk, I just got to the lift area and was told to come back "we need to keep a close on you. Oh, Bother! It was around 10:15 when I was moved to the cardiology ward bed 5, up twice cold feet cold body. 7:30 Tuesday tablets ready for Fairfield. A nice bunch of trainees came along with consultants and felt I was on a Hospital TV program. Had a good laugh one of the previous doctors came to announce the Boris Johnson Patient. Great laugh by all. I used my usual expletives regarding him, again more laughs. The ambulance crew had a sense of humour as I explained my non-human experiences over the years using a little Gaelic. Arriving at Fairfield at 10:05 changed into their attire and socks for the procedures Anna and Ann my nurses for the day. Later more monitoring and checks so updating the book while I wait. I had forgot the charger for the internet, so now getting bored with waiting. Restricted in what to do to entertain me?

Well, it was not till 2:40 I was wheeled down for the Anja-gram. What a lovely bunch of staff. Happy with each other, the banter flying back and forth. each person of the team explaining their part in what they were about to do after moving from the trolley to the table where Dr Mitchell also explained his part, oh dear from the wrist travelling through the vein to the heart was not such a bad experience but interesting when I adjusted my head to the monitor to see the route of travel. However, at the joint of the elbow, the pain came along with apologies and explanations of what the Doc was doing. "Work away Doctor" "Work Away" say's I with a counterfeited chuckle, as he says "not long now," "nearly there" Oh I thought never again. But the procedure was not long, about three-quarters of an hour from start to finish. 2 hours were spent under the supervision of Ann and Donna recovering, being monitored by Ann who reminded me of Marie (A long-standing friend) having near enough the same profile and a Gait that she was a younger version as she moved around the ward.

Donna who I assumed was the person in charge moving with alacrity from one bed to the next and the centre updating notes. She had me thinking of the actress from Mama Mia also with the name Donna examining bottoms? 5 pm saw the ambulance arrive to take me back to Crumpsall. Two girls this time and I was grateful it was a chair transport rather than the stretcher which plays havoc with the coccyx bone when going over the many potholes and legal bumps between Fairfield Heywood and North. Manchester. Arriving just in time for a naughty meat pie, mash, peas, and baby carrots that were more than welcome, even just warm as they were and sponge and custard all naughty but nice. I was feeling on the up as the procedure according to Doctor Mitchell, was a success and I could go home the next day Tuesday.

This now became the norm, with the nurses looking at my bottom daily and the consultant suggesting maybe the next day this went on for the rest of the week. Perhaps I should not have mentioned the scutters to which he wanted to know what I mean "me bowels are loose."

At the suggestion of blood, I raised my eyes and expressed on each occasion "I do not want to be a Tetley tea bag with 2000 perforations" well I suppose it was only half that in the long run. Now the one needle around tea time I said there were no worries as it was going through my cocoon.

Report to Doctor; Ali

Mr Clancy is a 68-year-old gentleman who was admitted to North Manchester General Hospital with a Troponin positive chest pain. His ECG showed inferior ST elevation which was fixed and hence he was treated medically and came forward to the Lab today for an angiogram? proceed.

This was performed via the right radial artery using a 6 French sheath and TR band closure, A diagnostic 5 French TIG catheter was used and the findings were as follows: Left main stem - Free from significant disease. LAD - Mild diffuse disease throughout. Circumflex - Large vessel with what looks like a long segment of moderate disease in the OM3 branch but this does look co-dominant. RCA - Mild to moderate proximal disease with a further moderate focal lesion in the mid to distal vessel.

Given the above findings, we opted to pressure wire the right coronary artery. I used a 6 French JR4 guide and passed a Pressure Wire X to the distal right coronary artery. This was covered with 10000 units of Heparin and the RFR was 0.99. This is a reassuring negative result and Mr Clancy was transferred back to North Manchester General Hospital for medical optimisation. I have suggested stopping his Saxagliptin and starting him on Empagliflozin. This is in addition to his other secondary preventative medications. I would be grateful if you could arrange for him to be followed up on a routine basis and should he continue to have any troublesome angina symptoms then please do not hesitate to re-discuss this gentleman's case with me and we may consider further intervention on his OM3 if necessary. At this stage, I will leave any subsequent follow up in your hands.

Diagnoses: 1. Type 2 Diabetes - Tablet controlled 2. Hypertension 3. Raised BMI 4. Recent NSTEMI 5. Negative pressure wire assessment of right coronary artery.

CHAPTER 15
THE CREDIT UNION YEARS

> *What is a credit Union?*
> *A credit union is a self-help co-operative whose members pool their savings to provide each other with credit at a low interest rate. To be part of a credit union you must share a common bond with other members. This is something you all have in common such as: living or working in the same area or for a specific Employer. https://www.findyourcreditunion.co.uk*

The first I heard of Credit Unions was on one of my many trips in the early 70s back to Dublin. My foster sister Dymphna telling me the only people to get paid first was her local credit union. Breda Ash a mentor of mine was a founder of Killarney Credit Union. Her sister Helen Walsh who looked after me when I was 16 and out of the industrial school became one of the first volunteer tellers and her Daughter Elma was also a teller as a paid employee at the credit union in the 90s.

I have been involved in the Credit Unions movement since 1988 and a founding father in 1990 of Metro Rochdale Employees Credit Union LTD. During the early years I was also part of study groups and have taken part in many meetings in pursuing a Credit Union for all the people of the Metropolitan Borough of Rochdale and this came to fruition in 2002 when Street Cred came into being albeit not because of anything I might have done.

I maintained contact with Street Cred as a member and encouraged sharing training via Julian Waldron's secretary and Chapter officer of the Association of British Credit Unions Ltd. (ABCUL) together with the other credit unions in Rochdale, Kirkholt Community Credit Union with 200 members and Metro Moneywise Credit Union. I graduated at the first Credit Union Development Education Program, Class of 2004 in Edinburgh and again DEEU in Liverpool 2014. The Program is an intensive six-day program on Credit Union uniqueness and social responsibility.

When on my late afternoon arrival, Marlene, the lead, says to let the class, 'know something nobody knew about me.' Well Panic set in but as usual the little people came to my rescue. I began facing the class in profile to explain "this is not a fat belly" as I patted my tummy, "but a Cocoon and inside my cocoon is a little person called Seamus, *'The Adventures of Seamus'* and when my time is up as a human being after 300years then out pops Seamus and he cannot return till three generations of humans have passed".

After my introduction a break became necessary as there was difficulty bring back order.

In September 2004 I was asked to help at Street Cred as a volunteer in helping to catch up with their accounts as they had a backlog and had not been audited for some time. It took till the later end of August 2007 to catch up with those accounts. Efforts were made in developing and presenting a rescue plan along with the association and other interested parties. It was not acceptable to the board and they decided to take alternative action. I had no choice but to resign the position of treasurer only taken up in January 2007 resigning in September of that year.

I have been a member of the Greater Manchester Chapter of Credit Unions since 2004 and have played an active part in the promotion of credit unions becoming Chapter treasurer from 2006 till 2014. As well as treasurer I coordinate training for Credit Union members of chapters around the region. I was active in encouraging RBH in supporting a new Credit Union for Rochdale. This was achieved in 2011 and now has Manchester Credit Union providing services to the borough.

The Credit Union "Metro Rochdale Employees Credit Union Ltd," came about in November 1988 when employees of RMBC were invited by Roger Baldry to a presentation at the Champness Hall on the top floor hall about credit unions. My attempts at trying to form a training co-operative tempted my curiosity and I had met a woman called Glenis at co-work, when I worked for the Methodist Church community program. The presentation was by Brian and his wife Christine McDonald from Merseyside buses Credit Union who had been running since 1984. The attendance was between 15 and 20 people from across the departments.

In 1989, a steering group was formed where study sessions were held with Len Nuttall at the beginning and later Lesley Bird both from ABCUL (Association of British Credit Unions). Metro Rochdale Credit Union for council workers was born. After nearly two years of meetings and training and visits to other credit unions, I suggested perhaps we should stop talking about it, throw a pound in the kitty and get the ball rolling.

The President and treasurer were proposed by myself and I was proposed by Roger as Vice president. Roger suggested Julian Waldron as the secretary in his absence and Pauline Hollows agreed as assistant treasurer all voted, and others took up positions for the various committees. We now had a basis to practice amongst ourselves the task of starting the Credit Union. There was a lot of support for the Credit Union and two attempts were required for the signing as not all Study group members could turn up for the signing due to work commitments and Holidays and I was one of those as it was a lunchtime signing and some of us worked far away from the signing venue in the Original Co-Op Building here in Rochdale home of the co-operative movement".

Metro Rochdale Employees Credit Union was open for business in August 1990, and since then the Credit Union has grown significantly in terms of membership, loans to member's interest earned, dividends, assets, and general reserves. A presentation was made by Jim Dobbin MP presenting me as Vice President of the Credit Union with a plaque at Castleton Comrades Club. The Credit Union first office was a small cleaner's walk-in cupboard in what was affectionately known as the Black Box (Mandela House). I argued for retired members to be allowed continued membership under the 10% rule, alas I lost, but a few years later it was agreed. It was not until November 1996 the Credit Union's first part-time employee was taken on, Lorraine, before that we all had specific jobs after work to complete.

The name was changed to Metro Moneywise in 1998. I ran a news article in the direct service newsletter under Andy Co-op promoting the Credit Union. Lorraine retired in 2017 exactly 21 years later to the date and Diane became the Finance manager. During those early years, I played devil's advocate and was not afraid to ask questions that caused me no end of grief over the years.

This led to statements being made to the board regarding those challenges and roles I played. A written statement in 2004 to the board that I was given years later when deciding to agree to help out another Credit Union that was having a challenging time:"

I congratulate Mr Clancy on his appointment, I am sure that with his vast knowledge of the Credit Union movement, his skills with 'Curtains for Windows© and Microsoft Excel,' he will be an able person for the task. Over the past few years, he has shown to be avidly interested in security, suspected errors and any other matter which would detract from the day to day running of our organisation. I would of course remind you that for the past 14 years we have never been out of balance and there has never been a cash shortfall. Unfortunately, according to the press, this cannot be said for another organisation and I am sure that with the obsessive attitude that Mr Clancy has for audit and security, he will be perfect for the post."

I must point out that this is an extract from a very long disparaging missive and the extract is meant to be sarcastic. "I think…" My time with Street cred was as a helper in catching up with their accounts, not as treasurer but I did attend board meetings to update them on progress with the catchup. I started the task around sometime in 2004 up until August 2007 when I felt the need to resign. It was from January 2007 when I took the position of treasurer as it was the only way to have a vote on a more sustainable proposal, I was professing to the board using the advice of the trade association A new person had taken on the supervisory role in January the same year and it was this person was advocating a desire to the two members of staff the takeover of the role of manager. Dictatorship does not go well with me hence the reason for me to step down. Two months later those members of the board that were left informed the FCA they were closing the Credit Union down. These were turbulent years for me and in hindsight perhaps I allowed my problems to lash out at those I perceived to be dictatorial and feathering their nests. It has never been my intention to be upset but to voice concerns and ask the questions that others felt difficult to tackle due to the fear of ridicule. Much has changed since those years and I achieved an even greater learning curve in the three years I spent with what can be said was a challenging managed credit union. I remained with the movement and voiced some of the observations and questions which are listed:

- Does the board act as one?
- Do all the board know what governance means?
- Are there more than one or two camps on the board causing conflict?
- Are there board members with personal agendas?
- Has the board had training in what a Credit Union is how it works?

- Has any training taken place before being a board member or co-opted on to a committee?
- Are they all aware of the basic rules of the Credit Union and committees?
- Is it a one-man-band and all are led?
- Are the rolls rotated so learning by doing can be achieved?

Since my return as a volunteer member in 2009 to Metro Moneywise at the multiple requests of the vice president and others on the board, I began a specific supervisor program that was executed over a month. The checks are a month behind the Credit Union accounts. All the selections are random from the previous transactions. Revolving credit, Loans, shares. Single Documents are checked when scanning weekly. Error anomalies and observations have been discussed with staff and in most cases, a satisfactory answer is given and not necessarily recorded or reported to the board.

Errors have been reduced however at times it can be difficult to accept when observations are made and it is found not to be acceptable. This appears to have been met with hostile words and retorted with enough mistakes are made when scanning which if it is the case should be informed so it does not happen again. This works two ways and hence the need for discussions and reports to the board. The consciousness of any findings that may cause upset should not prevent reporting, debating, or discussing the matter for awareness purposes to avoid repetition, repair or require policy additions. Suggestions that one would be well placed to attend the board leaves one to think that bringing attention to findings or observations is no longer required. If the internal audit is to be outsourced as is the case with several Credit unions, at a cost to accept that it will be done with 'considerable difference to what member Volunteers currently do.

When a change to revolving credit has been introduced for a member with less than one year of membership. The policy for revolving credit has been that a member can apply after a membership of one year. This being the case the changed policy of one-year membership being waived on revolving credit should be reported to the board and recorded in the minutes even if approved by the treasurer. The board is ultimately responsible and needs to know of the changes. It is not easy to make these reports and can be very stressful as to how to present and avoid causing upset. As a result of these pressures, it is possible to consider the position with the supervisory as one requires a very thick skin. Having said all that, the Credit Union in my opinion is the best in the Northwest and always has been because of the scrutinising. checks and balances performed by the many volunteers and now employees over the 30 odd years and through the 2020 pandemic endured by the membership. I have more than enjoyed the banter from my weekly involvement at the office, a wonderful set of people dedicated to serving the members and the understanding they showed me personally with transactions I required to my estranged children.

My motivation for applying to join the board of ABCUL comes from the Northwest forum meeting on Monday evening of the 12th of February 2018 as a concern there was not going to be anyone else willing to stand. Representation and commitment were important for the future of the movement as a whole and I offered my services till others from the Northwest would come forward and take part. However, as it happens the board was reduced to nine in 2021 which was when I decided at 70 to leave being in evolved with the movement but remaining a member until I go for a long sleep. I gained from being a member of the ABCUL Board a strong belief in the purpose of trade associations coming together, Respect that there are various points of view and ways to solutions and there is a variation of views, which is healthy. I learned to understand the need for directors and members for the role of staff in why they may be the preferred deliveries of projects, presentations, and board directions. My contribution to the Board I'd like to think is an overall consistent view of the whole movement with my exploration of the history of the four nations coming together.

My hope and aspirations for the youth of the movement are listening and learning to what they need. The Credit Union movement is changing more and more employees are part of the movement with their own Ideas aspirations and understandings of where the movement needs to go. Not what we old codgers who nurtured its beginning with volunteer participation, employees now moving the movement forward professionally. The town hall discussions conducted up and down the country in 2019 was at the right time for all concerned and can bring about positive innovations to the movement moving beyond 2025. But one must realise that the movement in the UK is unique to the UK and whilst innovation from other parts of the world may be helpful, they need to be the UK developed and owned. Not forgetting small can be sustainable as much as the mighty Any future director should after a comprehensive Induction and a review of previous minutes remember it is good to listen and if one has a point of view then make it as you will be with likeminded people. Canvassing with other directors on your thoughts and understanding of the associations. Enjoy the debates and learn by taking part, always remember what has been done in the past can help to move forward.

The British Credit Union Historical Society was established in 2008. There was little take-up from the wider movement. Five years later three former officers of the Manchester Chapter of credit unions recognised those steps had to be taken. "The First 50 Years" A4 booklet compiled by Martin Logan (CU Historian) for International Credit Union Day 2013 at Sheffield Cathedral to celebrate the first fifty years in 2014 of the movement in Britain. In 2012 Martin Logan Voyager Alliance and Frank Duffy Fallowfield Credit Union and I formed the British Credit Union Historical Society. The Society has the aims of "Preserving the Past, Educating the Present, Enriching the future and Promoting unity" The idea was to build up a comprehensive and accurate resource about the Credit Union movement in the United Kingdom, which everyone can use and benefit from. I offered to fund the booklet to celebrate the movement's 50 years from my work pension which I had just received. The society holds a lot of records from 1964 onwards gathered from UK credit unions, Credit Union trade associations and individuals. These records include documents, photographs, oral histories, and video recordings, newspaper clippings. The archives are an important historical resource for credit unions, researchers, and members of the community. Website: - cuhistoryuk.com. Both myself and Martin Logan have given presentations to international visitors at the Co-op College over the years on the Movement. Martin was much better at delivering than myself; he was a natural. The talks were always well received but for health reasons, it became more difficult for me. Abbie *e-mailed* me in August of 2019 because she had been engaged by the Credit Union

Foundation to develop a bid to the National Lottery Heritage Fund for a Credit Union oral history archive project. Since she left ABCUL she had completed a Masters in History and was currently volunteering with a similar project looking at protests over the past 100 years.

I was considering where a home of the Historical society could rest as we the founders were getting older and the work that had been done was endangered of being lost and may have been forgotten. Since Martin and myself were delivering presentations to overseas Credit Union visitors for a few years to the CO-OP College it became one of the first suggestions for a home.

Having co-opted to the board of ABCUL in 2018 I soon came to the opinion that the foundation was the best place if possible. This became more so with the new CEO of the association and secretary of the Credit Union Foundation after numerous casual discussions with the then President and CEO Robert and President Karen, who when first became president said "we are but stewards of the future" in relation to my many proclamations to not forget our young professional from the CU Futures programs and "How wonderful it has been for Karen, to have worked with such kindred spirit these past few years."

During all this time since 2018, I was rather busy transferring a lot of the history built up from the 2013 website funded by myself and with the help of Megan and George from Metro Moneywise Credit Union to their proposed more up to date website with an App hopefully to be completed by March 2021 when I planned to retire from the movement. So, with all this in mind, I wrote on behalf of the British Credit Union Historical Society to offer our support for the Save and Sound Project which was currently trying to get off the ground.

It was in such changing times for the Credit Union sector, it is more important than ever to make sure that the work of the pioneers and early volunteers is understood by those who have benefited from their work. We at the society were excited about the prospect of the development of a comprehensive oral history of the movement, ensuring that the memories of people who worked to bring financial services to their communities and workplaces were not forgotten. This work was vital to ensure that their unique stories were not lost forever. Having completed the transfer of data from the old website and the introduction of lockdown throughout the UK it seemed logical to release the website as something people could peruse during their time stuck at home. With that in mind, I wrote the following to all Credit Unions and trade associations/organisations: -

> *Your credit union's history is part of The Four Nations History Project. Please add the link to your website by exploring cuhistoryuk.com and search for your Credit Union now add YOUR CREDIT UNION history link to your website for the members to view on a phone, tablet, laptop, or computer.*

Following that post, all trade associations and organisations have responded favourable about letting members know about the New Historical website cuhistoryuk.com and the majority seem to be supportive of the wish to have the Credit Union Foundation as a home for the site. It is my wish as treasurer to transfer all the remaining funds of the society to the foundation for 'future renewal of the site. However, before that can happen Martin Logan history man would like a meeting with some members of the Foundation before approving the transfer. I will be taking a step back from the Society and the ABCUL Board as I will be reaching my 70th birthday and need a rest from thinking? Megan at Metro Moneywise is continuing with overseeing the website with me for the foreseeable future. I was looking for a future home for the BCUHS and saw that within the framework and structure of the CU Foundation. The foundation was happy to facilitate the necessary meeting with the society officers. Questions were asked for in advance from the BCUHS and discussion centre around them. As follows:

> *"What type of home would the Historical Society have within the CU Foundation, Would the name of the Society disappear? What sort of support could the Foundation provide to the Historical Society? How would the Historical Society be funded? How would any future research by the Historical Society be supported and funded? There is an online section and there is an archive section. What would happen to either or both?"*

I was fully aware of all these concerns that have transpired over the years since the published booklet and the development of the website. It was my belief that the foundation would resolve those concerns overtime and Martin as the last society man standing, with his continued participation in the Save & Sound project would enhance BCUHS recognition. As you can see the questions were put at the meeting and in principle a paper was be produced by the foundation in line with our discussions and duly received in mid-October of 2020 as agreed.

By November we were all happy with the draft agreement and through the support of a permanent home for the society with the Credit Union Foundation that the website can continue with the task of preserving the History of the British Credit Union Movement.

The work of the British Credit Union Historical Society was honoured at an online signing ceremony in December 2020, Society founders and Lord Kennedy of Southwark, Chair of the Trustee Board of the *Credit Union Foundation*, and Credit Union Foundation Secretary Robert attended the remote event. Lord Kennedy praised the officers of the Society for their considerable efforts and their many achievements.

The ownership of the collection, and the website I had developed transferred to The Credit Union Foundation ensuring that the work of Credit Union pioneers would not be forgotten.

CHAPTER 16
ANCESTRY A NEW ADVENTURE

It was August 2018 when I had contact with people who were born in the same home as me in the same year. Like meeting Geraldine Martin's sister, at Winifred's funeral wake it was a strange sensation and a feeling of solidarity with these people. A feeling of acceptance I did not have with my own family and of the previously found half-siblings back in Ireland. This was when the term "Crib Mates" really came into my vocabulary a very nice feeling of togetherness. I live in hope of contacting others from those institutions. Again, it is Paul J. Redmond who I shall forever be grateful for his investigation and commitment to perhaps unintentionally linking so many "Crib Mates" around the world. Thus, began my thoughts on getting around to completing ancestry, communicating with the many people on the adoption of Facebook sites. The crib mates reading and discussing their stories from Saint Patrick's Home.

Having met on my mother's side the half-siblings on more than one occasion since 2003 after the scattering of Sean's ashes in Inch Annascaul. It was time to complete the long-held desire to send presents to all those half extra nephews and nieces I had met since. With the coronavirus spreading around the world this I felt it was the right time to complete the task as it would be in my mind useful to those young people more than me.

My last port of call was to my older brother Oliver on my mothers' side. I explained to him I have been promising to do this for months now and this Coronavirus has put my mind in focus. All my half nephews and nieces so far that I have met at some stage on my mother's side have received gifts. This I wanted completed before I embarked on meeting a half-brother on my father's side and I was a bit obsessed with being fair to all. However, the offer was declined and with that, in sadness I found it difficult to communicate with him till months later with quite by chance a message received via 'WhatsApp' something I have not mastered to use.

On first receipt of my DNA top of the list was Liam my half nephew from Sean's side followed by Tess R then Kevin R and Niamh in fourth place, SA is in fifth next is Stuart McCormack in 6th and 7th is Caroline Jones as a 2nd cousin and Andrew Chapman coming in at number 14 also 2nd cousin others do follow over 3000 cousins.

It was as early as May 16 2019 that this was in my inbox from Andrew Chapman who comes from New Zealand but live in Victoria Australia, both his parents were adopted. He Began "Gad 'day, I thought I would reach out and say hello. I'm working on how you are connected at this stage I know which branch on my tree and unfortunately, it's at a brick wall, but I have a surname that I think maybe from our common ancestor, "M" as this is the surname that is in my top matches for us on ancestry"

I had just got back from a trip to Ireland with JGK and my DNA test came in whilst I was away so I had not got into any history stuff yet. The names meant nothing to me at this stage. Andrew was a 49% DNA relation to me sharing 1.5% DNA that is between 2nd and 3rd cousins. It was a hopeful start to searching for further evidence of where I may have come from and perhaps a link to finding out on my father side. The pandemic of 2020 in Andrew's was crazy around the area of Victoria where he lived mostly involving toilet paper?!

As for the fires, the family was mostly affected by smoke in Sydney. It was bad at times so he did not go to work and just closed the house up to keep the smoke mostly out. He also had a flood and was ordered to evacuate, but didn't as the water had started to recede at the time of the order. So, they have had a bit of everything and followed now by the virus. I kept in touch throughout the year and updated with any progress I made once emailing to say I found my father only to inform him it was not the case. we did agree that we are connected it seems to be through the M name.

On receipt of my own, DNA test results the highest matches for me were Kevin R 90% and Tess R 99% from Count Armagh, brother, and sister. These two people were also a match for Andrew in Australia. In the meantime, an email arrived in my inbox from Caroline Jones nee Corcoran:

"Hi James I see we are second cousins and I was trying to work out the connection. We are related on my Roscommon side of the family who has been in Cloonfad near Tibohine for centuries. My grandmother was from Galway but I don't see any family names I recognize. Have you any ideas?? Best wishes Caroline Corcoran"

Well, knock me down with a feather a Jones turning out to be a second or third cousin (ok a Corcoran) born in Manchester as the following e-mail explains:

"Hi James I never knew my mother or father and I traced them both the old-fashioned way via a massive paper trail lasting about 20 years. I think Irish families have more secrets than most. If you like I could try and help a bit. I see you live in the Manchester area, 'were you born there, as the Cloonfad family have a big connection with Manchester going back over a couple of generations. Might be a good idea to compare what relationship you have with my other cousins and work from there? Great to hear from you, Caroline"

So, Caroline is a second cousin from the Cloonfad side of my extended family. When two people have a DNA match, it means they inherited DNA from one or more recent common ancestors. The length of DNA we have in common is measured in centimorgans. The higher the number the closer the relationship.

The most frequent family names are Corcoran, Sharkey and Beirne I perceive with the help of Caroline at the time as shown in the picture from Ancestry Thrulines. One of the many things I have got out of the search is the fantastic discovery of the Cloonfad side. It may be daft but I feel very much part of the whole Clan. Tremendous!!

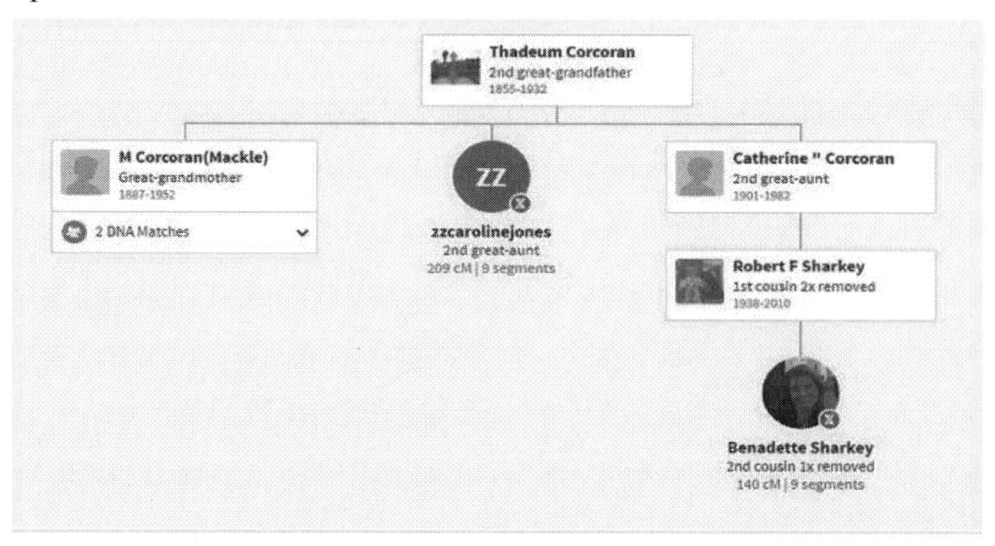

It was April 2020 when I finally realised, she was correct and Tessa R's mother Winifred M was my aunt, Jimmy M 1914 being her brother (how wrong all this was later to be). In the belief that Jimmy M was my father I searched on google for the name and up comes as suggested by Helena, 'a Glass shop in Dun Laoghaire owned by a Jimmy M. Well, I was gobsmacked surprised and at the same time shocked, frightened, and anxious as to whether I should contact him. There was an email address so with my stomach in my mouth I sent an email that read:

> "Jimmy, I have a connection to a Jimmie M and an Agnes Cullen. I wonder if you have also had a connection with this family from the early 1900s?"

The reply:

> "Yes, my father was Jimmie M. my mother was Agnes C"

I felt rather anxious now, more anxious with the reply. It was a bit of a shock but it should not have been given the DNA trail. Having started the search, I suppose I need to follow through and follow it through I did.

> "Jimmy, it is with difficulty I have written this e-mail repeatedly as I believe it may be very sensitive and hopefully will not cause any pain or upset. Please forgive my intrusion on your life because having received a DNA present from my nephew back in April 2019 and creating and investigating my family tree for the benefit of my children. it appears my great Grandfather is James M 1843 later discovering William M and Mary Anne Cocoran are my Grandparents. Rightly or wrongly. The Corcoran's and R have strong DNA shared links with me. I have concluded that we are related which surprises me as I lived in Blackrock in the mid-'50s as Jimmy Greene till '63 (I was boarded out from Stillorgan) then moved down to Tralee by the social till 1967 then Killarney and joining the army. Met my mother for the first time for about 10 minutes in 1990 after many years of searching and now this through DNA has me in a bit of a quandary. It may be wrong of me to ask but a DNA test from you could clarify the situation. I'm willing to send a test kit from Ancestry if you agree. I can send it to the Glass shop if you prefer. I have no wish to cause you or any of your family any problems.

What drove me on was the Picture of the Two girls sat on William M's knee with Mary Anne M Nee/Corcoran as they are the spitting image of my daughter at that age"

The reply was instant:

> "Good morning Jim Thanks for the reply, very fascinating. I would love to have a conversation with you regarding this. My contact house number 01280****, My mobile number is 086246**** Look forward to hearing from you soon.

We spoke several times over the phone and were both eager to meet he wanted to fly over I said no I would come to him and looked at flights in the meantime the world was facing a pandemic and both countries were in lockdown so that put an end to that plan. Jimmy agreed to do a DNA test with Ancestry we continued to speak on the phone and I began to get a bit of history on the family. His dad had an accident on the farm in Boston USA and lost an arm the family came back to Ireland. Jimmy (dad?) aged around twenty-two a carpenter by trade moved to Wales with his wife Agnes Cullen and lived in Rhyl. With the outbreak of war and young men being called up, Jimmy declared he was an American citizen and returned to Ireland. They had three children John 1936 Jimmy 1944 and Eamon 1947.

During this time in February, I looked at flights to Dublin for mid-week but had yet to book as I was concerned regarding the virus sweeping around the world. I was due at a conference in Manchester that weekend in early March. I had also booked to go to London for a First holy communion Sean's granddaughter Skye Elizabeth on the 25th of April Sean's birthday. I had been over the years to all of them and I was hoping there would not be a ban on travelling. So, in my conversations through Skype with Jimmy the new half-brother (I thought) it was looking like I might try Dublin in May if all would quieten down. It did not quieten down and all plans to meet were put on hold in the meantime I explored further the tree on the M side. Jimmy M received his DNA results and all that I thought was wrong as results show.

> *Centimorgans*
>
> *We know that a person has approximately between 6800 centimorgans (cMs) of DNA. Knowing this number helps us better understand the amount of DNA that we share with our relatives.*
>
> *For example, if we have 6,800 centimorgans and we inherited 50% of our DNA from each of our parents, it means that we inherited about 3,400 cMs from each parent. The number of total centimorgans that a person has can also help you easily use the number of centimorgans shared with someone to calculate the total percentage of DNA shared.*

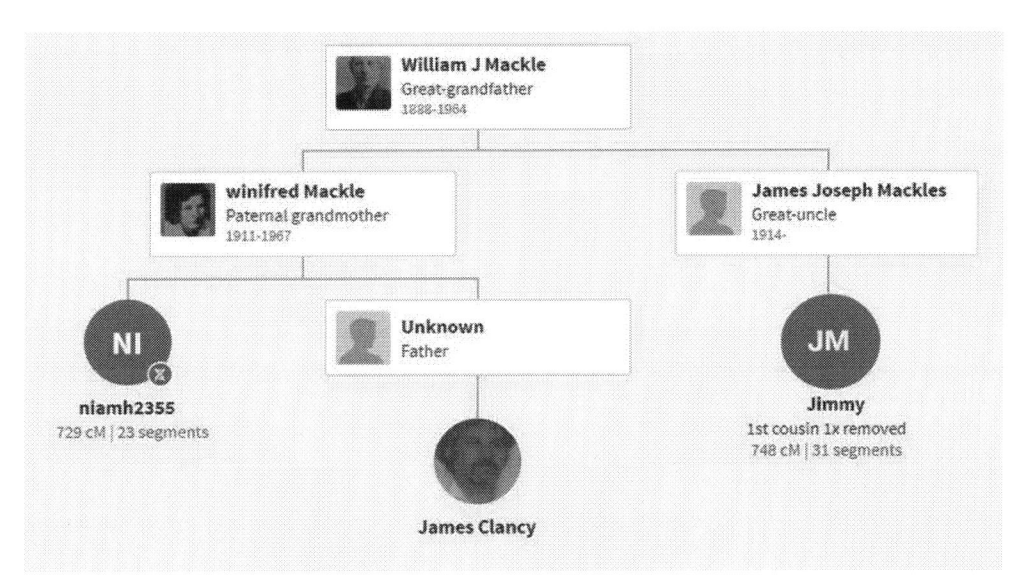

"Jimmy, I hope all is well with you and your family so sorry for dragging you into my search and hope it has not caused too much concern? It seems we are related but not in the way I thought for that I am truly sorry. So, you appear to be a first cousin through grandparents William M and Mary-Anne Corcoran. That same relationship is also with Kevin R, Tess R Niamh is a 1st cousin once removed, I think.

Well, a message from Liam S. Northern Ireland: -

"I'm managing the DNA test for my wife's father Kevin R (Family Tree is R/Fox) If you are a first cousin of Kevin, it would make sense that one of his uncles could be your father, however, we don't know anything about that. We've tried to fill in the M Family and the R family in case it helps you but (especially with the M side) we are relying on mostly word of mouth from my wife's father rather than hard documents."

Later I sent a message to Kelly C. USA I asked her about the photo of Michael R (grandfather) in her tree? The reply:

Michael R is the brother of my great grandmother, Teresa R. I don't have any information on him as far as who he may have married or if he had children.

A further message from her reveals: -

Theresa was born on 13 MAY 1875 • Elphin, Roscommon, Ireland and died 27 APR 1956 • Boston, Middlesex, Massachusetts, USA. One of her brothers was Bernard Matthew who married Katherine Fox. Their son was Michael R who married Winifred M. The story there is that Bernard came over to the US and lived with a couple of his siblings with the intention of bringing his wife and kids later. He never returned to his wife nor sent for her to come. Bernard was my great Uncle. Michaels kids (your first half cousins?) were/are: Teresa M R 1948– Bernard R 1952 – Leo R, Kevin R, Mary R, Kathrine R, Bernard R. I added Leo Bernard and Mary to my tree as I was not aware of them

154

More information came from Karen Anne Ohio USA: -

I see that you have Maxwell's in your family tree. Could you tell me how you might be related? Also, the Breslin name. I have been in touch with family in Ireland. This is the maternal side of my family. Breslin is the paternal side and this was my 'maiden name.

I replied later that year when I discover the Maxwell connection. Catherine Maxwell married Thomas Fox with a link to the R tree by my great-grandfather Bernard R through marring Kate Fox, Catherine being Kate' Mother my second great-grandmother.

Karen Anne returned with: -

Hi Jim - Thank you so much for the update. I have been in contact with a Maxwell relation in Ireland, who also has a Fox relationship (if I remember correctly) also. Some of the family still lives on Taddy Maxwell's property.

She was also able to confirm that Taddy (either Thaddeus or Timothy) did indeed marry a Mary Maxwell and that after having proved they were not related or distant enough in relationship, were married in the Catholic Church.

Karen Anne PS: -

I believe that one of the sons from Katie settled in England or maybe now that I think of it, it could be a Grandson. Now as to Winifred Breslin, I am still stumped. Some of my family went by Breslin, but also the name Bresnahan. Even my immigrant John used both names. But I do believe that the did come from the Roscommon area. It is true to say that Breslin/Breslan 1794 came from Elphin Roscommon but any details remain elusive in all the family tress explored by me and others. However, going back to the R side Mathias R my 'great 'great grandfather was an unflinching and determined Irishman. In 1879 he was one of the first to raise the standard and started a branch of the Land League in his town. He was also vice-president of the U.I. League in Elphin for his two last years. His [grand] father, Michael R my 3rd great grandfather also proved a true Irishman and fought for Ireland's freedom at the battle of Ballinamuck in 1798. The battle of Ballinamuck was fought on the 8th., Sept 1798 between the Irish and English in the battle field as it is since called beside the village of Ballinamuck. The French under General Humbert came to aid the Irish.

Now this Link came completely out of the blue the only cousin to communicate on my mothers' side to date. I discovered her on my heritage site in the august of 2020. I had to write to her with: -

"I am fascinated to know your link to John Clancy and Ellen Baldwin my Grandparents? I see you have a Bridgit Clancy on your tree as far as I am aware, she would be my Aunt Catherine/Kitty Clancy is my mother. I hope you can reply. If you can't see my tree then let me know?

Enter Kerri here in England she writes: -

Hiya, Bridget Clancy is my grandmother and her son Daniel is my father. Bridget married Denis Healy in 1950. My father told me that he has an aunt that went by the name of Kitty. I have struggled to find information on the Clancy side of the family unfortunately. Hopefully this information helps. Kerri-Ann.

I suggested to Kerri that she see my family tree to see extended family and if she knew of the Shinnicks? Her reply: -

I can see we match with the Clancy tree. Thank you for messaging me, honestly, it's been difficult to search that part of my tree. I only got to Ellen Baldwin and couldn't go no further back as I had no names nor areas in where to begin my search. With your family tree I can hopefully continue my search. The Shinnicks is not a name I am familiar with. I can ask my dad but he might not know.

I explained I had a problem with the Shinnicks for a full 2 years. Eliza or Elizabeth as John Clancy's wife was in some ways doubled up too. Not until Ed Cronin put me on the right track did, I end up with matching DNA with Liam my half nephew who I can blame for starting me on this journey of discovery. A fantastic experience learning where I came from and the link to so many people of the past and those of the present. Kerri Ann comes back with: -

I have asked my dad and unfortunately, he has no idea about the Shinnicks. As far as he is aware, Catherine married a Hale and had their children. I can see from your family tree that Catherine had 6 children and you said that you had recently met your mother. I have a DNA test on my heritage site that you could possibly compare but I'm not sure how it all works ha-ha.

I felt the need to explain my existence and that of others in my immediate family tree (much is already in the book) I conclude in the message to her: -

Kerri-Ann:

Hope all is well I have seen your DNA and your count of centMorgans to me is 637.6 Making you a 1st cousin once removed, as your dad is a first cousin to me. The circumstances of conception cannot be verified? Mother worked as a domestic in Dublin in the 50's. fathers' side. I except this may come as a surprise to your dad and you may wish to be careful as to what you tell him as I have no wish to cause alarm or shock.

The last reply is: -

It has come as a nice surprise, I'm fascinated with genealogy and due to your family tree, you have provided information for me to continue my search that I had recently given up on. I'm glad to hear you have met your half siblings and I hope this has helped you in your search. Unfortunately, we are not in constant contact with them, only funerals it seems. I will see if I can transfer my heritage DNA to ancestry. Kerri-Ann.

IT was the latter end of January 2020 when Heather's message appeared in my inbox from the Jones side of the Family Tree.

My reply was: -

That Samuel was my wife's uncle who I met several times and visited on his death bed with her in 1993/94. His sister was Claire Jones (nee Moore) my wife's mother. He was an active secretary of Hamer Working men's club in Rochdale.

He was a very nice man but I don't recall meeting is wife Joan so cannot comment. If I am correct then they had a son they had a son also called Sam. I'm not sure if it is the same Samuel Moore you are seeking?

Heather replies for more information: -

Aww this is lovely information. The Samuel Moore & Joan you refer to were my grandparents. I unfortunately didn't get the chance to meet my grandma and was only 5 when my grandad passed away in 1984. The son they had (Sam) is my Dad I am visiting my dad this weekend to show him our family tree. I'm sure he'll appreciate this a lot.

Do you know anyone who may have known my grandma Joan? Desperately trying to find out more about her. Thanks so much for this info.

OMG This is difficult but here goes: -

My ex, Maria Nee Jones Lives last I heard in Heywood, her brother Michael is in Shawclough and as far as I'm aware Rodney is in Sudden at the back OF SUDDEN CLUB. Roy is in France. Mind you your dad may Know more than me. Maria and Rodney Jones would be your best bet perhaps. I would advise caution in mentioning me to the Jones/Clancy as it was curiosity that had me investigate their family tree as both Clare Moore and Cyril were previously married with partners that had passed away. Some untrue accusation was invented to procure prosecution and an annulment to our marriage. So, take care and the best of luck. Rest assured your Grandad was a lovely man and I am pleased to have known him. kind regards Jim C.

Reply: -

Thank you ever so much for this information. Rest assured I shall tread carefully when researching and will certainly not mention your name. Appreciate your help very much. Thanks again Regards Heather. PS, it's so heart-warming to know my grandfather was a nice man.

JONES FAMILY TREE

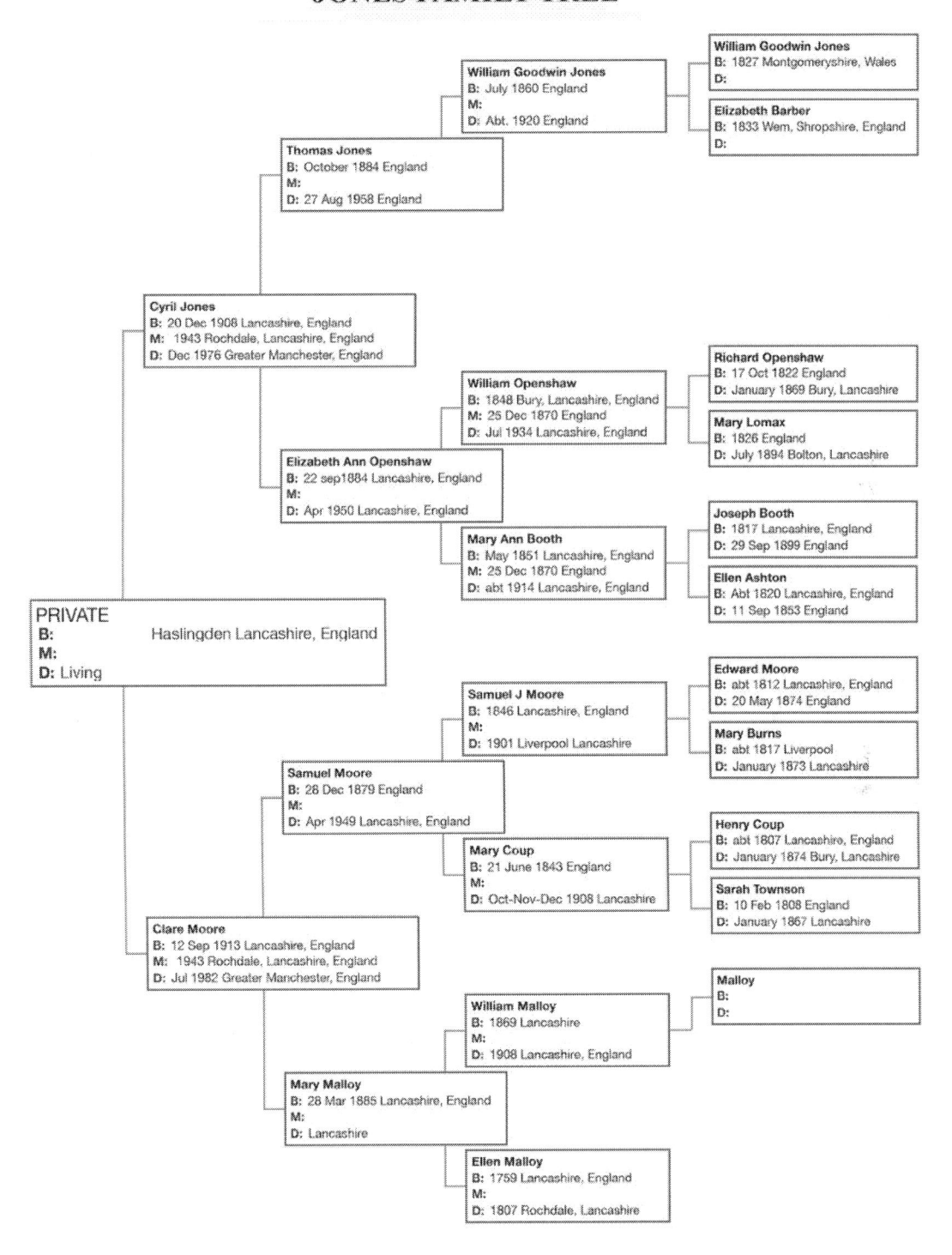

PRIVATE
B: Haslingden Lancashire, England
M:
D: Living

- **Cyril Jones**
  B: 20 Dec 1908 Lancashire, England
  M: 1943 Rochdale, Lancashire, England
  D: Dec 1976 Greater Manchester, England

  - **Thomas Jones**
    B: October 1884 England
    M:
    D: 27 Aug 1958 England

    - **William Goodwin Jones**
      B: July 1860 England
      M:
      D: Abt. 1920 England

      - **William Goodwin Jones**
        B: 1827 Montgomeryshire, Wales
        D:

      - **Elizabeth Barber**
        B: 1833 Wem, Shropshire, England
        D:

  - **Elizabeth Ann Openshaw**
    B: 22 sep1884 Lancashire, England
    M:
    D: Apr 1950 Lancashire, England

    - **William Openshaw**
      B: 1848 Bury, Lancashire, England
      M: 25 Dec 1870 England
      D: Jul 1934 Lancashire, England

      - **Richard Openshaw**
        B: 17 Oct 1822 England
        D: January 1869 Bury, Lancashire

      - **Mary Lomax**
        B: 1826 England
        D: July 1894 Bolton, Lancashire

    - **Mary Ann Booth**
      B: May 1851 Lancashire, England
      M: 25 Dec 1870 England
      D: abt 1914 Lancashire, England

      - **Joseph Booth**
        B: 1817 Lancashire, England
        D: 29 Sep 1899 England

      - **Ellen Ashton**
        B: Abt 1820 Lancashire, England
        D: 11 Sep 1853 England

- **Clare Moore**
  B: 12 Sep 1913 Lancashire, England
  M: 1943 Rochdale, Lancashire, England
  D: Jul 1982 Greater Manchester, England

  - **Samuel Moore**
    B: 26 Dec 1879 England
    M:
    D: Apr 1949 Lancashire, England

    - **Samuel J Moore**
      B: 1846 Lancashire, England
      M:
      D: 1901 Liverpool Lancashire

      - **Edward Moore**
        B: abt 1812 Lancashire, England
        D: 20 May 1874 England

      - **Mary Burns**
        B: abt 1817 Liverpool
        D: January 1873 Lancashire

    - **Mary Coup**
      B: 21 June 1843 England
      M:
      D: Oct-Nov-Dec 1908 Lancashire

      - **Henry Coup**
        B: abt 1807 Lancashire, England
        D: January 1874 Bury, Lancashire

      - **Sarah Townson**
        B: 10 Feb 1808 England
        D: January 1867 Lancashire

  - **Mary Malloy**
    B: 28 Mar 1885 Lancashire, England
    M:
    D: Lancashire

    - **William Malloy**
      B: 1869 Lancashire
      M:
      D: 1908 Lancashire, England

      - **Malloy**
        B:
        D:

    - **Ellen Malloy**
      B: 1759 Lancashire, England
      M:
      D: 1807 Rochdale, Lancashire

Cyril, Maria's father's first wife was Bertha Ashworth 1910 Crawshaw Booth, Lancashire her father was John Reacher Ashworth and Mother Mary J Ashworth of 790 Burnley Road, Rose Hill, Crawshaw Booth, Lancashire according to the census in 1911. Bertha Married Cyril Jones in July 1930 in Haslingden, Lancashire but died aged 33 January 1942 Littleborough, Lancashire with no Children. Cyril Lived at 404a Halcombe Road, Helmshore, with his Father Thomas Jones and his mother Elizabeth Anne Openshaw who had just the one child Cyril.

Clara Walton nee Moore Married in July 1936 Robert F Walton according to the 1939 census worked as General Labourer (Heavy) Cleansing. Robert Like many joined the Royal Navy with the declaration of war. On the 19th of December 1941. HMS Neptune hit a 'number of mines and quickly capsized, killing 737 crew members with only one survivor Norman Walton. Robert F Walton Rating STO 2nd Class Number D/KX 120732 of HMS Neptune is according to records is commemorated at UK Commonwealth War Graves at Tripoli War Cemetery. Clara Married Cyril a railway signal man in Rochdale around March 1943 according to family were married at St Patricks RC church. It seems the first name has been changed to Claire. So, we move on to what looks like the end of the search for my father?

When I first did my test in April 2019, I did not know what I would get in DNA matches, and I never imagined how much I would be able to learn from them. I wondered at first about imparting the knowledge I had gained and whether to be truthful about the DNA results if I am asked by new family members, and as to how I should approach the subject. This is the case that concerned me when first contact was made with Tess R who was top of the DNA list on my father's side. Would this truth cause upset to someone close or in the wider family of whom I knew nothing?

It was May 19th 2019 when I received the first results of the DNA via Ancestry which tells me that I have three very close first cousins with my nephew Liam on my mother side at the top of the list at 96% relationship, followed by another person at 99% and another at 97% and a fourth at 87%. So, with this information I decided to try another DNA sample with another company to give the paternal side and low and behold two of the above that I had tested with this company led me to understand that they were from my father's side. This was very exciting.

I messaged through to the Ancestry site and got a reply telling me the other was a brother and a daughter.

Teresa replied to my message:

> "I emailed you before but perhaps I'm mistaken. I think the connection is through my mother Winifred from Portadown Northern Ireland.
>
> I'd love to know what the connection is with you and your nephew the other is my brother. Look forward to hearing from you"

The following day I replied:

> I have no idea how we might be related all I can say is I was born in Dublin St Patrick's home the Navan Rd in 1951 out of wedlock. There is a chap in Australia called Andrew Chapman who also is related by 1.5% so far removed but he links your mother. I messaged again in October 2019 to further inform that through DNA we are related either by our parents or grandparents? April 2020, I messaged it has taken so long for me to get to this stage but I feel I should let you know that your suggestion of your mother Winifred is I'm sure my aunt and a Jimmy born in 1914 to a William or John and Mary Anne Corcoran are grandparents? All turns out in my mind to be true. Our relationship seems to be through a Michael Born 1910 and a Winifred 1914. I remember your brother 751cM and 729cM is his daughter. Jimmy 748cM is also related to Winifred being his aunt. So as far as I can make out, we are all 1st half cousins. So, when Jimmy completed the DNA test it transpires it is not possible for his dad to be my dad i.e., not enough Centimorgans but more than likely my uncle.

Oh! Dear me back to the drawing board! I again messaged that:

> I have come to the logical conclusion that my father is as a result of union of Michael and Winifred and it is only a matter of courtesy to let you know the revelations may conclude that search for my father as part of the book I am writing.

With that message I receive a reply:

> "Hi James, I think your father might be my brother or possibly my other brother. If you want some information, you can ring me on 353. *******. one brother is in hospital at present. I think I am your aunt. Kind regards…

"Well after introducing ourselves on the phone for the first time, I was asked where I lived, I said Castleton Rochdale twelve Miles from Manchester as this would be the most recognisable location. The conversation continued by proclaiming I have a relative in Manchester, Quentin an entrainer.

Well, there you have it, instant recognition I was related in the first sentence of our conversations. In a breath or two she declares she maybe my aunt.

I explained where I had come from on my mother's side and how I had had a few minutes back in 1990 with mother and her meeting my children who were in the car at the time. I then proceeded as to how I arrived at getting a DNA from Liam and this leading me to herself, and others in the listing below Liam. I was now certain that it was impossible for any of her brothers to be my father as a 1st cousin is confirmed with DNA all the way back through Michael and Johns grandparents and going further back to 1806 in line to 1790. The other side together are matched to the same descendants all the way back through Corcoran the M line to Daniel McConville 1801 and Betty Seaton 1805. Cavanagh and Kelly's 1800 to Cavanagh 1775.

The first to message me was Andrew Chapman and he led me on the Norther Ireland trail and I may not have reached this stage if young Jimmy had not done a DNA test. That is when the cat was, as I thought set amongst the pigeons. It would seem I am the grandchild of Michael and Winifred. Michael who was studying for the priesthood prior to marrying Winifred had a child (my dad) and may have had the child adopted. That is the consensus of the aunts and Uncles who are in their seventies now as am I. The strong suggestion is that my dad could be named on his mother's side? A marriage certificate was discovered by one of the uncles and Grandad and Grandmother were married in April 1936 in the Northern Ireland Portadown where Granma lived when the family came back from America because of Jimmy's accident in Boston. There are a lot of tales with this revelation and maybe more to come after I have further conversations.

My first uncle was born 1937 and is in hospital and has been for some time and at some stage I put this incentive questions to his Sister I asked does he have any children through Marriage and if so, could they be persuaded to take an ANCESTRY DNA Test? It would take a few months before being able to compare but it would solve the mystery if the test showed over 1600 to 2000 CentMorgans? This was very wrong of me as he was very ill after falling and his daughters should not be troubled with my concerns about who my father was. My second uncle born 1938 passed away in 2020 a teacher in a college in Northern Ireland. I learned his daughter wrote of my uncle in the local paper, "He was an astute political thinker and civil rights activist in the 60s, helping journalists get to marches and report the story. He even ran for SDLP office in the 1970's. A love of Ireland, justice and fairness always prevailed he had a passion for Gaelic Games. He was also an inventor and radical thinker. My eldest aunt born 1940 I'm told is still going strong and was a teacher as was my second aunt who was born in 1944 and passed away in 2016. She apparently immigrated to Canada in 1967 wrote several books her first one which I have read and had received an award in Canada. The book although fiction is based on her grandfather my great grandfather leaving his wife and small son to fend for themselves.

The true story as I have been told is great Grandfather had a dispute with someone about right of way on his smallholding, he assaulted the person and spent a short while in jail for the offence. On release in 1911 with his wife carrying his second child he sold a cow or a calf to buy his ticket to America to live with his other siblings promising to send for his wife and children later. It never happened. My great grandfather's sister would periodically write and send parcels. Later in life he did write to his eldest son Michael my grandfather.

Kitty and Michael are on the census 1911 as living with her father Thomas & Catherine a well-established family in the area. John Michael's brother was born later in that year of 1911. As far as is known both boys were reared by the grandparents. My third Aunt born 1948 went on to study law and became a barrister. My youngest uncle is a year younger than me, born 1952 he worked as an architectural draughtsman until 1976 later taking up painting. As a young unknown painter, he has had several solo exhibitions. I have managed to trace the Baldwins back to Matthew born 1811 married to Eliza Breen 1812 3rd great Grandfather and Grand Mother and on the Female side from Mary Condon 1869 to 4th great grandparents back to James Cotter 1810 and Mary Lyons 1819 some strands go back to the 1790s on DNA however even suggested further back to 1741 a James Barry an Artist buried in Westminster Abbey in London.

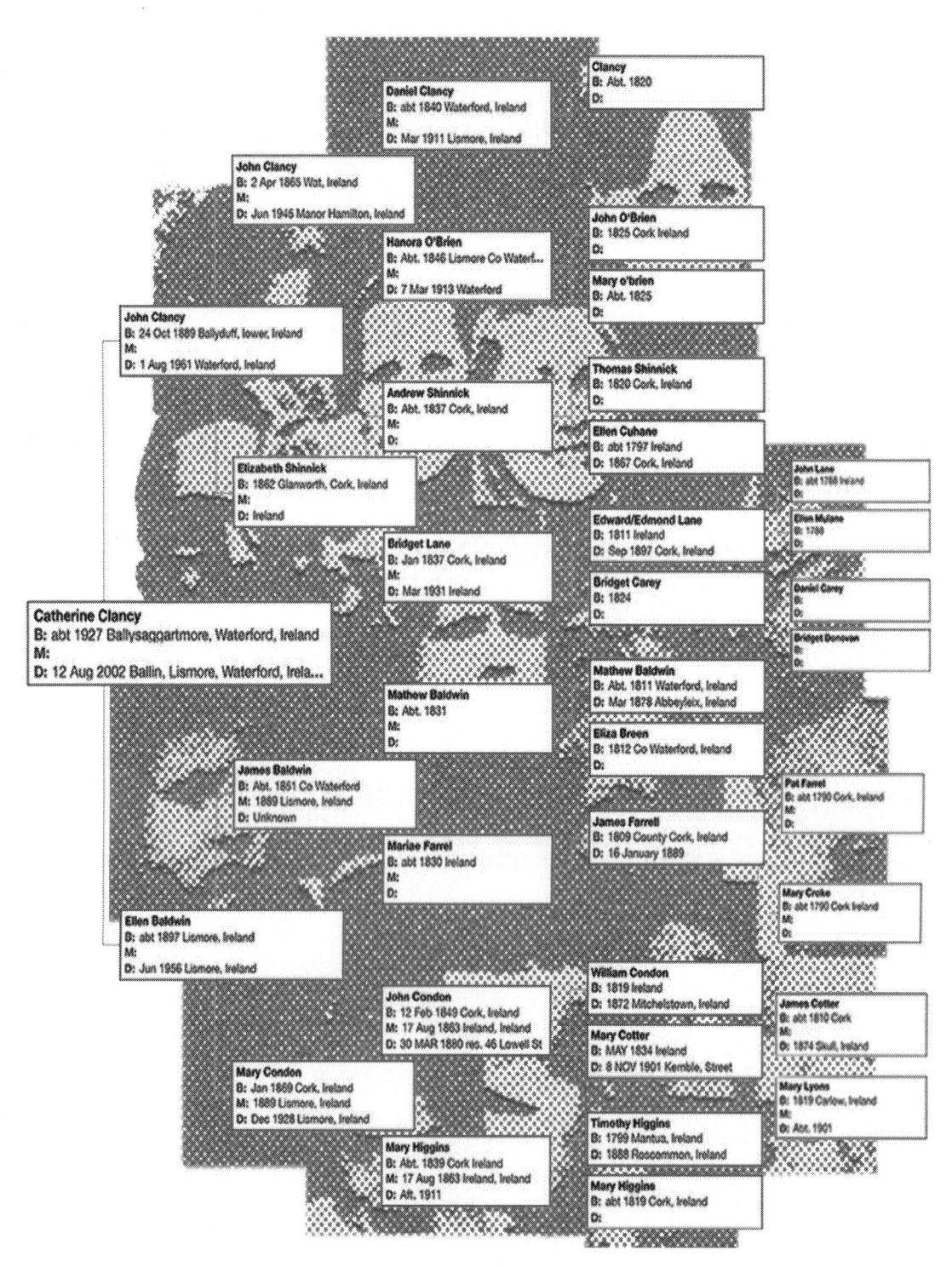

CLANCY TIMELINE

Daniel Clancy
B: abt 1840 Waterford, Ireland
M:
D: Mar 1911 Lismore, Ireland

Clancy
B: Abt. 1820
D:

John Clancy
B: 2 Apr 1865 Wat, Ireland
M:
D: Jun 1945 Manor Hamilton, Ireland

John O'Brien
B: 1825 Cork Ireland
D:

Hanora O'Brien
B: Abt. 1846 Lismore Co Waterf...
M:
D: 7 Mar 1913 Waterford

Mary o'brien
B: Abt. 1825
D:

John Clancy
B: 24 Oct 1889 Ballyduff, lower, Ireland
M:
D: 1 Aug 1961 Waterford, Ireland

Thomas Shinnick
B: 1820 Cork, Ireland
D:

Andrew Shinnick
B: Abt. 1837 Cork, Ireland
M:
D:

Ellen Cuhane
B: abt 1797 Ireland
D: 1867 Cork, Ireland

Elizabeth Shinnick
B: 1862 Glanworth, Cork, Ireland
M:
D: Ireland

John Lane
B: abt 1788 Ireland
D:

Edward/Edmond Lane
B: 1811 Ireland
D: Sep 1897 Cork, Ireland

Ellen Mulane
B: 1788
D:

Bridget Lane
B: Jan 1837 Cork, Ireland
M:
D: Mar 1931 Ireland

Bridget Carey
B: 1824
D:

Daniel Carey

Catherine Clancy
B: abt 1927 Ballysaggartmore, Waterford, Ireland
M:
D: 12 Aug 2002 Ballin, Lismore, Waterford, Irela...

Bridget Donovan

Mathew Baldwin
B: Abt. 1811 Waterford, Ireland
D: Mar 1878 Abbeyleix, Ireland

Mathew Baldwin
B: Abt. 1831
M:
D:

Eliza Breen
B: 1812 Co Waterford, Ireland
D:

James Baldwin
B: Abt. 1851 Co Waterford
M: 1889 Lismore, Ireland
D: Unknown

Pat Farrel
B: abt 1790 Cork, Ireland
D:

James Farrell
B: 1809 County Cork, Ireland
D: 16 January 1889

Mariae Farrel
B: abt 1830 Ireland
M:
D:

Mary Croke
B: abt 1790 Cork Ireland
M:
D:

Ellen Baldwin
B: abt 1897 Lismore, Ireland
M:
D: Jun 1956 Lismore, Ireland

William Condon
B: 1819 Ireland
D: 1872 Mitchelstown, Ireland

John Condon
B: 12 Feb 1849 Cork, Ireland
M: 17 Aug 1863 Ireland, Ireland
D: 30 MAR 1880 res. 46 Lowell St

James Cotter
B: abt 1810 Cork
M:
D: 1874 Skull, Ireland

Mary Cotter
B: MAY 1834 Ireland
D: 8 NOV 1901 Kemble, Street

Mary Condon
B: Jan 1869 Cork, Ireland
M: 1889 Lismore, Ireland
D: Dec 1928 Lismore, Ireland

Mary Lyons
B: 1819 Carlow, Ireland
D: Abt. 1901

Timothy Higgins
B: 1799 Mantua, Ireland
D: 1888 Roscommon, Ireland

Mary Higgins
B: Abt. 1839 Cork Ireland
M: 17 Aug 1863 Ireland, Ireland
D: Aft. 1911

Mary Higgins
B: abt 1819 Cork, Ireland
D:

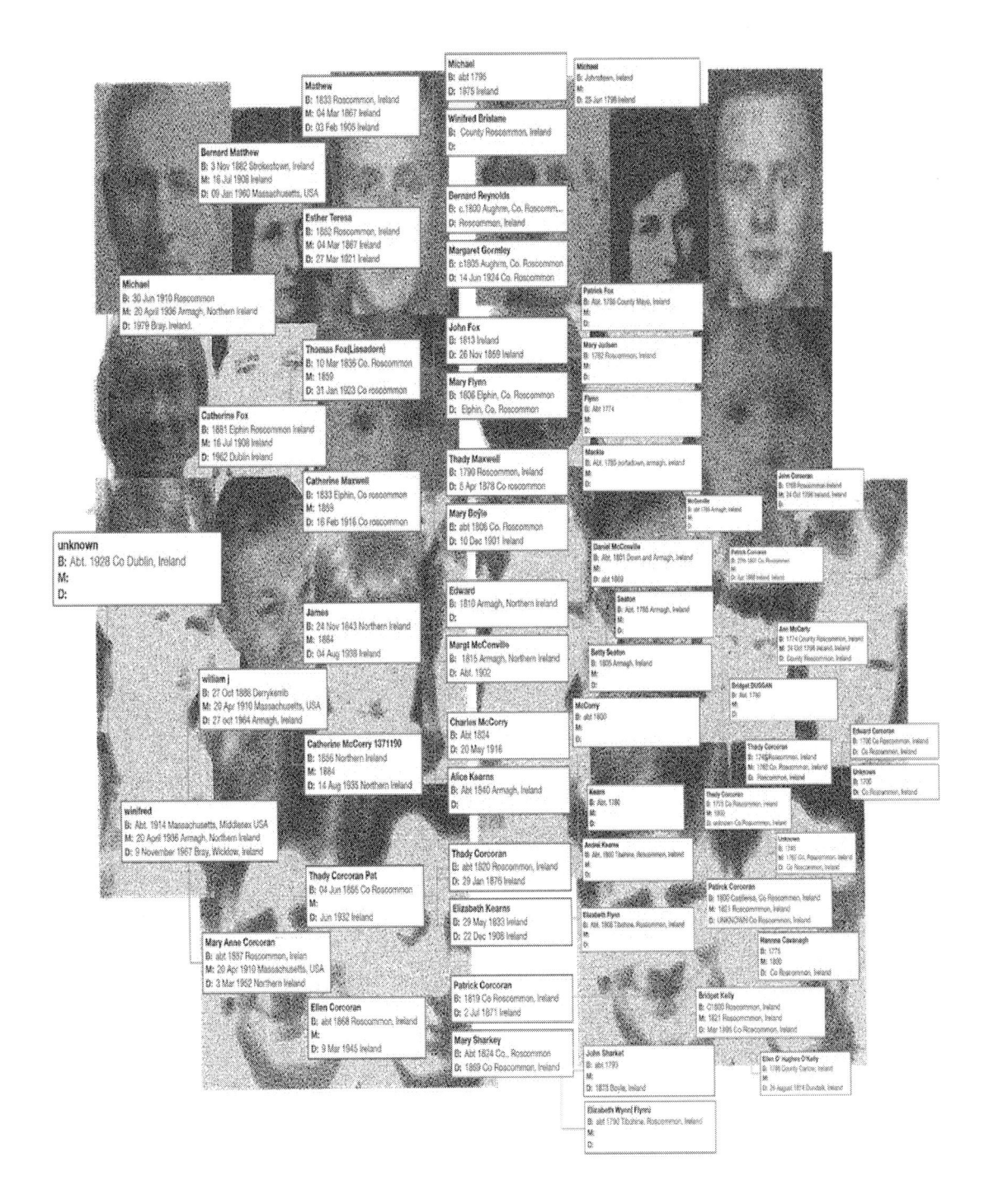

R/M TIMELINE

The family have been thinking a lot about this puzzle and discussing it with siblings and they keep coming back to the same conclusion, the only explanation is "if our parents" had a child a few years before they were married and then got together again. If people knew them this would seem very unlikely. Strange things happen and human nature is human nature. Father apparently studied for the priesthood so that will tell how religious he was! It seems the only explanation strange as it seems. I am told the rest of the family were absolutely amazed at my story and a brother is doing some research himself but it appears very clear that I am a lost nephew. It was nice to hear that, no one had any problems at all with this and nothing but the best wishes in my search. Tusla has been the suggested way forward. So, there you have it, Great Grandfather left his son and son left his son who in turn, left his son and under duress, he left his son, will it continue with Treacle-Pud, leaving his son? 'It remains to be seen?'

The evidence of this painstaking search of my parents was documented somewhere in Ireland, however, confirmation of my father's data eludes me. The census documentation of mother and father have yet to be found for that time prior to my conception. Such a challenge lies solely in the hands of current or future family interest. Notwithstanding my own further investigations curtailed by the travel restrictions of the era of the present-day pandemic.

I have enjoyed this journey as a realisation of how much we are wholly interconnected and the importance of being nice to everyone. Love is the sweetest thing; you must find it and hang on.

It is very hard to believe that I have found my roots and I have so many relatives around the world but like I tell everyone I meet I am 96% Irish and 4% Scottish thanks to the little people of this world?

DNA will give you clarity and confirmation of your existence, 'so do not give up! Upload your personal DNA results to GEDmatch which provides more applications for comparing your DNA test results with other people. *It's free!*

CHAPTER 17
UPSTAIRS DOWNSTAIRS AND COVID 19

In March 2020 I Attended the ABCUL AGM week ending the 15th having breakfast with Linda Dawn Morgan from *Crown Savers Credit Union* in London, a lady who I met in Edinburgh in 2004 on the first DEUK program in the United Kingdom. I had met up with her at various times on my trips to London. Dawn sadly died two weeks later; she was poorly and had recently been in hospital before coming to Manchester. The next few days received a phone call that Bonnar, a good friend had also passed away. Bonnar a musician who lived in Heywood was suffering from cancer, a frequent visitor to the Newtown club here in Castleton, and the third person to pass away was Jack Coates also a patron of the club who became a friend from the Farewell Inn days. Thus, began the 2020 lockdown.

This was my start to the lockdown of 2020 when I began to enjoy the company of the resident from downstairs chatting in the garden doing this new thing called social distancing and forgetting about all the other messed up feelings continuing to doggedly clog up my mind. Mother divine, she could talk but for me that was great, I could listen and not have to reply unnecessarily slowly basking in the sun for hours on end getting perhaps an overdose of vitamin D and a beetroot red cocoon to boot. Her Friend was a frequent caller during this time and was encouraging Drina and me as two peas in a pod. 'Drina and I began to visit Aldi's shopping purchasing flowers for Lily Mae's Grave and then heading to the cemetery as her daughter had passed a few years previous the anniversary being the eighth of May. We took a few trips out in the car going to the lake for Fish and Chips on a Saturday, ice cream at the Whitehouse Blackstone Edge, and other trips around the area finishing off with Kentucky Fried Chicken. Those early days as I got to know her, Drina sat in the back of the car as a safety precaution of the coronavirus.

In time and lots of texting between us, I have funny feelings that have escaped me for so long in the pit of my stomach. I have Drina withdrawal systems when her texts stop and a feeling of abandonment until the first text of the morning. Yes, I think my life is changing yet again and I am perhaps on a new journey one that I feel is without competition but a kind of melancholy perfect peace in my mind in contrast to the perpetual concern of conflict that was my marriage in always wishing to please and failing dismally. It was a joint decision to revamp the gardens as we conversed regarding the blanket of weeds spreading in both gardens and an overhaul was required thus agreed between the two of us. A few weeks passed and we continued to talk but not getting anywhere so I asked Carol to ask her fella if he wanted the job as he was self-employed and perhaps in need of work not being able to receive furlough payments during the pandemic of Covid 19. Well, he appeared on the phone to be keen and would access and quote a ballpark figure the following week. That did not happen so I was back to Square one. I emailed another person as I had viewed his work with Woodland View off Bacup road.

An agreement was reached with great expectations for all involved. The following week the work began with great gusto and in time the second garden was being cleared. For it is what Drina wanted. Eight-foot by twelve-foot decking for her garden furniture and leisurely hours.

Drina, bless her! and I fell out or perhaps it was my stubborn ways in so far as she was making suggestions to the chap doing the work not consulting me and I was beginning to feel used as before with a previous relationship. Having laid our cards on the table when I as usual had calmed down. Drina carried on being Drina and our cavorting came to a halt for a short while, resuming perhaps with more care later as the work progressed. I later realised she did not necessarily hear half of what was being said, missing keywords, that on occasion steered the conversation in other directions as she had yet to receive new hearing aids. The plan for the rockery with a cave for the hidden Lord Buddha didn't half cause me some pain as after assembly my mind would not accept what I had thought was the completed product. In the absence of the worker, I disassembled and reassembled several times, the rocks with the cave and put the lord Buddha further in hiding till my mind was at rest. Drina sat by my side whilst I rested and in deep thinking offering words of concern regarding my heart and back. Also, regarding my continuously lifting and shifting heavy rocks to and fro! The following day the worker arrives informing me the said rockery and cave was not finished and would require taking down and reassembling after the waterfall feature was fitted. Oh! Heck!!

In time the job progressed to a near conclusion. Not all I requested was delivered with reasons for executions not viable or possible? I was not convinced as easy in my opinion was the person's preferred option.

Throughout this time Drina and I were getting closer and the cavorting moving to a higher level. Elevenses became the norm each day along with the application of cream and massaging of my feet and legs and the request of higher, higher. Her fingers invoked a relaxing feeling of ecstasy and as the nuns would say impure thoughts. Those impure thoughts after watching the obligatory soaps did progress further with the multiple massages habitually performed, being magically sensual and many a rise to other expectations. I introduced her to my local club and arranged membership when the lockdown was lifted. This too was a joy and I felt at ease returning to enjoying a pint in the company of a woman after so many years.

We shared a meal or two both upstairs in my flat and downstairs in hers before our jaunts to the Newtown club. When Boris the gobshite allowed the opening of restaurants' we had lunch at a local eatery. Yes, I was getting closer and closer. Drina was having a get together with family and a very close friend on a Saturday and although I was invited, I was not ready to be involved or inspected by the family. I was pleased that her garden was completed as I had suggested it got priority for the occasion of her birthday. On that day I called at the Comrades Club here in Castleton for a glass of Guinness, and after an hour I went down to Middleton to sort out a Fencing quote for Jacqueline on my return I decided to be brave and see how the 'get together was going in the garden. Yes, all was well and I was offered a drink but requested orange juice and water which Drina's daughter had sorted being the perfect host she introduced me to her daughter, her aunt, cousin, and Drina's best friend who I had already met before. There was a bit of music being played on a mobile phone which was hardly audible. A selection of finger food was later brought out and duly consumed and Oscar the daughter' dog had taken to pinching the sausage rolls but had no interest in the Veggie offerings they were consumed by her daughter and cousin. The Chocolate cake was with Green and Chocolate Malteser absolutely to die for, beautiful, mouth-watering, delicious and all created by the hands of her sister as many more cakes before this one as stored on Drina's phone. The granddaughter had to attend a children's party so she left with her mammy.

By six o'clock the sun was retiring and the promised clouds were gathering above so a dash to the front room was achieved by all with the call to open the presents brought. Drina continued to open her presents and two of the parcels contained perfume and samples were being tried on all present. I smelled both and when asked if I liked them, I said no whilst others had proclaimed their love of the aroma. One of the girls I could feel was not best pleased with my reply but for the others it was refreshing to get a straight answer. More presents were opened and I could not help noticing they had all come from just the one person who seemed to require the approval of all present. The conversation steered to a jovial reason as to why Drina could not be contacted at various times of the evenings and I made some jocular comments as to the possible causes. At this stage I knew I was late for the club, bade my farewell and went upstairs to collect my bingo bag of prizes only to return knocking on the door to declare that one cannot do much with a periwinkle. Leaving them in what I perceived as polite laughter. Drina's birthday bash had been a success by all accounts and downstairs was in darkness on my return to my abode. Sundays had been established as a day of rest from each other in the early days of our cavorting as this was the day, so I completed my cooking for the week however I ceased to bake bread and cake halfway down what was becoming a mind distraction relationship.

Weeks later after the party Drina had been to Todmorden to meet her sister and after their jaunt around the Saturday market, they had a few jars and a good laugh in a pub that afternoon. I was coming to tea as usual and received a text informing me it would be late and we ate about 7:30. It was steak pudding mixed with little new potatoes, gravy. I said I think this is too much for me but I ate it all and enjoyed it as well. After, as was becoming the norm we walked round to the club it was a warm night and I was determined not to drink as much as on previous occasions. I started with orange and water Drina had a pint of lager. I was requested to call bingo which is 'my won't on a Saturday' and changed to a pint of lager before the first session of bingo.

Conversation flowed freely as did the drink between the gang of four in the far corner near to the bar throughout the evening as it has done since the introduction of Drina to my Saturday companions at the reopening of the club. With the drink, the discussion led to how the cavorting was going and as to how far we had gone and the suggestion came across that we should try getting closer together by spending the night with each other. All through the cavorting, we had returned to our beds every time which suited me fine as I toss and turn a lot and enjoy my sleep using the whole bed. So, when we left the club and got back upstairs-downstairs, I said we will try the night together upstairs at mine as I was feeling guilty for not trying and there would be no "hanky-panky" as we both had far too much to drink. Well, what a night I was up and down like a yoyo I just could not sleep. It was about four in the morning I was getting more and more agitated. In the end, I had to ask Drina to go back downstairs. She led me to believe she understood; in fact, she said so again when getting dressed and again when I went down to do the door. We kissed goodnight and I asked if she had got her key out and we bade goodnight again, even though it was early morning.

That morning it was late for me. I was up just after ten and decided not to wake Drina with texting and I would wait to hear from her. Nothing for most of the day and then a garbled predictive text of which I endeavoured to decipher and assumed she was the worst for the weather as none of it made any sense. Except that one line was I presumed she needed to stay in bed on Monday to catch up on sleep. It seemed reasonable to me so I got on with trying updating this book which I had neglected unconsciously making input errors because my mind was all a buzz thinking, not all was well downstairs. It was later that afternoon around two o'clock, 13:58 to be precise when one of the clearest texts the first I received in all the six months of cavorting was in near perfect Queen's English. "Good afternoon Jim bop… I am going to give Gail a help in hand with something she's collecting, selling, about tea-time love so I'll see Ya after Emmerdale + Corrie ok chuck" I replied "What happened to stay in bed all day? CHUCK"! a term she knew I did not like. It was then I realised something was up and it was confirmed by her reply two hours later where she was also going for a meal with Gail and "Lusa" afterwards.

Knowing something was wrong I left it alone for the night and woke up around Four in the morning with a tight chest laying there wondering what to do and eventually went searching for my spray which I found. After some time, it eased off and I fell back asleep. Waking that morning about eight-thirty with Drina on my mind and the stress I felt I decided to try a conciliatory text. "Morning Flower if you're up I'm going to collect a parcel from the Post Office. It seems the postie couldn't see the doorbell. Anyway, I'll call for a brew on the way back if that is allowed and perhaps a foot rub. Also, a clear up of all that missed Sunday and Monday XXX."

Well, I got no answer at all on my return and waited for a few hours in the hope of a favourable text but nothing came. This was stressing me out, so in the end, I went down the stairs unlocked the side gate and knocked on the back door which was as usual ajar, so as usual I called out on my way to the front room asking how things were. In the end, I said I sensed that something was wrong and would she tell me what? It was having to leave my flat in the night and return to her own. She had decided it was over "She had DUMPED ME". Well, I was so angry and upset I left saying that I had been used to procure her decking landscaping her garden at a large financial cost. She replied she paid for the decking but failed to mention the seventy-seven pound I had subscribed via her selling my treadmill and the purchase of the curtains she did not want or need. I was a fool and all week I felt a fool and further on I still feel a fool.

I told her I would no longer do her bins to return my key to the shed and took my cream that was allegedly lost and surprisingly turned up from the week before. Yes, I know everything I did that week was petty and the anger continued in my head for quite a while. Long drawn-out texts had continued all about being sorry for upsetting me, it was nothing to do with anyone else and wanting to remain friends, it was not me that was the problem, but something to do with her stomach and needing to talk to me further about it all. I accept that perhaps I was wrong but I vowed not to go back there but will endeavour to be civil and not be as petty as I had been.

I also decided that my cavorting days were over for good as much as I had enjoyed the relationship that had developed far too quickly. During the late summer months, I insisted to myself not to avoid using my garden when the sun shone and I erected a barrier between the shared path and my garden.

Thus, avoiding the visiting dogs from downstairs using it as a toilet and the intention of avoiding possible confrontation with Drina. Neighbours will have noticed the distance and barrier created between Drina and me as we both sat silently in our respective gardens. The anger rises and subsides time and time again but as autumn looms and the leaves begin to fall, I am mellowing; my thoughts and my mind's eye draws me continuously to the magical porcelain doll in a foetus position lying still on my bed reminding me of Greek or Roman marble statues void of any form of garments. Yes, it was a knee jerk reaction that I regret which I perceived to have left too long to come back from to feel comfortable and renewed.

I continue to console myself with the persistent thought of others who controlled Drina's absence from her life. In hindsight, my selfish actions that Sunday morning was so wrong and I could have tried to sleep in my reclining chair which often I had done in spouts of illness.

Moving on to January 2021 Covid 19 strains had begun to affect the young and Drina's daughter had the disease and then her niece. Now she was scared and decided the cavorting should stop for a while and I was fine with that but it lasted just a couple of days and by the weekend we were eating again together. More of her family contracted the disease but managed to recover in hospital.

Christmas came we had dinner together upstairs with all the trimmings with the odd can of larger and Drina occasionally with the pink gin. All in all, very peaceful and nice. Spring had been and gone and there was no sign of the waterfall being completed in my garden. At the time I was assured it would be fitted as soon as possible in the spring of the new year. The chap not being well and with a spell in hospital was unable to complete so I left it till the summer to make contact. It was early spring when I received this invitation regarding Lauren and Ryan a nice surprise, Lauren being the youngest of Sean and Kathleen's children getting wed?

The time has finally come
We have set a date
Ryan & I will say 'I' do'
and we 'really just can't wait!
We're sorry you can't join us
but Covid rules apply.
We ask you write a message on this Heart
And seen it by reply!
They'll be added to our Guestbook.

Your wishes on display.
Please raise a glass on 2nd June,
and toast our wedding day?

More recently, Drina and I continued seeing each other and enjoying each other's company during all this time. Visits together to the club had started back, albeit with Boris's permission. The May and the bank holiday availed us of the local pub restaurants in serving food again.

With the lifting of some of the covid rules Bernard and I embarked on an entertainment program for our Newtown club here in Castleton. Bernard spent some considerable time procuring suitable comedy shows music streams to present digitally on the Saturday. There was still a ban on live entertainment and this seemed away of bring back people together in a social setting whilst complying with the regulations. I collected the necessary equipment from JGK up Todmorden, and Bernard and I had a few run throughs to ensure a smooth and entertaining night out. Julie advertised on social media others phoned around and the concert room was back in action. Some dedicated Bingo members were the first to return along with a welcome bunch of girls who normally went to the Brickcroft in Rochdale that sadly had recently closed. The following week the audience was augmented with the return of our *Balderstone* friends whose own club had closed the year before lock down.

Introductory music was piped through the speakers via Bernard's iPad, the program itinerary was projected on to a white screen via laptop and Projector. The half hour or so comedy sketches replaced live entertainment followed by great applause. Music videos played whist setup for bingo, to whom some, consider is a comedy act by itself, and with the Clubs 'Open the Box game' with a prize of one hundred pounds culminated into a very enjoyable evening.

It was now Thursday the 17th of June when I was confirming on the phone my attendance at a Zoom meeting for Metro Moneywise at 5pm that evening. Also deliberating with the CEO with 'regard to points that I had just emailed to her, when the doorbell rang and through the 'monitor I could see two familiar faces' but could not comprehend that they could be outside my door. Flashes came to mind what were they doing here, it can't be them, could it, there mother would be going crazy! The shout came it's Millie and Masie "I thought flaming heck! they've learned to drive!" I fumbled with the monitor to open the door for them and failed. The shock I was not suitably dressed, "Hang on I'll come down" Dressed I went down saying as I opened the door "what are you two doing here" and then I saw Kathleen coming into view. Still a shock but relief they were not on their own, but a great and fantastic surprise. Having given my apologies to Ciara the CEO, I explained the shock of family visitors from Chatham and London arriving unannounced at the door. Apologies excepted, we all went off to the Newtown Club for an hour or so and then on to the Hopwood arms for a meal. In my absence from the meeting, I was elected as vice president which I had previously agreed.

Lauren my niece, had sent some wedding cake and a gift of Jameson whiskey my favourite and Polish lemon vodka. Both with labels saying *"TAKE A SHOT WE TIED THE KNOT"* - MR & MRS HICKEY The presentation box included a key and label saying *THE KEY TO HAPPINESS IS LOVE* (*and the ability to open a bottle*) Lauren & Ryan 02.06.2021.

On the way back to the club we called for Drina to come back to the club with us. An hour or two later they departed for the hotel to go swimming. Drina and I remained in the club, I 'was still mesmerised by the fact of their visit,' which I'm told was at the spur of the moment. The following day Emma their mother contacted me, she told me that she was just as surprised as me. Times, I thought to myself, had improved immensely, despite all that had gone before!

It has been an education throughout the many strands of life that I have confronted and combatted throughout the 70-year journey here on this earth. Along with Michelin and Seanin my fanciful companions and the numerous human beings I have met on the many paths I have trodden, my thanks for their bountiful support. Life has become somewhat better with the hook up with Drina. 12 months have passed and no cross words, all is peaceful and tranquil. New friends with the Tuesday bingo gang at the Newtown Club with the development of digital entertainment for the Saturdays after lockdown.

I continue to monitor Ancestry and Gedcom to see if any of my father's side have completed a DNA, and I now have requested unredacted data on my brother Sean and myself from the mother and Baby homes commission. Like Charles Dickens "No Great Expectations" except the long sleep!

> *If you would like to access your personal data which may be held on the records of the 'Mother and Baby Homes Commission of Investigation, you may be requested to fill out the Subject Access Request (SAR) form and email this to the following address sar@equality.gov.ie*

I finish with a poem (*with kind permission Carol Ellis*) which somehow reflects part of my life, the significance of which is now I feel I may have, at the very least, found a way to get over or around any wall.

Beyond the Wall

Vulnerable, abandoned, godforsaken and neglected
Impoverished, unfortunate and cruelly unprotected
The world outside oblivious, did no-one care at all?
Indifferent to the wretched stolen lives beyond the wall
Children raped and beaten and methodically brutalised
Sadistic violence commonplace but how come no-one realised?
Fatal beatings certified as accidental death
Impartial to their suffering, no point in wasting breath
A child who was a "runner" could expect a Brother's fist
Battered with the Hurley stick, a broken leg or wrist
Dragged back to their torment, locked behind the iron gates
A never-ending nightmare, only dreaded hell awaits
The mentally defective, wanton women, "whores" and "prostitutes"
Pregnant out of wedlock, adolescent girls and destitute,
Oppression, degradation, and a system that was punitive
The selling of their babies, diabolically lucrative
Toiling in the laundries, they were little more than slaves
Worked to death then cruelly cast aside in unmarked graves
A daily dose of silence, prayer, and gross humiliation
Spartan, cold, indefinite, their bleak incarceration
Alcohol and drug abuse, and mindless criminality
Help to numb the memory of terror and brutality
Misfits of society, they fight their private war
Shamefully betrayed absurdly locked away once more
Lies, deceit, conspiracies to cover up the truth
Wicked clerics free to rape and violate our youth
The Pope is in denial does he just not care at all?
Indifferent to those wretched stolen lives beyond the wall

Carol Ellis, August 2018
(Mrs Yorkshire the Baking Bard)

THE ADVENTURES OF SEAMUS

The Adventures of Seamus

A Story by James Clancy

With Graphics by Lindsey Duncan

Long ago in the land of Youth-En-Rin lived two brave "little people", Mise and Tatu. They had three children whom they loved very much. Youth-En-Rin has been the home of the little people since time began. In this happy land lived Elves, Fairies, Leprechauns, Gillydoo's, Gnomes and lots of magical little people from every planet in the Galaxy.

There was a time, however, when Youth-En-Rin was ruled by a wicked King who was known as the Poison Dwarf. Mise and Tatu fought a great battle with him. It was long and fierce, but in the end good won over evil and the Poison Dwarf was banished forever. But before he left, he cast a spell on one of the three children.

Today, just as in days long ago, there are little people amongst us, but unless you are a special human you may never see one. Seamus was a special person and he had always played with two little people friends for as long as he could remember. As he was growing up with other small children Seamus could not understand why they all lost the ability to see and play with his little people friends. This made Seamus awful sad.

These little people were called Michelin and Seanin who had come from the land of Youth-En-Rin on a secret mission. When Seamus got older, they begged him to build a place for them and their friends to visit. A holiday village for all little people.

The problem was to find a magical place …

They travelled North South East and West; Seamus discovered the perfect site. It was beautifully situated on the banks of a river which flowed gently through a green valley of shrubs and woods.

This holiday village would be a great adventure place for all children to visit.

An army of builders descended on the site and, with Seamus in charge, work began in earnest. Michalin and Seanin watched with happiness, sometimes giving a little magical assistance, as the buildings began to take shape.

There was the Town Hall at the top of the hill, a church in the valley, rows of houses and novelty shops. There were streams and waterfalls. There was a canal running alongside the model steam railway that went all the way around the village.

Tiny gondolas and barges floated down the canal and secret adventure tunnels criss-crossed underneath the village. The whole place was a maze of shrubs and flowers of every kind and hue, with slides, rides, and swings everywhere – a children's play paradise.

Now nearing completion, everyone awaited the grand opening of the village. Michalin and Seanin sent messages to all their little friends and relatives all over the galaxy.

A special Invitation was sent to the Princess Pudger of Youth-En-Rin, one to Princess Woppits who lived on Tir-Na-Nog, and another to Prince Treacle Pud from the magical Kingdom of Twee Tree.

Seamus was busy writing out invitations to friends and officials all over the world.

As the day of the opening grew closer, things started to go wrong. Tools and machines started to go missing. At first it was thought that somebody was playing a practical joke

The situation worsened. Whole buildings were rooted up and moved to a different site. The canal drained. The adventure tunnels filled with water. The church was standing on top of the hill where the town hall had been.

Everyone was baffled.

Some of the visitors from the galaxy were due to arrive the next day. "Well, my little magical friends" said Seamus, "At least they will understand our problem. They might even be able to help. Later that night Seamus made his way to the village to mull over what to do. All was very quiet, Seamus thought. Just a little too quiet. There was no breeze; rustling of the bushes had ceased, the insects and birds made not a sound. It was if the place was devoid of life, Seamus s was beginning to be frightened his hair was by now like a grovel hogs on the top of his head.

Suddenly! The earth Trembled, there was a great rumbling noise.

Seamus found it difficult to keep his balance. The wind was like a tornado and he was finding it hard to breathe.

Looking up a great ball of fire was hurdling at him. He tried to move but his feet were like lumps of lead, he could not move he thought his days were numbered.

The glowing ball of fire hurdling towards him stopped suddenly metres away. The fierce light forced him to close and protect his eyes. Seconds later as he opened his eyes this skeleton like figure was stood menacingly in front of him.

The creature stretched out his scrawny hands and a fierce battle raged. Seamus struggled and fell. Suddenly, the whole village lit up and a commanding voice began to bellow from above, "DWARF! This time you have gone too far"! The poison dwarf began to panic as the model of the parish church rose slowly off the ground and entombed the poison dwarf forever in the tower.

Michalin and Seanin had by now arrived at the scene followed by two of the new arrivals from youth-en-rin. They gathered round Seamus who still lay where he fell. The light above the village began to fade. The light narrowed to a beam like a ray gun, it passed over Sheamus going up and down his body. It disappeared as quick as it had arrived. Seamus opened his eyes, sat up, and looked around him. Michalin and Seanin shouted with glee and began to dance the hornpipe. They later introduced Mise and Tatu.

Seamus jumped to his feet shouting that the opening of the village was today and he must finish the preparations. Mise got hold of Seamus telling him not to worry and that everything was going to be grand. She sat him down beside Tatu and told him that Michalin and Seanin were his brothers and she was his mother and Tatu his father. Sheamus began to go smaller and smaller "it's true" he said, "I can remember everything that has happened". "That poison dwarf made me human" "That is right Seamus and we tried all the spells in the book to get you back," said Tatu, "but sadly it was not in our power to reverse the spell," said Mise.

"That is why your brothers were with you all this time and why you as a special person were able to see them".

Seamus hugged his family of little people, "I am very happy to have found you, but also very sad. I want to stay with you but I have a human family and we still need each other" Mise and Tatu looked at their son with pride. "You have made the right decision son," they said in unison. Little did they know who his human partner was none other than the Bacup *Banshee* a distant relative of the poison Dwarf?

People from all over the galaxy started to arrive all shapes colours and sizes and not all could see each other, not all were special people. That did not matter. This special place was built to bring all young people to one place in the galaxy to enjoy together even if they cannot see each other. Seamus was there, back in his human form with his human family.

The princess Woppits was the first of the little people to arrive, followed by prince Treacle Pud, Then the princess Pudger all here to represent the non-humans and those who cannot be seen. Human officials came and shook hands with Sheamus and his family congratulating him on a job well done. Sheamus was very pleased and his longing was fulfilled to see all the people of the galaxy together in peace love and harmony.

TATU is the Irish for "It's You" (the father) MISE is the Irish for "I am" (the mother)

ANTS AT ARMS LENGH
Arm's Length Management Organisation (ALMO)

The ant population in Midwoodale have for many years lived in relevant harmony. The attempts to destroy the normal day-to-day service providers [workers] of the hive had successfully been foiled.

Stability did not last for long as a new reign of doubt and deceit had begun to invade the hive. These lab ants were genetically modified to destroy the centre of the ant population in every ant colony for miles around.

Armadillos were imported and were contracted to improve

The structure, training, and performance of the hives. They began by eating away at the outskirts. Trimming back…

To streamline those services deemed not essential. The armadillos were in heaven and defended by brute force their status and income. The ants fled to save themselves. New smaller hives were created with their own elected leadership.

In the meantime, partnerships were formed with other species of ants. The first lot of partnerships were the jackal ants who wiggled and squiggled their way to greater remuneration from the king and queen's coffers. These jackal ants were dispersed North South and Centre. Soldiers and workers were dispersed to smaller hives in the east and west to deliver services, closer to all the ant communities. The armadillos were encouraged to move to another area with a cracking package and did not hesitate to do so.

The jackal ants increased in number whilst the service ants, worker ants, and soldiers were drastically reduced in number. The lab ants took over the centre. The king and queen were deposed and a new leader ship was formed called the partners. The jackal ants with the aid of bio technology evolved into cat like ants. They had nothing but contempt for the rest of the ant population and took to stalking and snooping on the lab ants.

The ants who had formed new communities became known as the co-ants and believed in their communities and started to run their own services for each other and the slogan displayed was 'not for profit' the co-ants set up centres all over the community. The struggle was very difficult and long. But small communities thrived and shared among themselves and others with the slogan "not for profit." Meanwhile the cat ants were chewing away at the lab ants and it was not long before they were consumed by greed and became distant from the needs of the whole community.

The final straw came sometime later when it was announced that the partners would evolve into a much-reduced concern and they soon became known as the fat cat ants. The former jackal ants became extinct and three new leaders were presented known as the chief fat cat ants of north south and the centre. East and west were left to the co ants who spread the slogan "not for profit" and the ant world became a better place to live. In time the co ants became stronger and stronger and with co-operation became known as the collective. The movement grew all over the world and many links were formed.

"Co-operation 'Co-operation'!! "Not for profit, not for profit" became the cry of many in the insect world. Dragon flies, Beetles, ladybirds. Bees, slugs, snails, worms, and many others threw off the mantle of oppression by their predators and embraced the theme of co-operation. Defiant.

BROTHER RYAN REPORT

ST. JOSEPH'S SCHOOL, TRALEE. (MONTHLY REPORT)

H/S. No. 117 NAME James Clancy
Admitted last November. 13 yrs.

CHARACTER and CONDUCT Honest, reliable and manly. Excellent in every way.

HOW ADJUSTED TO SCHOOL LIFE Mixes well and he is actively interested in the different spheres of school life.

STANDARD OF EDUCATION Std V. He has good ability — very interested in his work.

VOCATIONAL TRAINING Woodwork, which he likes very much and is getting on very well at it. Spends 1½ hours daily in this shop.

GENERAL CONDITION OF HEALTH He enjoys excellent health — he has got very big and sturdy.

HOBBIES Outdoor games — Reading & Music. Plays the trumpet and he shows great promise on that instrument.

OTHER PERTINENT INFORMATION He never receives a letter from his mother. This boy promises to turn out very well.

SIGNED J. L. Ryan
Resident Manager

DATE 27th May 1964

REFERENCE I

[form image]	*[form image]*
Entry Form into home for mother, note missing details	Chickenpox and Weight could be questioned
[form image]	*[form image]*
Vaccination Record	To Baby unit Saint Patrick's Home possible ration book. Ration books ended in December 1951

Note two different forms and all the information deleted. Cruel!!

REFERENCE II

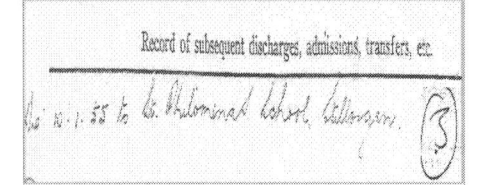

Record of subsequent discharges, admissions, transfers, etc. *As 10.1.55 to S. Philomena's School, Stillorgan.*	19 SEP 1958 — 28 Castlebyrne Park, Newtown Park Ave, Blackrock I have been to St Philomena's home and picked Jimmy Clancy Yours Sincerely, (Mrs) Mary Greene
Discharged 1955 where is all the data	Selected By Ma Greene

AF/EF — 25th September, 5
 	
The Sister in Charge,
St. Philomena's Home,
Stillorgan,
Co. Dublin.
 	
Re: Jimmy Clancy.
 	
A Chara,
 	
    I am directed to inform you that Mrs. Mary Greene, 28, Castlebyrne Park, Newtown Park Avenue, Blackrock, has informed me that she selected the above children to be boarded out with her.
 	
    I am to request that you let me have the necessary information in regard to the children indicating dates of birth, birth certificates and medical reports in respect of the children.
 	
Mise, le meas,
 	
Leas Runai.
	AF/EF — 15th October, 57
	
	The Secretary,
	Dublin Board of Assistance,
	1, James's Street,
	Dublin.
	
	A Chara,
	
	    I am directed to inform you that Mrs. Mary Greene, 28, Castlebyrne Park, Newtown Park Avenue, Blackrock, has applied to the Board to have the children James Clancy boarded out in her home. It is noted that your Board is maintaining ____.
	
	    The necessary report forms have been completed by the Board's Children Acts Inspector and I am enclosing copies of same for your information. I am also to inform you that the Board have a further child in this home and before placing the two children it will be necessary for me to obtain the sanction of the Department of Health.
	
	    Awaiting hearing from you in this matter.
	
	Mise, le meas,

Nuns Informed at Saint Philomena's	Fantastic revelation in 2021 that Frankie is also boarded out.

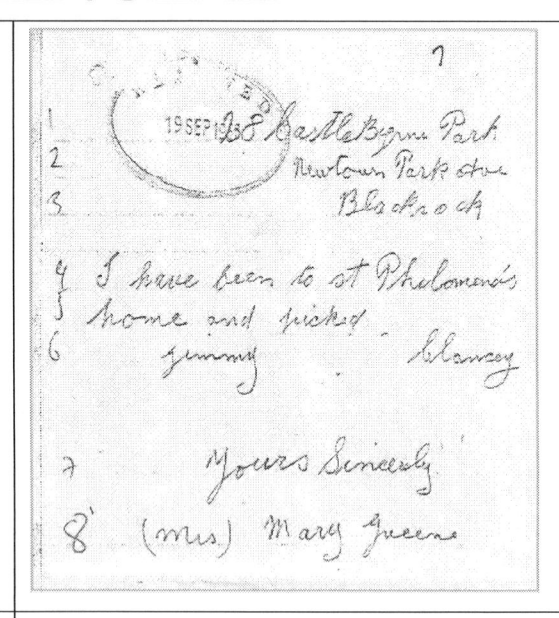

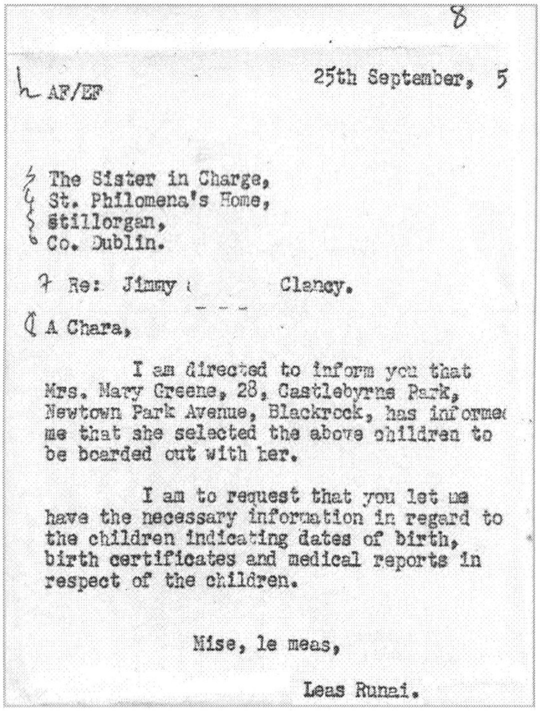

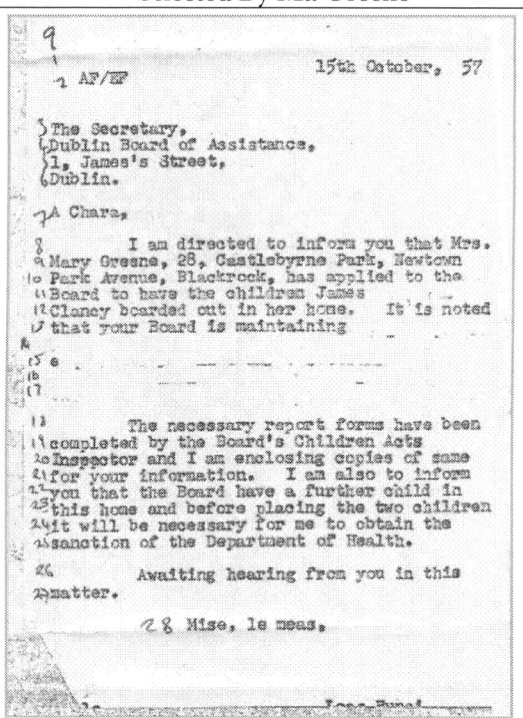

(Certificate of Baptism)	Ma-Greene requesting Sean and I for boarding out
Permission granted	Sleeping arrangements suitable

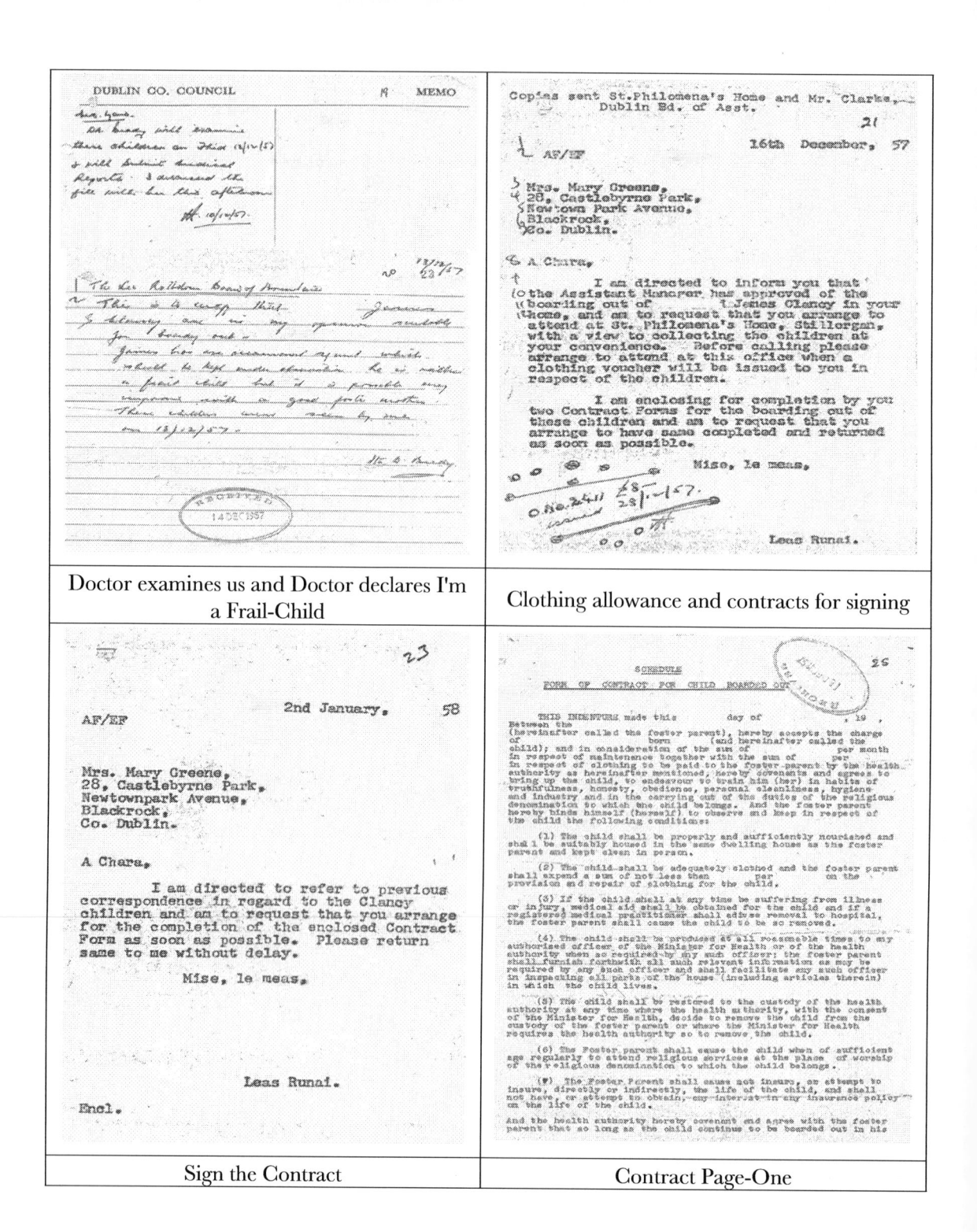

Doctor examines us and Doctor declares I'm a Frail-Child

Clothing allowance and contracts for signing

Letter dated 16th December, 57 to Mrs. Mary Greene, 28, Castlebyrne Park, Newtown Park Avenue, Blackrock, Co. Dublin:

A Chara,

I am directed to inform you that the Assistant Manager has approved of the boarding out of James Clancy in your home, and am to request that you arrange to attend at St. Philomena's Home, Stillorgan, with a view to collecting the children at your convenience. Before calling please arrange to attend at this office when a clothing voucher will be issued to you in respect of the children.

I am enclosing for completion by you two Contract Forms for the boarding out of these children and am to request that you arrange to have same completed and returned as soon as possible.

Mise, le meas,

Leas Runaí.

Sign the Contract

Letter dated 2nd January, 58 to Mrs. Mary Greene, 28, Castlebyrne Park, Newtownpark Avenue, Blackrock, Co. Dublin:

A Chara,

I am directed to refer to previous correspondence in regard to the Clancy children and am to request that you arrange for the completion of the enclosed Contract Form as soon as possible. Please return same to me without delay.

Mise, le meas,

Leas Runaí.

Encl.

Contract Page-One

SCHEDULE
FORM OF CONTRACT FOR CHILD BOARDED OUT

THIS INDENTURE made this day of , 19 , Between the (hereinafter called the foster parent) of (and hereinafter called the child); and in consideration of the sum of per month in respect of maintenance together with the sum of per in respect of clothing to be paid to the foster parent by the health authority as hereinafter mentioned, hereby covenants and agrees to bring up the child, to endeavour to train him (her) in habits of truthfulness, honesty, obedience, personal cleanliness, hygiene and industry and in the carrying out of the duties of the religious denomination to which he belongs. And the foster parent hereby binds himself (herself) to observe and keep in respect of the child the following conditions:

(1) The child shall be properly and sufficiently nourished and shall be suitably housed in the same dwelling house as the foster parent and kept clean in person.

(2) The child shall be adequately clothed and the foster parent shall expend a sum of not less than per on the provision and repair of clothing for the child.

(3) If the child shall at any time be suffering from illness or injury medical aid shall be obtained for the child and if a registered medical practitioner shall advise removal to hospital, the foster parent shall cause the child to be so removed.

(4) The child shall be produced at all reasonable times to any authorized officer of the Minister for Health or of the health authority when so required by any such officer; the foster parent shall furnish forthwith all such relevant information as may be required by any such officer and shall facilitate any such officer in inspecting all parts of the house (including articles therein) in which the child lives.

(5) The child shall be restored to the custody of the health authority at any time where the health authority, with the consent of the Minister for Health, decide to remove the child from the custody of the foster parent or where the Minister for Health requires the health authority so to remove the child.

(6) The Foster parent shall cause the child when of sufficient age regularly to attend religious services at the place of worship of the religious denomination to which the child belongs.

(7) The Foster Parent shall cause not insure, or attempt to insure, directly or indirectly, the life of the child, and shall not have, or attempt to obtain, any interest in any insurance policy on the life of the child.

And the health authority hereby covenant and agree with the foster parent that so long as the child continues to be boarded out in his

189

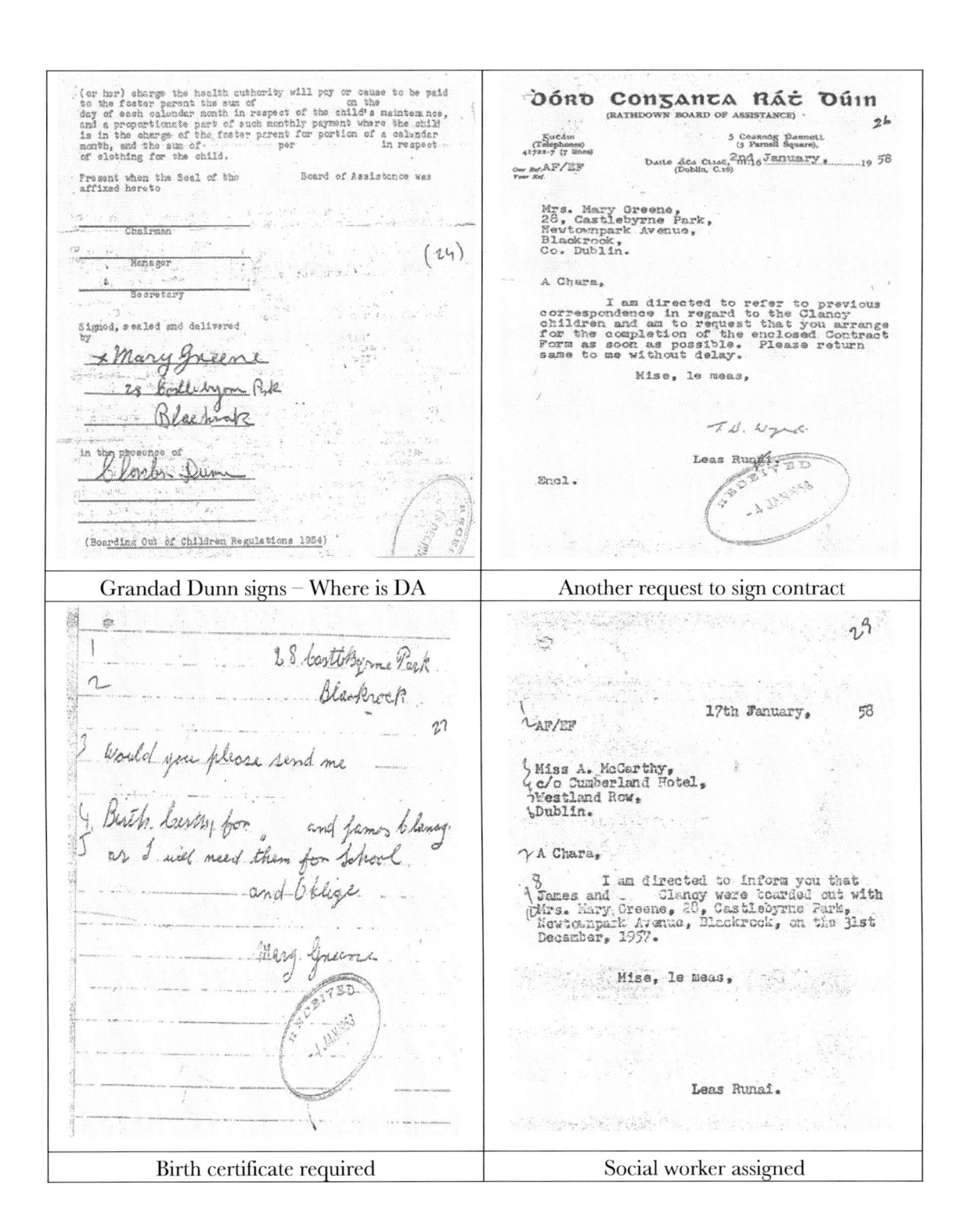

(or her) charge the health authority will pay or cause to be paid to the foster parent the sum of on the day of each calendar month in respect of the child's maintenance, and a proportionate part of such monthly payment where the child is in the charge of the foster parent for portion of a calendar month, and the sum of per in respect of clothing for the child. Present when the Seal of the Board of Assistance was affixed hereto _____ Chairman _____ Manager _____ Secretary Signed, sealed and delivered by × Mary Greene 28 Castlebyrne Pk Blackrock in the presence of E. Foster Dunn (Boarding Out of Children Regulations 1954)	**Bórd Congantá Rát Dúin** (RATHDOWN BOARD OF ASSISTANCE) Sucán (Telephone): 41721-7 (7 lines) 5 Cearnóg Pharnell (5 Parnell Square) Our Ref: AF/EF Baile Átha Cliath, 2nd January, 1958 (Dublin, C.16) Mrs. Mary Greene, 28, Castlebyrne Park, Newtownpark Avenue, Blackrock, Co. Dublin. A Chara, I am directed to refer to previous correspondence in regard to the Clancy children and am to request that you arrange for the completion of the enclosed Contract Form as soon as possible. Please return same to me without delay. Mise, le meas, T.J. Wynn Leas Rúnaí Encl.
Grandad Dunn signs – Where is DA	Another request to sign contract
28 Castlebyrne Park Blackrock Would you please send me Birth Certs for and James Clancy as I will need them for School and Oblige Mary Greene	AF/EF 17th January, 58 Miss A. McCarthy, c/o Cumberland Hotel, Westland Row, Dublin. A Chara, I am directed to inform you that James and Clancy were boarded out with Mrs. Mary Greene, 28, Castlebyrne Park, Newtownpark Avenue, Blackrock, on the 31st December, 1957. Mise, le meas, Leas Rúnaí.
Birth certificate required	Social worker assigned

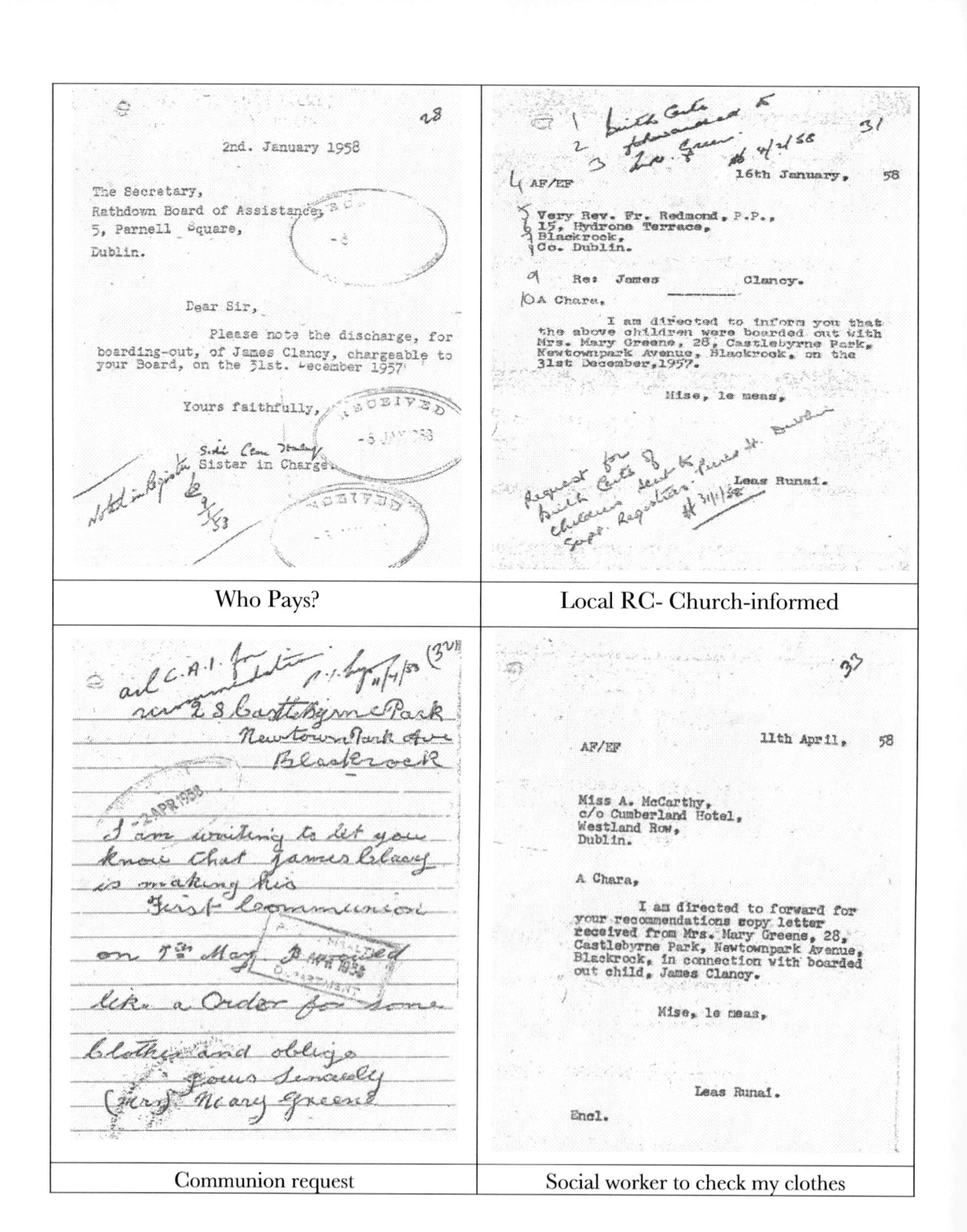

2nd. January 1958 The Secretary, Rathdown Board of Assistance, 5, Parnell Square, Dublin. Dear Sir, Please note the discharge, for boarding-out, of James Clancy, chargeable to your Board, on the 31st. December 1957. Yours faithfully, Sister in Charge. **Who Pays?**	16th January, 58 AF/EF Very Rev. Fr. Redmond, P.P., 15, Hydrone Terrace, Blackrock, Co. Dublin. Re: James Clancy. A Chara, I am directed to inform you that the above children were boarded out with Mrs. Mary Greene, 28, Castlebyrne Park, Newtownpark Avenue, Blackrock, on the 31st December, 1957. Mise, le meas, Leas Rúnaí. **Local RC- Church-informed**
28 Castlebyrne Park Newtownpark Ave Blackrock I am writing to let you know that James Clancy is making his First Communion on 7th May. Would like a Order for some clothes and oblige Yours sincerely (Mrs) Mary Greene **Communion request**	11th April, 58 AF/EF Miss A. McCarthy, c/o Cumberland Hotel, Westland Row, Dublin. A Chara, I am directed to forward for your recommendations copy letter received from Mrs. Mary Greene, 28, Castlebyrne Park, Newtownpark Avenue, Blackrock, in connection with boarded out child, James Clancy. Mise, le meas, Leas Rúnaí. Encl. **Social worker to check my clothes**

REFERENCE III

1960-April – Da writes to remove us	Social worker informed
Social worker requested to report	Recommendation & Complaint Social worker response

AF/JH. For the attention of Mr. McGuirk. The Secretary, Dublin Board of Assistance, 1, James Street, Dublin. 1, Meitheamh, 1960. Re: Clancy Children: c/o Mrs. Greene, 28, Castlebyrne Park, Blackrock. A Chara, I wish to refer to the application of Mrs. Greene to have these children removed from her custody. I shall be obliged if you will let me know what progress is being made in this matter. Mise, le meas, Leas Rúnaí	*(handwritten note re: Mr. Donoghue, S.O., rang Mr. Dawson, Cherry Orchard, who confirmed that James Clancy was admitted there on 10/5/60 as suspected meningitis. (not yet confirmed). 12/5/60. Mr. Dawson rang. Confirmed Influenza. Still a patient in Cherry Orchard. 20/5/60.)*
1960-May – The board assisting	Doctor sends me to Hospital
(handwritten note: Re: James Greene. Interview with S.A.O. — We should consider whether this child should ever be allowed to remain in present Foster Home — ask Mr. McGuirk to seek one in Ireland. 31/5/60.)	Notification received from Dublin Fever Hosp. 20/5/60. JAMES GREENE, 28 CASTLEBYRNE PARK, BLACKROCK on 8/5/60 admitted suffering from ? MENINGITIS Confirmed as INFLUENZA. *(further handwritten notes, 21/5/60, 23/5/60)*
Note about me as James Greene	Flu 'realised

193

XXXXXXXXXXX
RATHDOWN

46

28th June, 60

AF/EF

Miss A. McCarthy,
c/o Cumberland Hotel,
Westland Row,
Dublin.

Re: Clancy children boarded out with Mrs.
Greene, 28, Castlebyrne Park, Blackrock.

A Chara,

I am directed to request that you arrange to keep these children under constant supervision and submit a detailed report every three months as to their progress.

Mise, le meas,

Leas Runai

1960 June - Social worker to monitor us

45

13th June 60

The Secretary,
Dublin Board of Assistance,
1 James's Street,
Dublin

Re: Clancy Children c/o Mrs. Greene,
28 Castlebyrne Park, Blackrock.

A Chara,

I am to refer to my letter of the 1st inst. in regard to above and am to request a reply as a matter of urgency.

Mise, le meas,

Leas Runai

Reply ASAP

49

Mrs. Mary Greene,
28, Castlebyrne Park,
Newtown Park Ave.,
Blackrock,
CO. DUBLIN.

Dear Madam,

With reference to your letter received here on the 4th October, 1962 and to Miss McCarthy's visit to you I have to inform you that the Health Authority will be prepared to take the children in care while you are visiting your daughter in England. It is noted that you will be away for about 4 weeks. You should arrange to take the boys along to St. Philomena's Home on Monday next the 15th October, 1962.

Yours faithfully,

gueg/bo'c.

1962-Oct - Returned to home Granted

50

28 CastleByrne Park
Blackrock

5 NOV 1962

Dear Sir
 I am writing this to let you know I will be unable to take the boys back as the Corpoation has allocated me a smaller house they have told me there is not enough room to house any more than one child I'm very sorry I could not have the boys but with my family all gone I could not keep this house any longer.
 Yours Sincerely
 (Mrs) Mary Greene

1962-Nov - Ma's intervention requested

194

Social worker says new home ok

For attention of Mr. C.J. Murray

G. C. McIntyre Esq.,
Town Clerk,
Town Hall,
Dun Laoire.

Dear Sir,

Two children James Clancy (born 16.1.51) ... were placed with Mrs. Mary Greene, 38, Castlebyrne Park, Newtown Park Ave., Blackrock on a boarding-out basis on the 31st December, 1957. During the past year, at the request of the foster-parent, the children were taken in care in St. Philomena's Home to enable her to attend the marriage of her two daughters in England. Recently the foster-parent informed the Authority that she had moved to a smaller home at 62, Brookfield Place, Blackrock and would not have sufficient accommodation for these boys. According to her the Housing Department, Dunlaoire County Borough would not be prepared to allow her to take the boys in the new home. The Authority's Children Officer has visited the foster-parent at her new address and she is of the opinion that in view of the fact that the children with Mrs. Greene are all boys sufficient accommodation is available in the new home. The foster-parent has now stated that she will be prepared to take the two Clancy children back to live with her if sanction is forthcoming from the Dunlaoire Borough Housing Department.

I shall be obliged, therefore, to know whether any objection will be raised by you to these two boys residing with the foster-parent at the new address.

Yours faithfully,

gmcg/bo'c.

1963-Jan – Ma has typed letter sent

/Copy/

62, Brookfield Place.
8. 1. 63.

Sir,

I have just come back from England and I hear there is a 4 roomed house with Bathroom at 33, Castlebyrne Pk. Miss McCartty tells me that ^ and Jimmie Clancy are not settleing down. If I could get above house I would gladly take them back I think if you were to explain to the housing office they might let me transfer there I have not asked them yet. I would like you to see what chance there is and then I would apply myself. This house I am in has only 3 rooms and they would not allow the boys to come here. I am realy sorry for letting them go when I hear that they are not happy.

I hope to hear from you soon so that I can try to get the house.

Yours sincerely,

Mrs. Mary Greene.

Passed to authority

For attention Mr. C. Murray: 11th January, 1963

G.C. McIntyre Esq.,
Assistant City Manager & Town Clerk,
Town Hall,
Dun Laoghaire,
CO. DUBLIN.

Dear Mr. McIntyre,

I refer to my letter of the 3rd January, 1963, and I enclose herewith for your information a copy of a letter received from Mrs. Mary Greene, 62, Brookfield Place.

Yours faithfully,

gmcg/bo'c.

1963-Mar – Ma Visits home.

62 Brookfield Place
10-3-63
11 MAR 1963

Dear Sir,

I'm writing this to ask what happened about the Clancy boys as my husband was wondering he did not hear from you anyway I would like to ask you if I could take James but as I was up to see them one Sunday and James got very upset when he seen me so I did not go since I know you like them kept together but as the sister told me James is

getting big, now he will be 12 year old this month and I thought it would be nice for him to make his Confirmation in Blackrock which will be in May. so if you would be so kind as to let me know and oblige. Yours Sincerely (Mrs) Mary Greene	23rd March, 1963. The Sister-in-charge, St. Philomena's Home, Stillorgan, CO. DUBLIN. Reverend and dear Sister, I enclose herewith, for your information, a copy of a letter which was issued to Mrs. Greene, regarding James and Clancy. Yours faithfully, aa/bo'c.
Ma wants me for Confirmation	Sisters informed
23rd March, 1963. Mrs. Mary Greene, 62, Brockfield Place, Blackrock, CO. DUBLIN. Dear Madam, With reference to your letter of the 10th March, 1963, I understand from Miss McCarthy that you intend taking James back to your home from St. Philomena's, Stillorgan. You may make arrangements with the Sister-in-charge, St. Philomena's regarding the matter. Yours faithfully, aa/bo'c.	9th May, 1963. Mrs. Mary Greene, 62, Brockfield Place, Blackrock, Co. Dublin. Dear Madam, With reference to your letter of the 10th March, 1963, I wish to inform you that James was confirmed on Tuesday the 7th May. The boys appear to be very attached to you and your home and are constantly enquiring when they will be going home. As we are anxious to provide for the future of these children, I should be obliged if you will get in touch with the Authority to discuss the question. The telephone No. is 54264, ext. 105. Please ask for Mr. McGuirk, Staff Officer. Yours faithfully, aa/yod
Sisters informed	1963-May – Alleged, 'we want to go home'

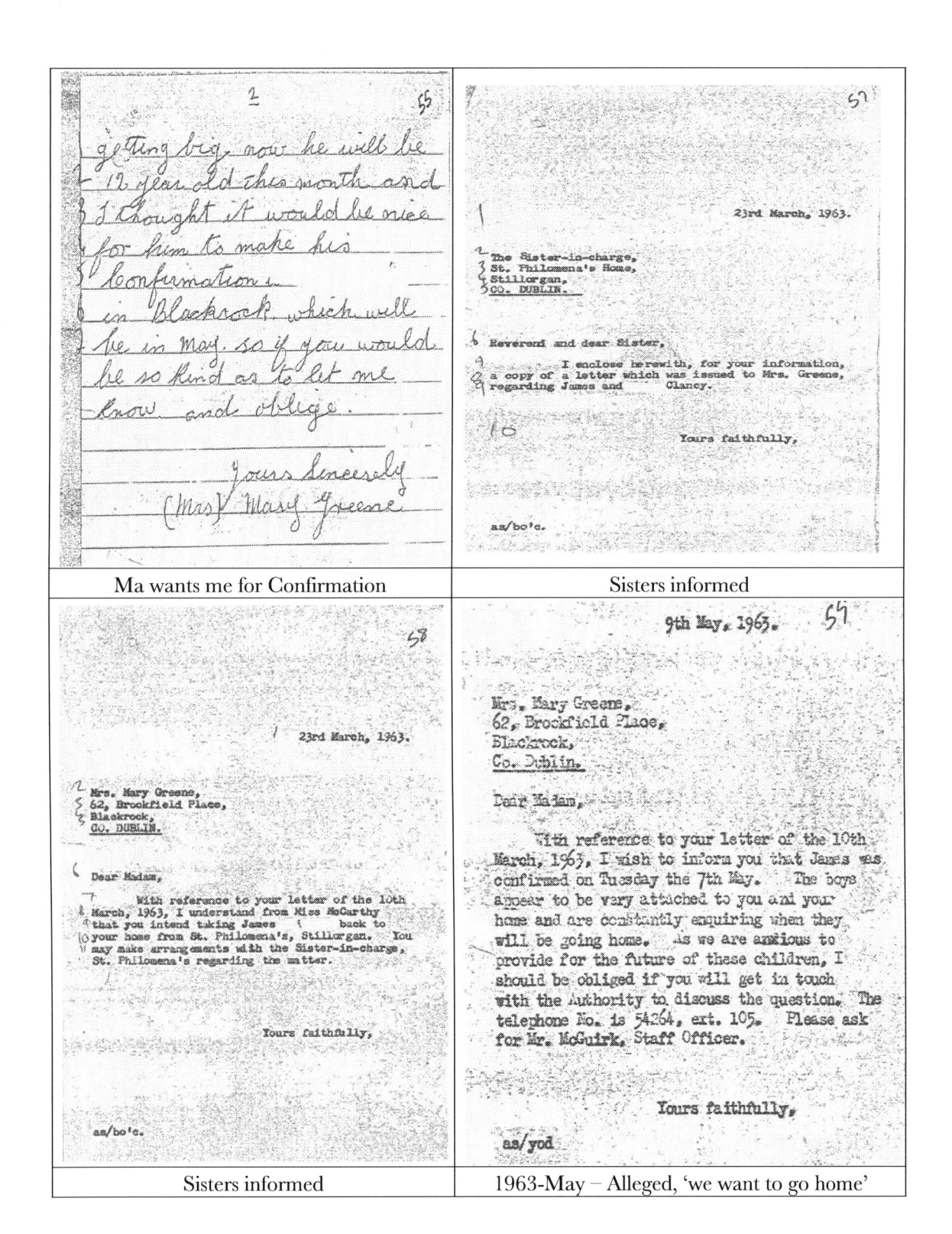

Again, Ma declines having us

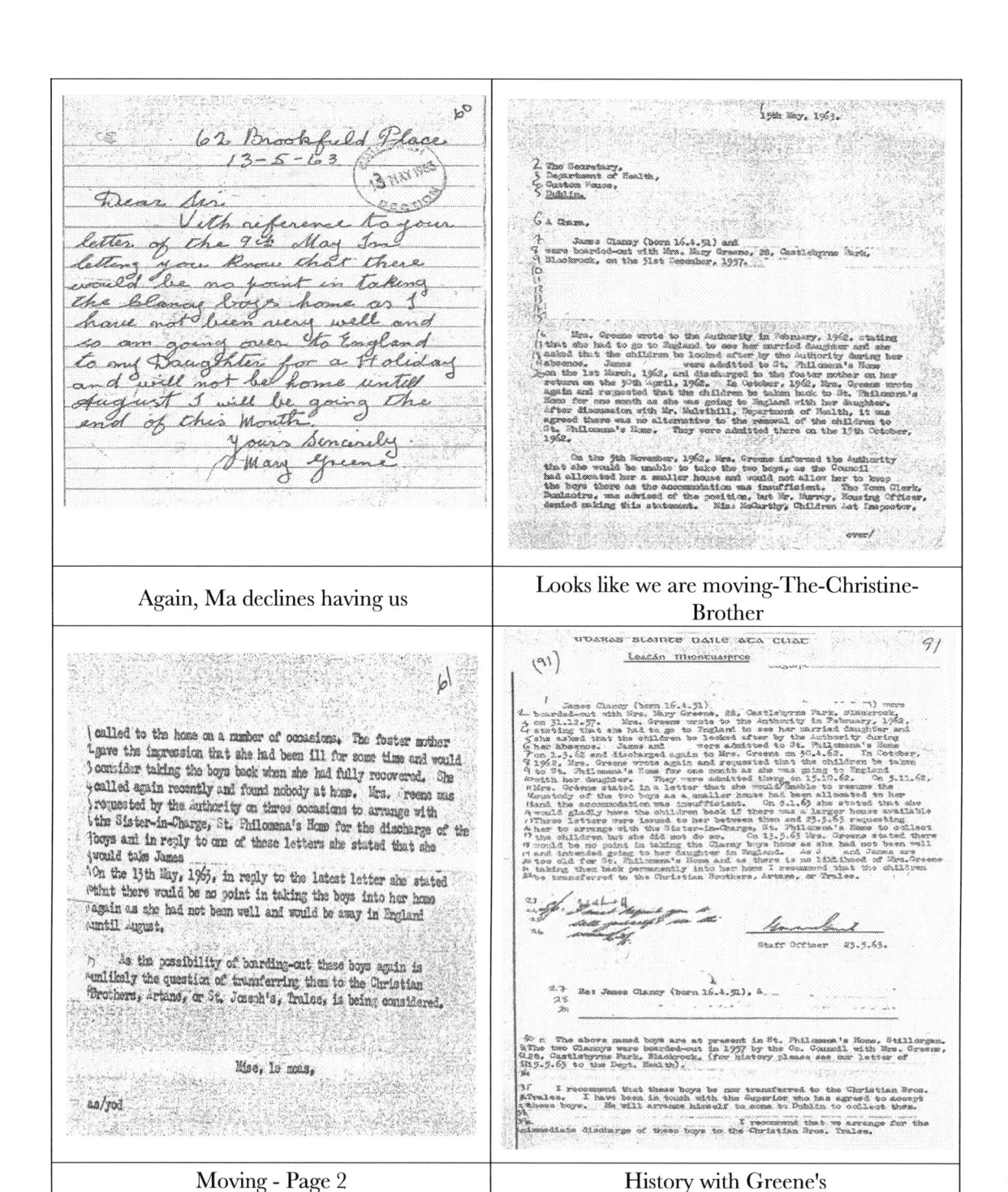

> 62 Brookfield Place
> 13-5-63
>
> Dear Sir,
> With reference to your letter of the 9th May I'm letting you know that there would be no point in taking the Clancy boys home as I have not been very well and so am going over to England to my Daughter for a Holiday and will not be home until August. I will be going the end of this Month.
>
> Yours Sincerely
> Mary Greene

Looks like we are moving – The-Christine-Brother

19th May, 1963.

The Secretary,
Department of Health,
Custom House,
Dublin.

A Chara,

James Clancy (born 16.4.51) and _____ were boarded-out with Mrs. Mary Greene, 28, Castlebyrne Park, Blackrock, on the 31st December, 1957.

Mrs. Greene wrote to the Authority in February, 1962, stating that she had to go to England to see her married daughter and she asked that the children be looked after by the Authority during her absence. James and _____ were admitted to St. Philomena's Home on the 1st March, 1962, and discharged to the foster mother on her return on the 30th April, 1962. In October, 1962, Mrs. Greene wrote again and requested that the children be taken back to St. Philomena's Home for one month as she was going to England with her daughter. After discussion with Mr. Underhill, Department of Health, it was agreed there was no alternative to the removal of the children to St. Philomena's Home. They were admitted there on the 15th October, 1962.

On the 9th November, 1962, Mrs. Greene informed the Authority that she would be unable to take the two boys as the Council had allocated her a smaller house and would not allow her to keep the boys there as the accommodation was insufficient. The Town Clerk, Dunlaoire, was advised of the position, but Mr. Murray, Housing Officer, denied making this statement. Miss McCarthy, Children at Inspector,

over/

Moving - Page 2

called to the home on a number of occasions. The foster mother gave the impression that she had been ill for some time and would consider taking the boys back when she had fully recovered. She called again recently and found nobody at home. Mrs. Greene was requested by the Authority on three occasions to arrange with the Sister-in-Charge, St. Philomena's Home for the discharge of the boys and in reply to one of these letters she stated that she would take James

On the 13th May, 1963, in reply to the latest letter she stated that there would be no point in taking the boys into her home again as she had not been well and would be away in England until August.

As the possibility of boarding-out these boys again is unlikely the question of transferring them to the Christian Brothers, Artane, or St. Joseph's, Tralee, is being considered.

Mise, le meas,

as/yod

History with Greene's

James Clancy (born 16.4.51), & _____ were boarded-out with Mrs. Mary Greene, 28, Castlebyrne Park, Blackrock on 31.12.57. Mrs. Greene wrote to the Authority in February, 1962, stating that she had to go to England to see her married daughter and she asked that the children be looked after by the Authority during her absence. James and _____ were admitted to St. Philomena's Home on 1.3.62 and discharged again to Mrs. Greene on 30.4.62. In October, 1962, Mrs. Greene wrote again and requested that the children be taken to St. Philomena's Home for one month as she was going to England with her daughter. They were admitted there on 15.10.62. On 5.11.62, Mrs. Greene stated in a letter that she would be unable to resume the custody of the two boys as a smaller house had been allocated to her and the accommodation was insufficient. On 6.1.63 she stated that she would gladly have the children back if there was a larger house available. Three letters were issued to her between then and 25.5.63 requesting her to arrange with the Sister-in-Charge, St. Philomena's Home to collect the children but she did not do so. On 13.5.63 Mrs. Greene stated there would be no point in taking the Clancy boys home as she had not been well and intended going to her daughter in England. As _____ and James are too old for St. Philomena's Home And as there is no likelihood of Mrs. Greene taking them back permanently into her home I recommend that the children be transferred to the Christian Brothers, Artane, or Tralee.

Staff Officer 23.5.63.

Re: James Clancy (born 16.4.51), & _____

The above named boys are at present in St. Philomena's Home, Stillorgan. The two Clancys were boarded-out in 1957 by the Co. Council with Mrs. Greene, 28, Castlebyrne Park, Blackrock. (for history please see our letter of 5h.15-5.63) to the Dept. Health).

I recommend that these boys be now transferred to the Christian Bros. Tralee. I have been in touch with the Superior who has agreed to accept these boys. He will arrange himself to come to Dublin to collect them.

I recommend that we arrange for the immediate discharge of these boys to the Christian Bros. Tralee.

REFERENCES IV

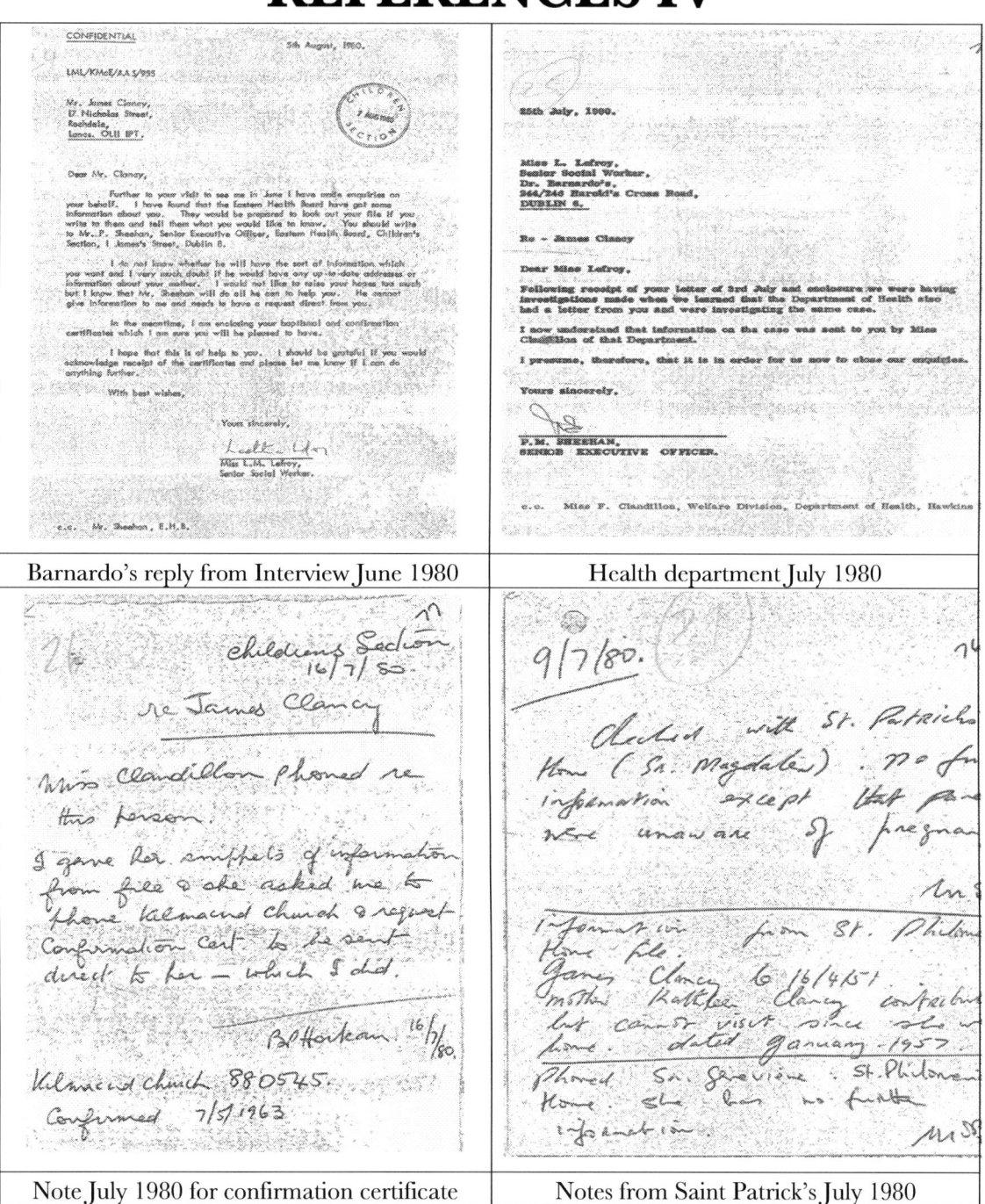

Barnardo's reply from Interview June 1980	Health department July 1980
Note July 1980 for confirmation certificate	Notes from Saint Patrick's July 1980

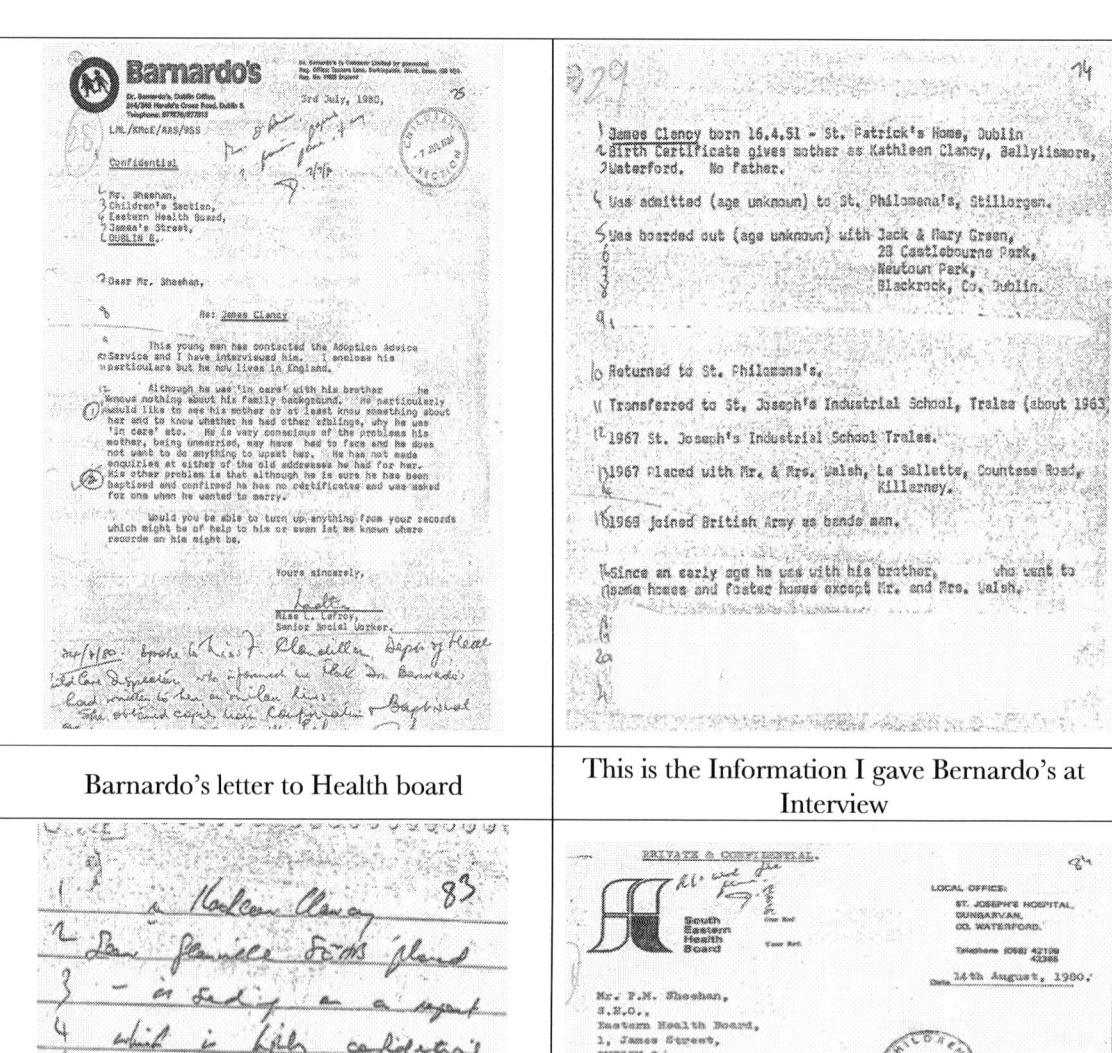

Barnardo's letter to Health board	This is the Information I gave Bernardo's at Interview
Sadly, a request highly Confidential no Further Action	Confidentiality about Mother - Not sure why?

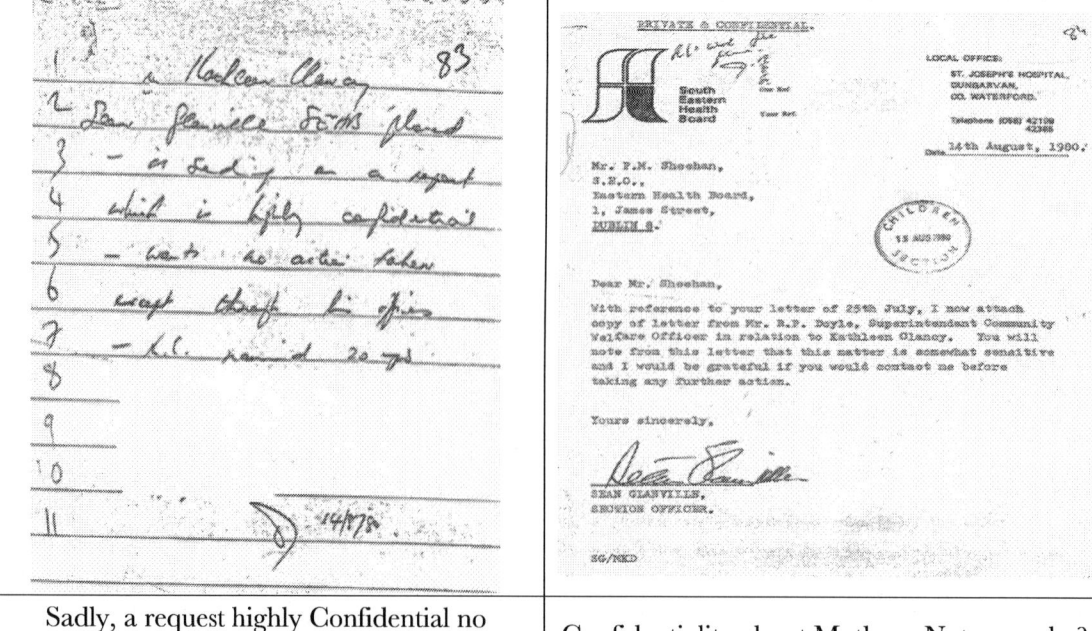

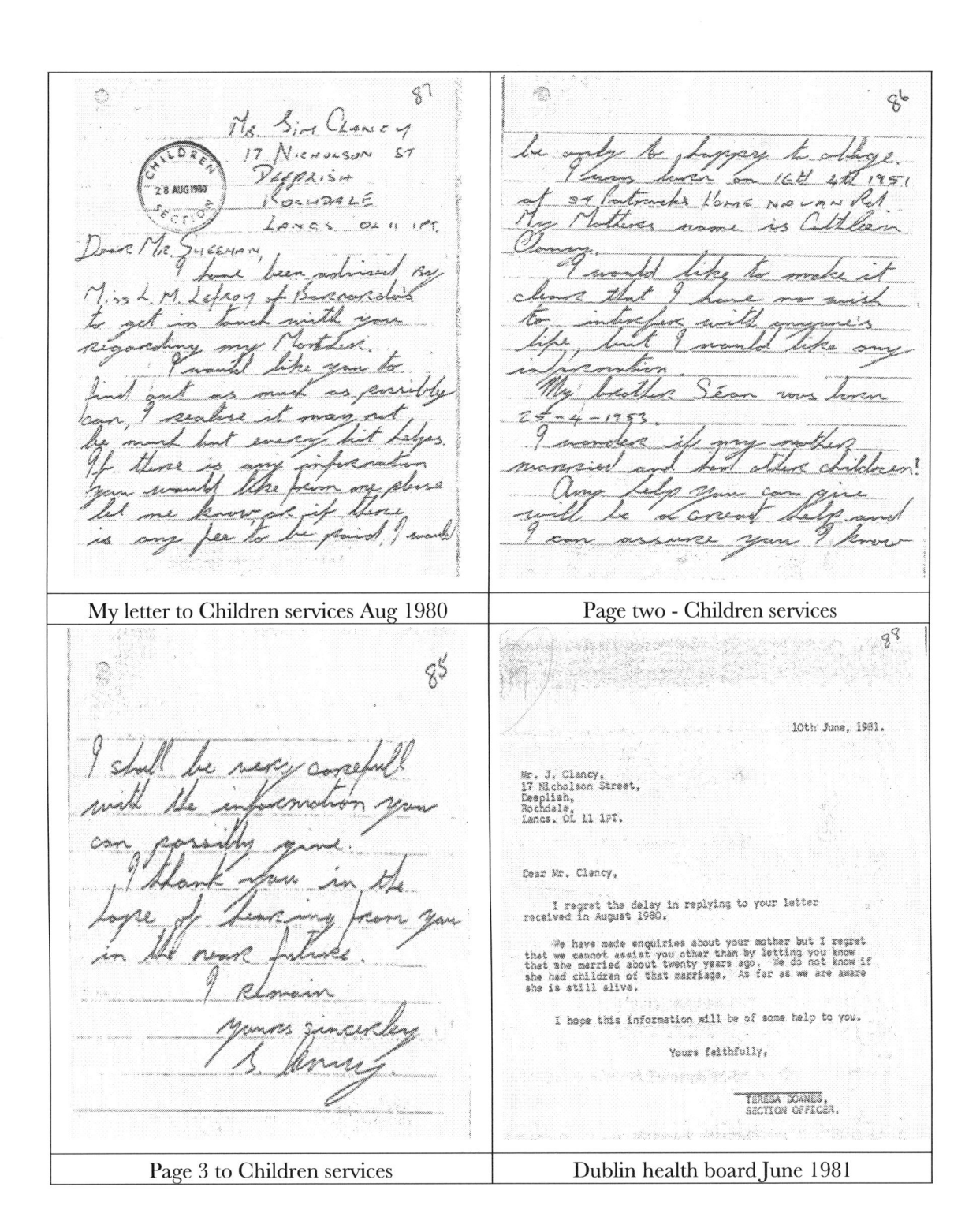

Mr. Sean Clancy
17 Nicholson St
Deeplish
Rochdale
Lancs OL11 1PT

[CHILDREN SECTION 28 AUG 1980]

Dear Mr. Sullivan,

I have been advised by Miss L.M. Lefroy of Baccarat[?] to get in touch with you regarding my Mother. I would like you to find out as much as possibly can, I realise it may not be much but every bit helps. If there is any information you would like from me, please let me know and if there is any fee to be paid, I would

My letter to Children services Aug 1980

be only too happy to oblige. I was born on 16th 4th 1951 at St Patrick's Home Navan Rd. My Mother's name is Cathleen Clancy. I would like to make it clear that I have no wish to interfere with anyone's life, but I would like any information. My brother Sean was born 25-4-1953. I wonder if my mother married and has other children? Any help you can give will be a great help and I can assure you I know

Page two - Children services

I shall be very careful with the information you can possibly give.

I thank you in the hope of hearing from you in the near future.

I Remain
Yours Sincerely
S. Clancy

Page 3 to Children services

10th June, 1981.

Mr. J. Clancy,
17 Nicholson Street,
Deeplish,
Rochdale,
Lancs. OL 11 1PT.

Dear Mr. Clancy,

I regret the delay in replying to your letter received in August 1980.

We have made enquiries about your mother but I regret that we cannot assist you other than by letting you know that she married about twenty years ago. We do not know if she had children of that marriage. As far as we are aware she is still alive.

I hope this information will be of some help to you.

Yours faithfully,

TERESA DOWNES,
SECTION OFFICER.

Dublin health board June 1981

REFERENCE V

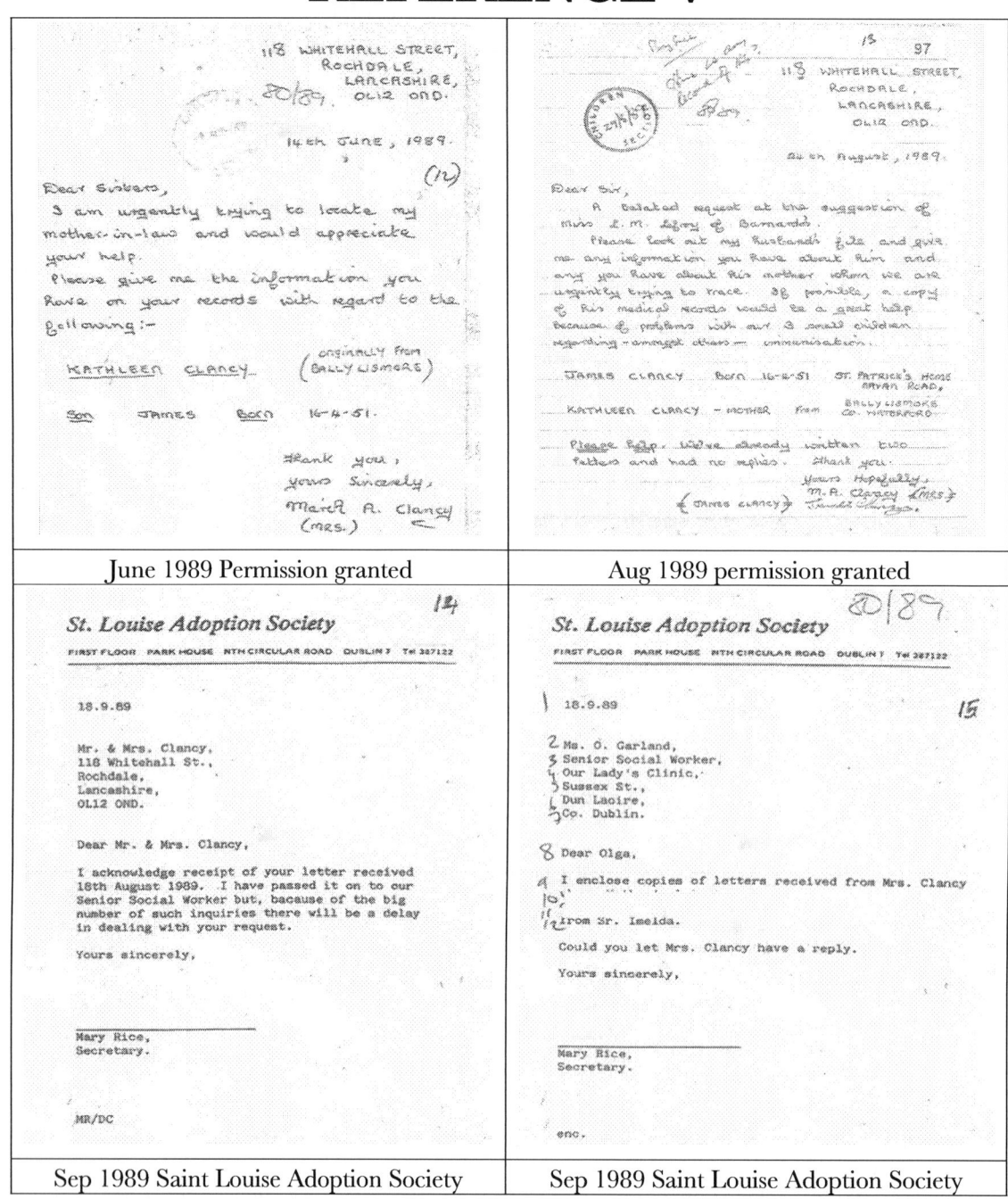

---

118 WHITEHALL STREET,
ROCHDALE,
LANCASHIRE,
OL12 0ND.

14th June, 1989.

Dear Sisters,

I am urgently trying to locate my mother-in-law and would appreciate your help.

Please give me the information you have on your records with regard to the following:-

KATHLEEN CLANCY (originally from BALLYLISMORE)

Son JAMES BORN 16-4-51.

Thank you,
Yours sincerely,
Mary R. Clancy
(Mrs.)

June 1989 Permission granted

---

118 WHITEHALL STREET,
ROCHDALE,
LANCASHIRE,
OL12 0ND.

24th August, 1989.

Dear Sir,

A belated request at the suggestion of Miss L. M. Leroy of Barnardo's.

Please look out my husband's file and give me any information you have about him and any you have about his mother whom we are urgently trying to trace. If possible, a copy of his medical records would be a great help because of problems with our 3 small children regarding — amongst others — communication.

JAMES CLANCY Born 16-4-51 ST. PATRICK'S HOME BRYAN ROAD,

KATHLEEN CLANCY - MOTHER from BALLYLISMORE CO. WATERFORD

Please help. We've already written two letters and had no replies. Thank you.

Yours hopefully,
M. R. Clancy (Mrs.)
{ JAMES CLANCY }

Aug 1989 permission granted

St. Louise Adoption Society
FIRST FLOOR   PARK HOUSE   NTH CIRCULAR ROAD   DUBLIN 7   Tel 387122

18.9.89

Mr. & Mrs. Clancy,
118 Whitehall St.,
Rochdale,
Lancashire,
OL12 0ND.

Dear Mr. & Mrs. Clancy,

I acknowledge receipt of your letter received 18th August 1989. I have passed it on to our Senior Social Worker but, because of the big number of such inquiries there will be a delay in dealing with your request.

Yours sincerely,

Mary Rice,
Secretary.

MR/DC

Sep 1989 Saint Louise Adoption Society

St. Louise Adoption Society
FIRST FLOOR   PARK HOUSE   NTH CIRCULAR ROAD   DUBLIN 7   Tel 387122

18.9.89

Ms. O. Garland,
Senior Social Worker,
Our Lady's Clinic,
Sussex St.,
Dun Laoire,
Co. Dublin.

Dear Olga,

I enclose copies of letters received from Mrs. Clancy from Sr. Imelda.

Could you let Mrs. Clancy have a reply.

Yours sincerely,

Mary Rice,
Secretary.

enc.

Sep 1989 Saint Louise Adoption Society

(17) 118 Whitehall Street, Rochdale, Lancashire, OL12 0ND. 5th March, 1991. Dear Mrs. Pine, You may remember me from last June when I was searching for a relative and called to see you. Forgive me for writing to you but I do not yet know if we will be able to visit Ireland again this year. The lady we are searching for is called Kathleen or Catherine or Kitty and worked as a domestic for the people at no. 42. She would be in her 20s, possibly 25 years old and that would be 1949 to 1952. Please cast your mind back and see if you can remember anything. You mentioned the O'Keefe family. Would they have lived at no 42 at the time? Do you know where they are now or where they went to? I'll gladly refund any postal costs. Please help if you can. Thank you, yours sincerely, Maria A. Clancy	(18) 45 Eaton Square Terenure, Dublin 6W 9.4.91 Dear Sr Catherine, Enclosed please find the letter & envelope to which I referred this morning. I am posting a letter to Mrs. Clancy this evening, giving her your address and stressing that she give full details when writing to you. Thank you for being so helpful. Yours sincerely, (Mrs) B. Pyne.
Mar 1991 Maria writes to Mrs. Pine	Reply Mrs. Pine
23 118 WHITEHALL STREET ROCHDALE, LANCASHIRE, OL12 0ND. 30th April, 1991. Dear Sister Catherine, I'm not sure why I've been referred to you but please help if you can. I'm trying to locate a family called O'Keefe with regard to a domestic who worked for them in the 1950's in Eaton Square. The domestic was called Kathleen or Catherine Clancy and may have been known as Kitty. She was or is, my husband's mother. We'd like to know which part of Dublin and for whom she was working before she went to the O'Keefe family.	2 I don't know what records you have access to — perhaps you could tell me — or what other information you need but please help if you can. We are willing to refund any postage for you. Thank you, yours hopefully Maria A. Clancy (Mrs)
Maria's letter to sister April 1991 page 1	Maria's letter to sister April 1991 page 2

202

118 Whitehall Street, Rochdale, Lancashire, OL12 0NJ. 22nd May, 1991. Dear Sister, Thank you for your reply to my letter. Let me first explain something to you. All letters that leave our household are written by myself simply because my husband is not a "letter writer" and he prefers it that way. My husband is fully aware of the content of them all and whenever I say I'm writing on his behalf then I'm doing just that. If, however, you feel it still necessary, I can ask my husband to write himself. If you have the records from the Navan Road then you must have	2 all the information my husband seeks. His name :- James CLANCY Born St. Patrick's, Navan Rd. on 16-5-51. Mother Kathleen (Kitty) CLANCY domestic. Do you also have the records for St. Philomena's children's home, Stillorgan? Jim was transferred there at some stage. Please let us know if we can have photo-copies of the records or if you can give us all the information contained therein or if my husband would be able to see them for himself. There are an awful lot of barriers in Ireland with regard to information,
Maria 2nd letter to Sister May 1991	*Maria 2nd letter to Sister May 1991 Page 2*
3 It's a pity we cannot break them down! Thank you, Yours Sincerely, Maria Clancy (MRS)	2 Sherwin Way, Castleton, Rochdale, Lancashire, OL11 2UZ. 14th October, 1993. Dear Sister, I understand you have access to the records from St. Patrick's Home, Navan Road. I was born there on 16-4-51. My brother, Sean was born at St. Kevins Hospital on 25th April, 1953. Please let me have any information you have on your records about myself and my brother. I respect my birth mother's right to anonymity therefore I'm only asking for the information you have with regard to Sean and myself. Thank you, Yours faithfully James Clancy
Maria 2nd letter to Sister May 1991 Page 3	*Maria signs J Clancy! in 1993*

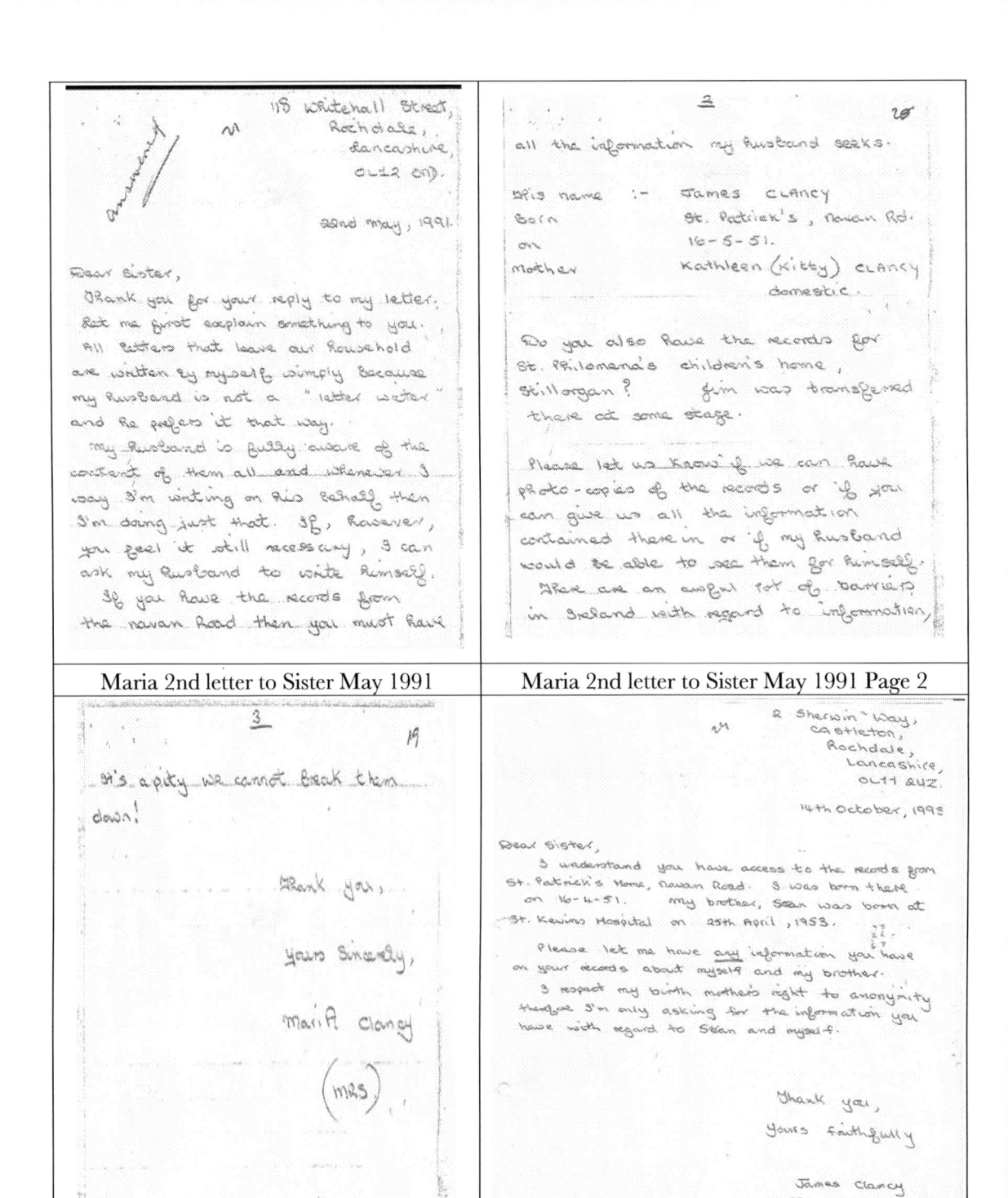

203

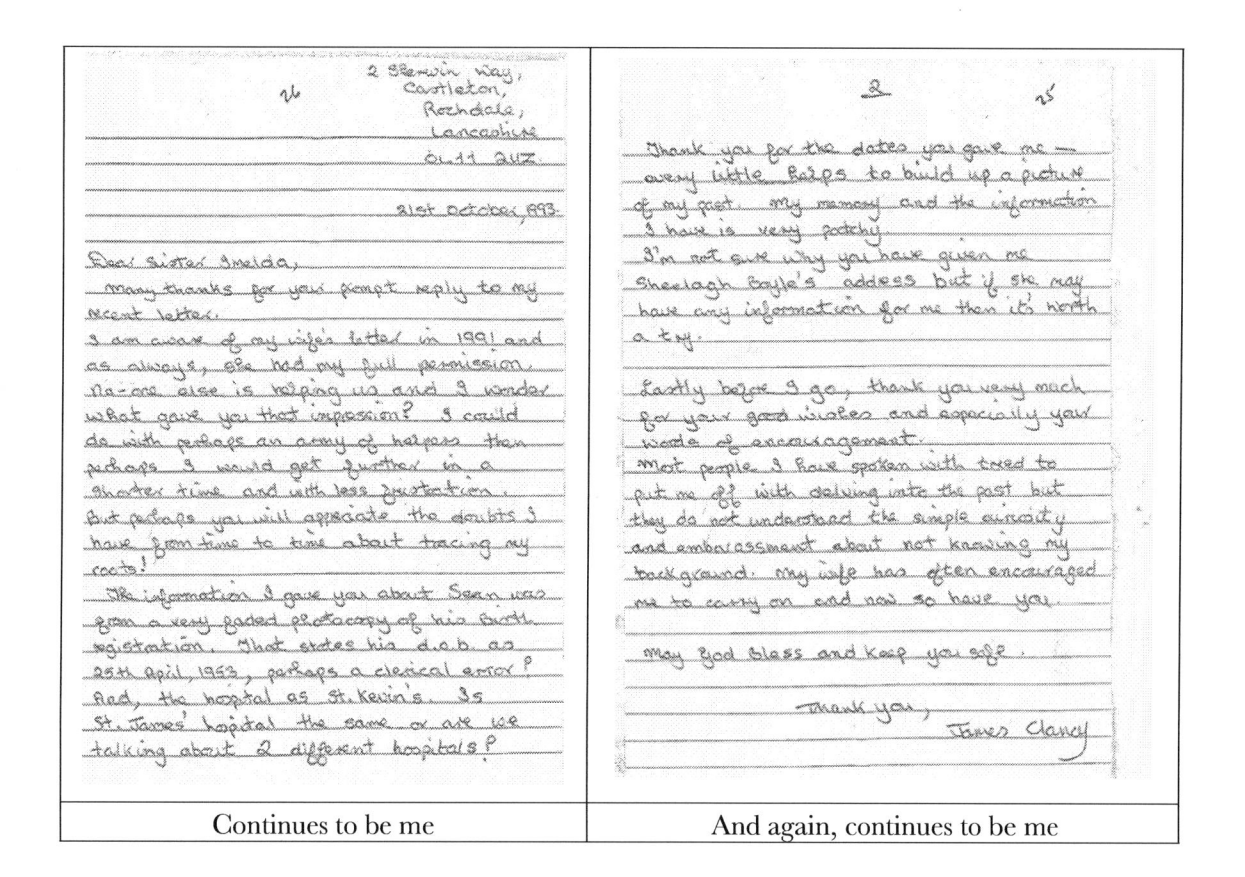

2 Sherwin Way,
Castleton,
Rochdale,
Lancashire
OL11 2UZ

21st October, 1993.

Dear Sister Imelda,

Many thanks for your prompt reply to my recent letter.

I am aware of my wife's letter in 1991 and as always, she had my full permission. No-one else is helping us and I wonder what gave you that impression? I could do with perhaps an army of helpers then perhaps I would get further in a shorter time and with less frustration. But perhaps you will appreciate the doubts I have from time to time about tracing my roots!

The information I gave you about Sean was from a very faded photocopy of his birth registration. That states his d.o.b. as 25th April, 1953, perhaps a clerical error? And, the hospital as St. Kevin's. Is St. James' hospital the same or are we talking about 2 different hospitals?

Thank you for the dates you gave me — every little helps to build up a picture of my past. My memory and the information I have is very patchy.

I'm not sure why you have given me Sheelagh Boyle's address but if she may have any information for me then it's worth a try.

Lastly before I go, thank you very much for your good wishes and especially your words of encouragement.

Most people I have spoken with tried to put me off with delving into the past but they do not understand the simple curiosity and embarrassment about not knowing my background. My wife has often encouraged me to carry on and now so have you.

May God bless and keep you safe.

Thank you,
James Clancy

| Continues to be me | And again, continues to be me |

REFERENCE VI

Brother Manning's Report 1

FOR THE ATTENTION OF: ▓▓▓▓▓
FROM: Jack Manning,
Tel.: ▓▓▓▓▓
MY YEARS IN TRALEE: August 1963 / August 1969

Residential Institutions Redress Board
RECEIVED 16 NOV 2003

STANDARD OF FOOD:

Even though it was not directly my responsibility, I took an active interest in all of this.

FARM: potatoes, wide variety of vegetables, apples, pears, cows, milk, butter, hens, eggs, pigs, pork, bacon, sheep, lambs, mutton, turkeys.

BAKERY: white loaves of bread, brack, slabs of sticky currant buns.
The children got all of the above.
Extra bread, potatoes were freely available.

OUTSIDE SUPPLIERS: meat, beef, corned beef, cooked cold meat, corned beef, meat rolls, sausages, rashers, pudding, chickens, cheese.

Butter, jam, tea, sugar, soap powder, gravy mix, flour, oranges, bananas, dried fruit, large tins of biscuits, jars of sweets, variety of minerals.

MEAL TIMETABLE:
Breakfast: 8.30 am
Dinner: 1.00 pm
Afternoon snack: 4.00 pm
Tea: 6.30 pm

The above timetable is roughly as I remember it.

CONTENT OF MEALS: Breakfast: porridge, tea, milk, sugar, bread, butter, jam.
regularly: boiled egg, sausages, fried bread.

I can personally remember doing a survey of the local shops to find out the cost of rashers and pudding. I then persuaded the Superior that the children should get a substantial cooked breakfast every Sunday morning.

This consisted of: fried egg, sausages, rasher, pudding and fried bread.

Brother Manning's Report 2

Dinner: soup, bread,
meat, stew, mince, shepherds' pie, sausages,
potatoes, vegetables, chips, peas, beans,
dessert, rice, semolina, bread and fruit pudding, custard,
jelly, ice cream, cooked apples, tinned fruit.

Afternoon snack: tea, bread, jam, brack, fruit buns, biscuits.

Tea: tea, bread, butter, jam.
regularly: chips, fried- scrambled- boiled eggs, cheese,
cold cooked meat, salad.

VARIETY: I can clearly remember, with Brother Price and Brother Dowling, drawing up a seven- day weekly menu to ensure there was sufficient variety in the meals being served.

SPECIAL DAYS: cakes, biscuits, sweets, fruit, bottles of minerals.

CHRISTMAS DAY: full traditional Christmas dinner: turkey, ham, roast potatoes, Stuffing,
plum pudding, nuts.

large Christmas party in the recreation hall: large bottles of minerals, sweets, chocolate, bars, cakes,
biscuits, selection of fruit.

all above served out in individual portions.
also a bag to take away what could not be eaten.

Because most of the boys in the school were orphans and in an effort to help them better enjoy the Christmas period, we deliberately gave them an over abundance of goodies at this party.

OTHER PARTIES: major feasts: New Year, 6th January, Easter, St. Patrick's Day, Holydays,
bank holidays, first communion, confirmation etc. etc.

Brother Manning's Report 3

STANDARD OF CLOTHING:

BACKGROUND: *Tailor's Shop:* suits, trousers, jackets, overcoats, shirts;
work overalls / uniforms, football shorts;
night shirts, sheets, pillow cases, towels etc.;
band uniforms for wet and dry weather; -
were made and repaired here.

Shoemaker's Shop: boots, shoes, bags etc. made and repaired here.

OUR APPROACH TO CLOTHING: The children should be warm, dry, comfortably and respectably dressed.

When I arrived in Tralee - August 1963 - the school was a relatively open institution.
Many children regularly went, unaccompanied, into the town on various errands.

More and more of the children went each day - again unaccompanied - to the local Technical and Secondary Schools.

On September 1968, the remainder of the children attended the local Primary School.

All above were dressed as the "town" children attending these schools.

From 1965 onwards we gradually changed from the practice of the tailor's shop making 50+ suits from the same bale of cloth to stocking up a large store room with various styles, colours in readymade suits, overcoats, jackets, pullovers etc.

REFERENCE VII

DIOCESE OF SALFORD
SALFORD DIOCESAN TRIBUNAL Tel: 0161 817 2202

JONES – CLANCY   J1 – 06/14

Mr James Clancy
33 Ajax Street
Rochdale
Lancs
OL11 3HN

31 March 2014

Dear Mr Clancy,

Maria Ann Clancy (nee Jones) has approached the Catholic Church about the possibility of investigating her marriage with a view to seeking a declaration of nullity in Church Law.

Maria Ann Clancy was married to James Clancy, and we are not sure if you are this person. The only purpose of this letter is to safeguard the rights of the former spouse of Maria Ann Clancy.

If you were formerly married to Maria Ann Clancy, naturally, you have the right to take part in these proceedings. However, until you confirm that you were married to Maria Ann Clancy we are unable to give more details at present. We would, of course, keep your address completely confidential.

We should be glad if you would please return the enclosed form in the stamped addressed envelope, or telephone this office.

With kind regards and every good wish.

Yours sincerely,

Rev Christopher Dawson

DIOCESE OF SALFORD
SALFORD DIOCESAN TRIBUNAL Tel: 0161 817 2202

JONES – CLANCY   J1 – 06/14

Mr James Clancy
33 Ajax Street
Rochdale
Lancs
OL11 3HN

7th April 2014

Dear Mr Clancy,

I am writing to ask if you would be prepared to help us in the following matter.

Your former wife, Maria Anne Clancy has approached us to investigate the possible invalidity of your marriage, which took place on 28 August 1982 at St. John's Church, Rochdale, Lancs.

Having received this request, we are obliged to respond, and so we are writing to ask if you would be willing to make a statement regarding the circumstances and events relating to the marriage. We would be happy to arrange an appointment for you here at the Tribunal, or if it suits you better, arrangements can be made for you to be seen locally.

Please be assured that we are not seeking to apportion blame to either party for the breakdown. This enquiry is purely a matter concerning the Catholic Church and has no implications in civil law.

I enclose our information sheet, and a reply slip, which I should be grateful if you would complete and return, indicating whether or not you wish to be involved in these proceedings. Your co-operation will be very much appreciated to enable us to come to an objective assessment of the situation.

With kind regards,

Yours sincerely,

Rev. Christopher Dawson

DIOCESE OF SALFORD
SALFORD DIOCESAN CHANCERY OFFICE
T. 0161 817 2202 E. tribunal@dioceseofsalford.org.uk

JONES – CLANCY   J1 – 06/14

Mr James Clancy
33 Ajax Street
Rochdale
Lancashire
OL11 3HN

6 October 2015

Dear Mr. Clancy,

I am writing concerning the petition for nullity of marriage which your former spouse, Maria Anne Clancy, brought before this Diocesan Tribunal. The case was recently examined by the judges of the Tribunal, who found in favour of the nullity of your marriage.

However, as a marriage can only be declared null once there are now confirming judgements favouring nullity, the case is now to be forwarded to the Metropolitan Tribunal in Liverpool, so that they can examine it and make a judgement. If this judgement also favours nullity, then your marriage will be declared null.

Before the case is sent off to Liverpool, Church Law requires that, in addition to communicating to you the judgement of the Tribunal here in Salford, we also extend to you the opportunity to read the sentence (the deliberations of the Tribunal by which it arrived at the judgement, written by the Tribunal judges) once it has been written.

Accordingly, please find enclosed a response form, which we would ask you to return within the next 21 days. If you indicate you wish to inspect the sentence, then we will arrange a convenient time for you to visit the Cathedral centre to read it. If you indicate you do not wish to read it, or do not return the form, then it will be forwarded to Liverpool without further delay.

Given the heavy workload of the Metropolitan Tribunal, it is not possible to estimate how soon your case can be judged there, but as soon as we receive their reply, we will inform you accordingly.

As these documents are private and confidential they have to be seen here in the offices in Salford.

With kind regards and every good wish,

Christopher Dawson
Rev Christopher Dawson, J.C.L.
Judicial Vicar

SALFORD DIOCESAN TRIBUNAL
Cathedral Centre, 3 Ford Street, Salford M3 6DP

Information Sheet for Respondent

1) The accompanying letter indicates that your former spouse has asked to have the religious status of your marriage examined. The nature of this investigation will determine whether a further union will be possible in the Catholic Church.

2) Such an investigation seeks to examine in some detail the nature of the consent (and your own ability to give that consent) at the time of the marriage. This involves the Petitioner (your former spouse) in making a detailed statement; and you are also invited to do so. This can be done here at the Tribunal offices or locally. It goes without saying that your participation is earnestly sought to allow for a fair appraisal to be made.

3) The Petitioner is required to produce the names of persons who can throw light on the marriage (both before and during it); and you are also invited to name persons who you think could also be of help in this regard.

4) If you are agreeable an appointment will be arranged to enable you to make a statement.
You will also be informed of the nature of the petition, which has been presented by your former spouse.

5) When all information has been received it will be available for inspection here.

6) You will also be told of the outcome of the case. Following a decision (given at First Instance at Salford) there is always a mandatory appeal to a second instance Tribunal namely the Metropolitan Tribunal of Liverpool.

7) You are asked to inform this office if you change your address so that contact may be kept with you.

S.R.C.D.T. REGISTERED CHARITY No. 250037

ACKNOWLEDGEMENTS

Although it was primarily written with my children and grandchildren in mind it has gained a wider interest since the search for extended family.

This book is dedicated to my children and grandchildren so they may know who their *grandad really was*, and yes even Maria, my annulled ex-wife.

My thanks to those in the *County of Waterford*, half siblings on my mother's side, for their understanding and welcome over those years of discovery.

With the breakthrough of my aunts and uncles and numerous cousins, on my paternal side, a whole-hearted wish in the future to meet with them all. The transient families between the various institutions for their impact in my life.

The people of the various help groups on facebook who offered support to those who have similar experience. To the many new found cousins who responded to my quest on the various ancestry sites.

My merits go to *Bernard Wilds* for his patience and perseverance when dealing with such a demanding idiosyncratic and finicky person such as myself.

All these people helped in their own way, unknowingly through being part of my life, helped me to be a survivor and possibly the driver to keep going till I can rest in the long sleep.

Peace, love, and happiness to all.

Jim Clancy

Printed in Great Britain
by Amazon